Minnesota on Paper

Minnesota on Paper
Collecting Our Printed History

MOIRA F. HARRIS and LEO J. HARRIS

With Essays by BARRY CASSELMAN and ROGER G. KENNEDY

UNIVERSITY OF MINNESOTA PRESS
Minneapolis · London

MINNESOTA

Published by the University of Minnesota Press
111 Third Avenue South, Suite 290
Minneapolis, MN 55401-2520
http://www.upress.umn.edu

Printed in China

The University of Minnesota is an equal-opportunity educator and employer.

14 13 12 11 10 09 08 07 06   10 9 8 7 6 5 4 3 2 1

Library of Congress Cataloging-in-Publication Data

Harris, Moira F.

Minnesota on paper : collecting our printed history / Moira F. Harris and Leo J. Harris ; with essays by Barry Casselman and Roger G. Kennedy.
    p.   cm.
Includes bibliographical references and index.

ISBN-13: 978-0-8166-4555-8 (pbk. : alk. paper)
ISBN-10: 0-8166-4555-8 (pbk. : alk. paper)

1. Printed ephemera--Minnesota--History. 2. Printed ephemera--Collectors and collecting--Minnesota. 3. Advertising specialties--Collectors and collecting--Minnesota. 4. Minnesota--History--Sources. I. Harris, Leo J. II. Casselman, Barry. III. Kennedy, Roger G. IV. Title.

Z1029.5.H37 2006

769.5--dc22

2006008300

Contents

Through the Rooms of History

BARRY CASSELMAN

THE WORD *EPHEMERA*, AS IT IS APPLIED TO the paper objects that are now so widely collected in all parts of the world, is profoundly misleading. The word in the singular is *ephemeron*, and almost all of its synonyms suggest brevity, transitoriness, and temporary conditions—or to paraphrase the commonplace, here today, gone tomorrow. But paper ephemera, items that do so much to capture certain moments in our history and culture, are anything but objects that disappear. This is the inherent paradox of the phenomenon—ephemera are the most permanent kind of impermanence. And this is true because we are compelled to collect them.

As a child I began to collect stamps and coins. My family went to Florida when I was 10 years old, and I spent days walking up and down Collins Avenue in Miami Beach collecting postcards from every hotel. Then I saved all the letters sent to me, my school essays, my report cards. Next it was maps and brochures from places we visited. I kept the menus from restaurants we dined in. When I went away to college at the University of Pennsylvania, I began to keep the books and the magazines I read. I saved beer coasters. In downtown Philadelphia, near the campus, I walked into a curio shop one day, and discovered autographed letters and inscribed first editions. When I moved to the Twin Cities and began publishing a small newspaper, I began to save the ubiquitous printed political material, including broadsides, bumper stickers, buttons, and posters, that appeared every election year. I also accumulated the remarkable local posters for art events and museums. Of course, I saved all the editions of my publications, including the newspapers I edited and the magazines that published my poems and short stories. I also kept the programs from every concert, opera, play, lecture, dance performance, convention, and program I ever attended. By the time I began to attend national political conventions, I realized that it was getting out of hand. But self-awareness didn't stop me. My collection of national convention memorabilia since that time fills boxes and bookshelves.

When I moved recently, I finally realized the enormity of what I have been doing. Friends who helped me move made me promise to throw out or give away myriad paper ephemera and other collectibles I had accumulated. Needless to say, I was able to discard only some of it. My youth is long gone, and now I have to think of what will become of all of this. I have begun to donate my collections of political ephemera to museums and historical societies. To throw it away would be, after all, unthinkable.

But I have also begun to try to understand what this lifelong fever has been about. I realize now that, far from being an isolated collector, I have been doing what millions of my fellow citizens have also been doing all these years. If you doubt it, go to eBay and other Internet sites where various kinds of ephemera are sold, bought, and traded. Read the many books about the categories of ephemera or the magazines that come out each month with the latest news about the pastime.

There is also, if you will permit me to say so, a very serious and philosophical side to the preserving and collecting of ephemera. This aspect reveals an essence of that peculiar social animal, the contemporary human being living in a free and creative place, including our state and our country. Ephemera is real history, not an abstraction. You can look at it, hold it, display it, and relish it. It is a record of the most serious work we have done, yet it is filled with glorious minor details and gossip. It is a continual celebration of human lives moving through the rooms of history. We love stories. In one part of my life, I create and write stories. Each story I write is formed and crafted into an object to be read. Each item of ephemera, however, tells a story of its own. A collection of any ephemera is really a special kind of library.

Although saving and preserving ephemera is as old as the ephemera itself, the widespread collecting of it is relatively recent. The printing press is less than 500 years old, and the modern technology for producing ephemera in quantity is less than 200 years old. Perhaps that is why the United States of America is apparently the most democratic, i.e., universal, in its collectors, who come from all social, cultural, and economic backgrounds. This country began a bit more than 200 years ago when its original states came together to form a political union, and the individual character and personality of each state remains with us today. I think it is only fitting that the authors of this book have begun with the ephemera of one state, Minnesota, which is old and rich enough in its history to have an extraordinary selection to present, and young and vibrant enough so that a reasonably comprehensive selection can fit into its pages. Some items from my little collection are featured here, as are items from collections much larger and more important than mine. This book is, if you will, a diary in visual paper forms of the events, passions, triumphs, disasters, interests, and creativity of the people of this state for the past 150-year period, which parallels and reveals as well the history of our whole remarkable republic in its journey to the temporary and brief time we now call our own.

The Compost of Our Lives

ROGER G. KENNEDY

SOME TRUTHS ABOUT THE EPHEMERAL MAY last longer than the illustrations offered to support them. But all messages of importance are mixed. So here is a book about ephemera. Aspiring to longevity, we have before us an artifact about the anti-artifactual—calling our attention to the bravery of the authors in seeking to add some increment of value to the world, though they know that nothing granular or entire or discrete is likely to last. What we do know is that nearly everything that does last manages to associate itself with other things that last, and thus, together, as a new composite, become an organism adapting to change. Otherwise they die, decay, and disappear.

So what have we before us? A book about deliberate expressions of how someone or some set of persons in Minnesota wished to be thought to be, though not aspiring to be thought to be so for a very long time. For instance, the trade cards distributed by my grandfather and great uncles to express how romantic it would be to go skating on Kennedy Brothers' skates were not in aid of their being per-

ceived as purveyors of elixirs of love, but, instead, of the means to engage in healthy outdoor, though sexually charged, activity. Nor in its shotgun advertising did the Kennedy Brothers Arms Company desire to be considered merchants of death, like the proprietors of the Skoda Works or I.G. Farben or Krupp, but, rather, as friendly neighborhood encouragers of outdoor exercise. They were aspiring to be thought to be something nice. Ephemeral though those impressions might be, they were not trivial to continued success at Fifth and Minnesota Streets in St. Paul.

The one-story-high shotgun that once ornamented that building is now gone, ephemeral as it was. So is the building. The notches in its limestone side (which, my grandfather assured me, recorded the last urban shoot-out between the Sioux and Chippewa) are gone. But, of course, they were interesting as voids rather than solids, anyway. Life is change; certainly it is change at Fifth and Minnesota Streets. I was back there again a year or so ago, joining Michael Graves, the architect, in judg-

BROS.
rs for
s, Snow Shoe
and General
oods,

Manufacturers provided colorful stock designs for the envelopes and stationery of retail establishments. In this case the firearms were for sale at Kennedy Brothers, a longtime sporting goods store in St. Paul. The envelope is postmarked August 6, 1904. Courtesy of Tom Reiersgord.

ing plans for the replacement of a grain-handling tower beside the Mississippi River with some sort of celebratory expression of the role of St. Paul as a river port. I wanted to suggest a memorial to the rowdy, raucous life on that levee, but the passage of time had been so brief, and the memory of past lives so fleeting, that the serene civic garden proposed for so raunchy an area seemed a little, shall we say, ephemeral.

Sic transit gloria mundi. Melancholy reflections on ephemera have been a convention of literature, especially since the destruction of the last vestiges of the feudal system in the French Revolution. This book does not have a caption from *The Ruins, or Meditation of the Revolutions of Empires,* by Count C. F. Volney, so important to Thomas Jefferson at the time, or from Shelley's "Ozymandias," but those who were not present for that design competition at Fifth and Minnesota Streets might find suitable sentiments in either. Indeed, I didn't happen to need either Volney or Shelley because I had the building itself. We sat around in a vast, desolate space where once I practiced banking, a space I helped create at the end of the 1960s, after my father and grandfather's store building, and its super shotgun, had been torn down. I was employed by the Northwestern Bank, lastly as chairman of its executive committee (there's an ephemeral title for you!) and presided over the design and construction of the building in which nobody now banks. Ephemera now blow across the banking floor that replaced the main retail floor of Kennedy Brothers, where for fifty years before 1950 the customers' sales slips whizzed across the ceiling in little baskets, on wires, to the cashier. It was the pre-computerized world.

Reflections upon ruins? The building at Fifth and Minnesota is not yet a ruin, and I would hate to think that the Northwestern Bank of St. Paul is totally forgotten. Still, all buildings are as ephemeral as paper, from a geologist's point of view. One man's rubble is another man's yellowed paper. Buildings like paper ephemera ask, How do I look? Will you accept me, or should I go home and change? And, of course, as the words are uttered, the utterer changes. That's biology as well as psychology.

"Change and decay all around myself I see, oh thou who changes not abide with me." Plato sought release from his sense of the ephemeral in a world that was disappointing him, and so may we. Or, on the other hand, we may find some solace in the knowledge that we are in a company of the ephemeral, making our own tiny contributions to the detritus. All the while, our poems, our songs, our doodles, our worn-out pencils, our failed aspirations, and our lost loves participate in the ongoing life of humanity and beyond humanity in the lives of the living things with whom we share this wondrous earth. One life's ephemera are the compost for other lives.

Now then, here's a book about cigar wrappers and playbills and advertisements for one-day sales in 1878 and other hot opportunities that cooled a century ago. Makes you think, doesn't it?

On this trade card for Kennedy Brothers, a sporting goods store, the gentleman wears a costume typical of the St. Paul Winter Carnival marching clubs of the 1880s. Courtesy of the Hennepin History Museum.

Acknowledgments

IT WOULD NOT HAVE BEEN POSSIBLE TO PRODUCE this book without the gracious assistance of a number of persons and the organizations they represent. Organizationally speaking, we were aided by the Minnesota Historical Society; the Special Collections and the Children's Literature Research Collections of the University of Minnesota Library; the archives of the library of the College of St. Catherine; the Tweed Museum of the University of Minnesota–Duluth; the Ampersand Club; the Banta Corporation; the Paper Collector of St. Cloud; the H. M. Smyth Printing Company; the Walker Art Center; the Minneapolis Collection of the Minneapolis Public Library; the Minneapolis Athenaeum; the American Philatelic Research Library; the History Museum and Historical Library of the Minnesota State Fair; the James J. Hill Library; the Goldstein Galleries of the University of Minnesota; the Cloquet Historical Society; the Stearns History Museum; the Watkins Corporation; the Art Instruction Schools; the 614 Company; the Ramsey County Historical Society; the Saint Paul Riverfront Corporation; and the Hennepin History Museum.

Individually speaking, we are grateful for the assistance of a number of professionals (archivists, librarians, or curators) who deal on a daily basis with ephemera in its various forms. We are equally indebted to many private individuals, whether collectors or dealers, who opened their collections of ephemera to us. These kind persons include Mark Quilling, Rachel and Chuck Salloway, Mike Schwimmer, Rosemary Furtak, Adam Scher, Linda McShannock, Karen Nelson Hoyle, Julian G. Plante, Clark B. Hansen, Tim Johnson, Gregor Campbell, Wilber Schilling, Bill Stein, Thomas O'Sullivan, Bob Jackson, Peter Spooner, Sister Margery Smith, Rob Rulon-Miller, Terry DiNovo, Nancy Viking, Paul Hemple, Jan Bankey, Larry Dingman, Ernie Haemig, Barry Casselman, Eileen McCormack, Sandy Schwartzbauer, Edward Kukla, Adam Johnson, Jill Vetter, Nancy Cyr, Ellen S. Stuter, Elon J. Piche, Mark McManus, John W. Decker, Jack Kabrud, Michaeline Raymond, Glenn R. Wiessner, John Goplen, Sarah Harris, Steve Unverzagt, Priscilla Farnham, and Fred Foley.

Worthy of special mention are Todd Orjala, acquisitions editor at the University of Minnesota Press, who planted the seed from which this project resulted; Patrick Coleman, acquisitions librarian of the Minnesota Historical Society, whose wise counsel and great enthusiasm helped nurture the project; Floyd Risvold, who provided significant assistance with his impressive collections of American ephemera; the late Tom Reiersgord, postal historian extraordinaire; Paul "the paper man" Schoenecker, whose immense stock of paper ephemera opened our eyes to further topics for research; and Patty Dean, who opened the museum archives of the Minnesota Historical Society for us.

We are especially grateful to Roger Kennedy, museum administrator and historian, and Barry Casselman, writer, editor, and collector, whose fine essays begin our book. The subject, as we know, is huge, and we appreciate their thoughts and guidance.

Moira F. Harris
Leo J. Harris
St. Paul, Minnesota

Introduction

Minnesota on Paper: Collecting Our *Printed History* is about design and printing, advertising and collecting. Many printed paper items, ephemera, to give them their proper name, were not intended to last beyond an original one-time use. Once they had communicated their message, promoting a business or cause, or explaining a product, oblivion was their expected fate. But that was not always the case. Some items, for example, trade cards, poster stamps, *cartes de visite*, or postage stamps, were designed to be saved in albums.

Many items of printed ephemera were made in the thousands, and in the thousands they were discarded. Fortunately for anybody interested in social, business, or design history, at least some examples have been saved in both private and public collections. What follows is a look at some of the preserved treasures that we have discovered, items that were either produced in Minnesota or have a Minnesota connection. That is the geographic scope of our study; *Minnesota on Paper: Collecting Our Printed History* will additionally consider the Minnesota history and related popular culture necessary to fully understand the ephemera.

Ephemera has been the subject of scholarly examination and of museum exhibits, both internationally and in the United States.[1] There are collector societies that examine ephemera generally, such as the Ephemera Society of America, begun in 1980, or on a category by category basis. We are not aware, however, of any previous book to consider ephemera related only to a single state.

As can be expected, scholars have sorted paper ephemera into grand categories. We can simplify this list to four groups, based on their origin:

- Governmental (e.g., paper money, postage stamps, ballots, forms and receipts, security documents, notices and broadsides, etc.)
- The political process and patriotism (e.g., election campaign materials, posters, bumper stickers, badges, etc.)
- People, their rites of passage and associations (e.g., birth, marriage, and death announcements, programs, tickets, etc.)

- Advertising (e.g., products, services, tourism and business facilitation, bookseller promotion, playbills and programs, sheet music, menus, match covers, postcards, maps, letterheads, stationery, billheads, corner cards, etc.)

Note that all ephemera is not advertising, and all advertising is not printed paper ephemera. Bookplates and postage stamps fall into the non-advertising category, while that wonderful staple of Minnesota highways, the Burma-Shave sign, is printed or painted advertising yet it is not paper. So there are things to include and exclude, leaving, nonetheless, a long list of possible categories.

Human endeavor covers nearly infinite areas, and printed ephemera bears witness to them all. In this book we have selected categories of interest to us, categories that are visually significant and tell a story about Minnesota's past. This is not to say that there are not other categories of ephemera of equal or even greater importance. For example, we could have explored ephemera relating to organized sports, fishing and hunting, the professions, higher education, tourism, gambling, agriculture, mining, lumbering, the utilities, manufacturing, organized labor, and such destinations as zoos, museums, and carnivals. The fact that these are only hinted at or completely ignored means only that there is a lack of space, not a lack of interest. They can and should be addressed in a sequel to this work by other more energetic harvesters and writers.

An interesting recent exhibition showed how ephemera could be linked to one topic. Christian Peterson, associate curator of photography at the Minneapolis Institute of Art, realized that his department was rich in intriguing examples of ephemera. Letterheads of professional photographers, envelopes, postcards, advertisements on the backs of cartes de visite, trade catalogues, invitations to shows, and packets of camera lens tissues were among items on display in his show "Fabulous Photographic Ephemera" (2005). Minnesota ephemera included the work of photographers Norton & Peel of Minneapolis, the Lee Brothers of both St. Paul and Minneapolis, John Runk of Stillwater, and Kenneth Wright of St. Paul.

For each category of ephemera mentioned here, there is usually a beginning date and, often, a period that some would term its "Golden Age," during which the best examples were designed and produced. But even if a peak of achievement was reached, and collectors maintain that anything done later in time was in decline, printed ephemera continues to emerge.[2]

Often, but not always, collectors are lured by types of ephemera only when their use is curtailed and suddenly seems rare. Thus, although our study begins with ephemera prior to Minnesota's territorial days, there is no terminal date. Ephemera lives, and the most intriguing examples may yet be printed.

Change is significant in the field of ephemera. Blotters, for example, became extinct once the ballpoint pen replaced the fountain pen and its dripping ink. Bumper stickers were born only when automobiles were fitted out with bumpers. Matchbooks gave up most of their appeal when smoking lost its allure. Steamboat advertising materials disappeared when these vessels chugged into the sunset. Streetcar transfers, schedules, and related advertising were no longer needed when streetcars themselves vanished, although it might be argued that the new Minneapolis light rail system is a stepchild of the streetcar or tram, and may yet generate exciting ephemera. Among the newest pieces of ephemera are the PLU (price look-up numbers) stickers found on fresh fruit and vegetables. Recent ordinances banning smoking and allowing guns to be carried caused businesses to post signs declaring their premises smoke free and gun free. These signs will certainly become a new form of ephemera. Political ephemera, finally, gain new examples with each election. The problems in preserving such items were noted in a recent newspaper story about the October 7, 2003, gubernatorial recall election in California. Museum curators and archivists were faced with the challenge of saving representative ephemera from 135 candidates.[3] All of these changes, over time, are an important part of the story.

In short, for each category, we will when possible explore the reason for its creation and design, its historical and popular culture content and imagery, and finally, suggest the sources for its continued study.

However, we will make no attempt to determine value of the paper items described. Instead, our focus is on the items themselves, their content, their designers or printers, and the clients for whom they were made.

Aiding our search for Minnesota ephemera have been curators, collectors, and dealers. Ephemera research can be done in long-slumbering attics; facts can be uncovered in obscure newsletters, magazines, and newspapers. Some popular collecting fields—postage stamps, postcards, matchbooks, and calendars—have long attracted collectors. Collector groups name their fields of specialization. Those who study matchbooks call it phillumenology. The study of beer bottle labels becomes labelology, postcard collecting is deltiology, and collectors of Camembert cheese labels call their hobby tryroemiophily.[4] A person with a baggage label collection is an aerotelist. However, collecting is seldom strictly limited, so a bottle collector may be intrigued by a label or a philatelist by a postcard or a luggage tag. Clubs (and their newsletters, Web pages, and magazines) exist to support the specific interests of collectors. They offer camaraderie through meetings and conventions. In their magazines they exhibit or publish the new discoveries of collectors.

Other ephemera items find places within larger collecting areas. Beer labels, for example, are collected by many who also covet beer cans, bottles, and other forms of breweriana advertising. Noncollectors preserve ephemera by displaying it in their homes simply because the designs appeal to them. Magazine ads, calendar images, posters, and even labels may in this way serve as interior decorations. Thus ephemera, although considered to be an object of brief use, can often acquire longevity and permanence.

The same image may be found printed in several ways: on a calendar, postcard, playing card, blotter, or poster stamp. The Winold Reiss portraits of Blackfeet for the Great Northern Railroad are an example of this. A style of design familiar in one format may appear in another. For example, the large letter style of linen-look postcards found its way onto postage stamps in 2002 when the United States issued a sheet of fifty Greetings from America stamps. Each state name was set in large letter style against a background of appropriate images. A loon swam in Minnesota's lake design, with downtown Minneapolis behind the state name.

Two frequent ephemera subjects are unique to Minnesota. One is Minnehaha Falls, with its once awesome cascade, sometimes showcasing either Hiawatha or Minnehaha. The Falls of St. Anthony, wider, shorter, yet many times more important to the economic development of the state, has never rated a similar amount of artistic interest. Both falls were common destinations for Minnesota's explorers, tourists, travel essayists, and painters. St. Anthony Falls, crossed by bridges and harnessed by a dam, appealed with its sense of power. Minnehaha Falls, less transformed, retained its beauty and romance thanks to Henry Wadsworth Longfellow's "Song of Hiawatha." Another subject is Charles A. Lindbergh of Little Falls. Lindbergh

MINNE-HA-HA.
"Here the Falls of Minne-ha-ha,
Flash and gleam among the oak trees,
Laugh and leap into the valley."

WHITNEY'S GALLERY. SAINT PAUL

Cartes de visite were small photographs mounted on cardboard, which sometimes carried advertising messages on the reverse side. Subjects could be individuals, landscapes, or streetscapes. Joel Whitney, Minnesota's pioneer photographer, produced over twenty views of Minnehaha Falls from different angles and in various seasons. Courtesy of Clark Hansen.

The back cover of A Guide for Immigrants *(1857) carried advertisements for two important St. Paul businesses: R. F. Slaughter, a real estate agent, and the Pioneer & Democrat, steam printers, who printed the* St. Paul Pioneer *newspaper. Courtesy of Rob Rulon-Miller.*

became an instant hero and lifelong celebrity after he completed his New York to Paris flight in 1927. He, and his airplane, The Spirit of St. Louis, were featured on myriad forms of paper ephemera, usually without Lindbergh's involvement or approval. The state's Great Seal is yet another common element found in ephemera designs. Paul Bunyan, the storied figure who logs his way through the myths and ephemera of various northern forests, isn't strictly Minnesotan, however, despite his frequent use.

One of the earliest forms of advertising ephemera for Minnesota involved the campaign to encourage settlement. Emigrant guides, published in English, German, and Swedish, were widely circulated. Land was available nearly everywhere; the soil was rich, the timber plentiful. Just come, the guidebooks begged and, especially in the boom years of the 1850s, the emigrants did.

Once the emigrants arrived, the printing press followed. There were newspapers to be published, but also an enormous quantity of official documents and ephemeral items to be printed. At least one man had the foresight to suggest that those unofficial bits of ephemera be preserved. Thus, the first librarian of the Minnesota Historical Society, J. Fletcher Williams, begged members to save and donate these artifacts of history:

The Minnesota Historical Society

Again begs leave to call to the attention of its members and friends, to the importance of saving and collecting for it

Everything of a Printed Nature,

which they do not care to preserve, such as pamphlets of all kinds, documents, reports of institutions, catalogues, magazines, religious or political addresses and essays, almanacs, old city directories, and all other publications of that ephemeral nature, such as are usually

Thrown into the Waste Basket,

or cast aside or got rid of, as of no value. Most, if not all such publications (especially those relating to this State,) although not prized now, will become very scarce in a few years, and valuable for many reasons, if preserved in the manner we are trying to do, classified and bound,

And Kept for Reference and Use.

We therefore request our friends to save and send us every thing of this kind which they can spare, or (if in the city) notify us that the same are at our disposal, and they will be sent for.

—J. F. Williams Librarian[5]

What Mr. Williams suggested has long been an appropriate course of action, so it is probably thanks to his wise advice that a great deal of Minnesota ephemera exists in collections.

Throughout the book the names of collectors appear, and the question could be posed, Who collects and why? Maurice Rickards, himself a collector, wrote about early "ephemerists" in his *Collecting Printed Ephemera*.[6] To most people, Samuel Pepys is known for his diary, but he is known in ephemera circles as somebody who saved examples of printing from businesses within walking distance of his home. What Pepys preserved was not only specialized but, like this book, an attempt to celebrate the local.

Rickards's collection is now housed in the Centre for Ephemera Studies at the University of Reading. The collection was the basis for his *Encyclopedia of Ephemera* (2000), which was completed after his death by Michael Twyman, who was assisted by Sarah du Boscq de Beaumont and Amoret Tanner. The Rickards examples and the John Johnson Collection in the Bodleian Library (Oxford) are two of the finest and most extensive British ephemera collections.

Two of the most important and influential American ephemera collectors were Bella Landauer and Jackson Burdick. Mrs. Landauer began by collecting bookplates; Mr. Burdick started with cards inserted into cigarette packages. Both preserved many other types and examples, wrote about them, and donated their collections to public institutions.

Michael Twyman, director emeritus of the University of Reading's Centre for Ephemera Studies, wrote that women amateur collectors often preserved ephemera in scrapbooks, along with much else related to their own lives.[7] Such scrapbooks are often donated to local historical societies. The McLeod County Historical Society (in Hutchinson) has a large collection of such scrapbooks and is attempting to catalogue their contents to make the ephemera useful to researchers. A second category noted by Twyman includes the workbooks kept by printers, businesses, or government agencies. The latter often contained, for example, product labels accumulated for trademark protection. As Twyman notes, such workbooks were often jettisoned when firms closed, moved, or merged. Fortunately, some of these records do exist in archives and in a few museums that have been opened by the businesses themselves, such as that of the Watkins Company in Winona or the Hormel Company's Spam Museum in Austin.

Minnesota collectors we have met include Elon Piche, who became interested in railroad materials because he had once worked for the Great Northern. Several breweriana collectors began by saving advertising items from the breweries where they worked, so the job-related collection is not unusual. Another collector saves paintings and ephemera that have images of Minnehaha Falls because, like Samuel Pepys and his London material, the Falls are near to this collector's home. Fred Foley, whose huge collection of flour milling artifacts is displayed on the walls of his Copper Dome Pancake House, began his search with flour bags. Foley told a reporter, "I thought flour bags would look good on the walls of a pancake house. Once I started, I fell in love with history. It's become an obsession."[8] Some St. Paul Winter Carnival collectors began saving the buttons or medallions that were issued each year and then expanded by seeking paper ephemera, costumes, and much more. Other collec-

tors had marched in the Carnival parades or taken part as Carnival royalty, so they saved items from their special years.

Many collectors trade or sell duplicates from their collections at club meetings. Most of the large exhibits selling antiques and much else, held at county and state fairgrounds, have paper ephemera dealers; however, except for postcards and philately, ephemera is seldom displayed or organized as we had hoped. One woman at an antiques show who had albums of trade cards simply threw up her hands at our request. Her specialty albums held cards with cats, dogs, cute children, or holidays, but no album was reserved for Minnesota material. Another dealer who specializes in paper ephemera, "Paul the Paper Man," aided our search immeasurably with knowledge he had gained as an employee of the Louis F. Dow printing firm.

Early in our research a holiday trip to France suggested what a localized study of ephemera could be. The French city of Lyon has a long history as a printing center, boasts an institute devoted to the history of the book, and maintains a fine printing museum. That museum had acquired the archives of several local job printers and, in 2001, mounted an exhibit called "Ephemera. Les imprimés de tous les jours. 1880–1939." Invitations, posters, labels, stationery, bookplates, and mourning envelopes were on display, along with an explanation of relevant printing techniques, all revealing the manners, customs, and history of Lyon. Inspired by the Lyon exhibit, we returned to investigate the tale of printed ephemera in Minnesota.

CHAPTER ONE

Who Made Ephemera?

Discussing printed paper ephemera without considering those who designed and produced it would be a mistake. Thus we begin with a look at Minnesota printers, commercial artists, and agencies who devised advertising campaigns to use these printed ephemera pieces.

Printing as Gutenberg or Caxton or even Benjamin Franklin knew it would not have seemed strange to Minnesota printers circa 1850. Within the next few decades, lithography, chromolithography, and photomechanical means of reproduction would test the skills of local printers and transform and widen the nature of printed ephemera.

The printing industry has played an important part in Minnesota history and economic life. This certainly is due in part to its abundant natural resources, such as forests and waters. These resources made the production of paper products feasible. And as Minnesota flour mills, breweries, and railroad companies grew and sought markets beyond the local borders, many forms of paper advertising were soon required, and printers were quick to produce them. As a result of these factors the Minnesota printing industry is said to rank among the ten most important nationally.

The Printers

When James Madison Goodhue boarded a steamboat bound for St. Paul in 1849, printing, both of newspapers and of commercial jobs, was about to begin. Goodhue, born in New Hampshire in 1810, educated at Amherst College, and trained as a lawyer, had previously found employment as editor of the *Grant County Herald* in Lancaster, Wisconsin. But the new territory of Minnesota beckoned with a vision of new opportunities. So Goodhue ordered a press and type, and arrived at St. Paul's lower landing aboard the *Senator* on April 18, 1849.[9] Ten days later the initial issue of the *Minnesota Pioneer* appeared; it was the first newspaper ever printed in Minnesota Territory.

Goodhue proved to be an energetic and enthusiastic immigrant whose "bright and glowing pictures of life in the new Territory" attracted many others to settle.[10] "His journal," wrote J. Fletcher Williams, "was an institution inseparably connected with the word Minnesota." His illness and death in 1852 were thus a great loss to the community. Goodhue's newspaper, in the hands of Joseph R. Brown and then Joseph Wheelock, survived his death, as did his commercial printing venture. Through mergers and consolidations, the *Minne-*

sota Pioneer (now the *St. Paul Pioneer Press*) became the city's principal newspaper; Pioneer Printing is the oldest component of the Banta Corporation, a conglomerate printing firm headquartered in Wisconsin.

Before turning to the subsequent history of printing in Minnesota, a word should be written about the printing press that Goodhue brought to Minnesota in 1849. Writing about the early history of printing in Minnesota, Mamie R. Martin stated that the Goodhue press was a Washington hand-press built in Cincinnati in 1836.[11] It was purchased by the new proprietors of *The Visitor* (Iowa's first newspaper, located in Dubuque). From Dubuque the press was sold to Goodhue's newspaper in Lancaster in 1842. Seven years later Goodhue took the press north. Later in its long life it would be used in Sauk Rapids, in Sauk Centre, and in Lindstrom, with a change of languages, to print the *Medborgaren*, a Swedish-language journal, in 1897.[12] Eight years later the *Pioneer Press* purchased the press and gave it to the Minnesota Historical Society.[13] By 1909 the *Minnesota Pioneer* had absorbed many of its rivals, including the *Daily Press*, the *Daily News*, the *Daily Minnesotian* and, finally, the *Dispatch* in 1938.[14] In the course of time its name changed, becoming the *St. Paul Pioneer Press*.

During Goodhue's brief tenure as newspaper publisher he printed books and served, in 1850, as printer for the territorial government. Marjorie Kreidberg, writing about early Minnesota printers, commented that "public printing might have

An early printing press, manufactured by the Hoe Company, and used by the Pioneer Press Company. Courtesy of Banta Corporation.

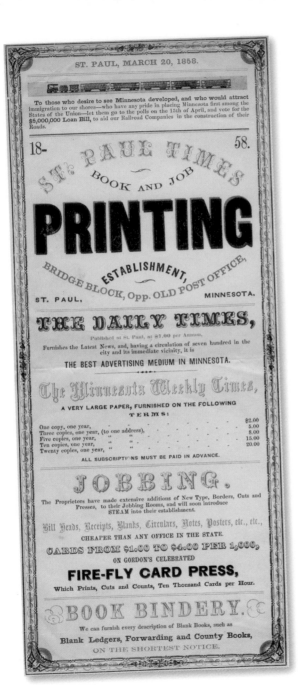

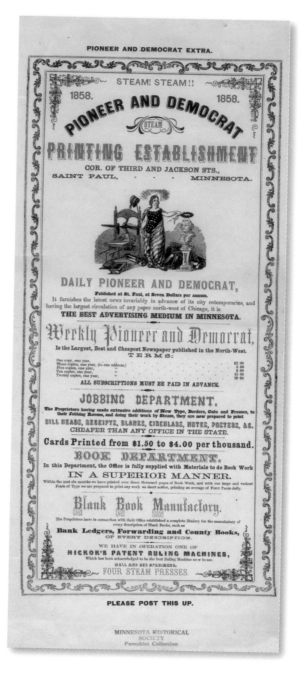

been the 'loaves and the fishes,' but job printing was undoubtedly the 'meat and potatoes' on most printers' tables. The major providers were early Minnesota business establishments, religious, educational, community and social groups, and the work of a few writer-publishers."[15]

The *St. Paul Times* used a broadside, dated March 20, 1858, to list their daily and weekly newspapers; the billheads, receipts, circulars, and posters they could print; and their services as a book bindery. This broadside, like that for the *Pioneer & Democrat* for the same year, not only showed what could be printed but used some of the decorative, ornamental borders, fonts, and stock images they had available to make any printed item more attractive.

Surveying the field of job printing in the Twin Cities during the decade after the Civil War, Robert Staehlin noted that 68 percent of the work was accomplished by five companies: Johnson & Smith and the Tribune firms in Minneapolis and Pioneer Printing, Press Printing, and David Ramaley in St. Paul. Only Johnson & Smith and David Ramaley were not also newspaper publishers.[16]

As the flyer for Ramaley, Chaney & Company indicates, this firm printed the entire gamut of business stationery as well as railroad timetables. David Ramaley was another early arrival in Minnesota, coming from Pittsburgh in 1855. Before founding his own firm in 1863, he worked as a reporter and editor on the *St. Paul Pioneer*. With H. P. Hall he published the *St. Paul Evening Dispatch* from 1868 to 1871 before returning to job printing.[17]

Fred L. Smith was born in Maine in 1843 and came to St. Anthony at the age of fourteen. An early

An 1872 rate card and calendar for Ramaley, Chaney & Co., specialist in commercial job printing. The opportunities for printers to specialize in many forms of business printing had grown as quickly as the transportation industry. By 1872 eight railroad lines served St. Paul. Courtesy of the Minnesota Historical Society (Museum collections).

Card showing views of West Publishing Company's St. Paul headquarters alongside the Mississippi River. The company moved to Eagan in 1992. Courtesy of the Minnesota Historical Society (Museum collections).

job was to serve as a newsboy for that town's *Falls Evening News.* He later worked for the *Pioneer* in St. Paul before beginning a commercial printing plant, the first in Minneapolis, in 1871. Smith's partners in this venture were Colonel C. W. Johnson, city editor of the *Tribune,* and Lewis Harrison. The firm would be known as Harrison & Smith for most of its history. A seventy-fifth anniversary publication noted that among their customers had been the First National Bank, General Mills, Cream of Wheat, Bemis Bro. Bag Company, Janney Semple Hill, and Munsingwear (for whom they printed the sets of Munsingwear paper dolls).[18]

By the end of the nineteenth century the job printers and the newspaper publishers had begun to separate and specialize. The printers who once advertised their ability to print everything from letterheads to news sheets and books reduced their lists. Those who printed books were known as publishers. Bookbinders could be separate firms or departments of the presses. Some early bookbinders' marks are found in the following chapter.

One early bookbinder was Peter J. Giesen who came to St. Paul from Cologne, Germany, in 1851. He worked as a printer on the *Minnesota Pioneer* before joining David Ramaley in a bookbinding venture. A major client was West Publishing, which had

specialized in law books since its establishment in 1872. Eventually the Giesen-Ramaley firm was purchased by West. Giesen would later become president of the German language newspaper, *Die Volkszeitung.*[19]

As the careers of men such as Ramaley, Smith, and Giesen suggest, working on the *Minnesota Pioneer* and the *St. Paul Pioneer* was part of many printers' careers. Later, job printing firms themselves proved to be a useful training ground as Harvey Blodgett recalled in a 1944 speech. Blodgett's firm began as Brown and Treacy in 1881. The Brown was Hiram Brown, whose loan of funds and name helped a printing salesman from Iowa to start another business. As Blodgett put it, "early in the nineties a young man appeared in our office and introduced himself as Herbert H. Bigelow. He said he wanted to start a calendar business.... Mr. Brown took a shine to Bigelow and the upshot was

Invitation to a Brown & Bigelow party for employees, 1928.
Courtesy of the authors.

the firm of Brown & Bigelow. On Brown's death [in 1904], Bigelow succeeded to the interest, but wisely kept the name, as we have done in our business. There has been no Brown money in either business for about 40 years." [20]

Brown & Bigelow grew to be one of the nation's largest producers of calendars. As part of its Remembrance Advertising program, the firm printed postcards, poster stamps, blotters, playing cards, and greeting cards. Logically, a company anniversary would rate an attractively printed card.

Lithography was invented in Germany by Alois Senefelder in 1796, but did not appear in the United States until 1835, and did not come in to widespread use until about 1850. Senefelder's famous technique made use of limestone blocks from his

region of Bavaria and their ability, when wet, to resist ink. The image was drawn on the stone with a lithographic crayon, fixed with an acid solution, moistened, then inked with a single color. Each color needed a separate stone, as many as seventeen for a chromolithograph of Eastman Johnson's painting *Barefoot Boy.*[21]

Chromolithography was used for printing trade cards, posters, and point-of-purchase materials while billheads, invoices, and other business stationery would be printed by one-color lithography. More than one image could appear on a lithographic stone, and images could be ground off when no longer needed. Printers stored their stones in specially built shelves with the job number visible. When commercial lithography was replaced by newer technologies the stones were discarded. Some became patio pavers while other stones, according to rumor, joined more plebian rocks underneath the street paving of downtown Minneapolis.

Writing about printing in Wisconsin, Alan E. Kent notes that lithography began in Milwaukee with the arrival of Henry Seifert in 1851. Seifert would later be joined by Julius Gugler.[22] Both the Gugler name and that of William Berlandi appear on labels created for Minnesota breweries.

In Minnesota, men with lithographic training

arrived slightly later. Isador Monasch, another German, established his lithography business in Minneapolis in 1868. A 1910 article about this firm noted that they did color work for the milling companies and produced the advertising cards used inside the Lake Minnetonka–bound streetcars.[23] The Monasch firm was acquired by Brown & Treacy in 1892.

In his 1944 talk Harvey Blodgett commented that early lithographic work in St. Paul was handled by the H. M. Smyth firm, founded in 1877. Frederick Henry Warnick, who joined Smyth in 1886, was regarded as St. Paul's Father of Lithography. He was probably involved in producing the sheet music covers and programs that Smyth printed

Lithographic workshop, 1900–1915. The stones are filed in slots against the wall. On the table next to the bearded workman is a stone ready to use. Under his arm is a bucket of water used to cleanse the ink from the stones after printing. Courtesy of Banta Corporation.

A printer could place more than one image on a lithographic stone, as these cuts for different businesses illustrate. The X indicates that the images were no longer needed, and the stone could be ground down for reuse. Courtesy of the Minnesota Historical Society (Museum collections).

Two lithographers at work, 1900–1915. Note the beer poster on the back wall, as well as calendars and portraits, all of which they may have prepared. Courtesy of Banta Corporation.

Poster with examples of beer, liquor, and soft drink labels lithographed by the Pioneer Press Company, circa 1900. Courtesy of Banta Corporation.

for the first St. Paul Winter Carnival in 1886. Smyth would later become a specialist in food and beverage labels produced for such Minnesota firms as Hormel, Green Giant, and the Summit brewery.

As noted above, the nineteenth century witnessed the beginnings of the printing industry in Minnesota. Men with handpresses opened businesses offering job printing alongside weekly and daily newspaper production. Toward the end of the century, firms began to specialize. The following decades and the next century would witness growth and consolidation. The firm begun by Charles McGill and Eli Warner in St. Paul in 1897 purchased the Pioneer Press of St. Paul in 1909 and Cootey, Blodgett of Minneapolis in 1912. Cootey, Blodgett had developed out of Isador Monasch's firm, first acquired by Brown & Treacy. Thomas Cootey was manager and then part owner; Harvey Blodgett was an early partner. In 1907 Cootey, Blodgett acquired one of the first offset lithographic presses in the country, another important technical advance in production. Later investors and owners of McGill-Warner were Donald McNeely (1953), Norman B. Mears (1963), and Frank Beddor (1976). Eventually McGill-Warner (then owned by Frank Beddor) merged with the George Banta Printing Company in 1988.

The Banta Corporation, a Wisconsin firm founded in Menasha in 1901, could thus claim to be the oldest continuous business in the state of Minnesota, the first to publish a newspaper (Goodhue's *Pioneer*), and the first to have a department of lithography west of Chicago. Banta printed university and college catalogues, academic journals, and specialty magazines. It now publishes direct marketing pieces and catalogues for Betty Crocker and Home Depot.

While larger Minnesota companies often had art or design departments, printing was not usually accomplished in-house, except in Winona. From the early years until 1988, the J. R. Watkins Company maintained its own print shop, "the largest west of Chicago," according to a researcher for the W.P.A. guide to Minnesota. The former print shop now houses the Watkins Heritage Museum.

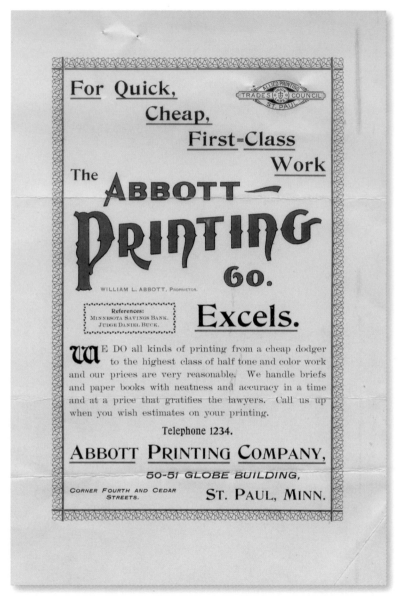

Flyer for the Abbott Printing Company. The logo on the upper-right corner clearly indicates it is a union shop. Courtesy of the Minnesota Historical Society (Museum collections).

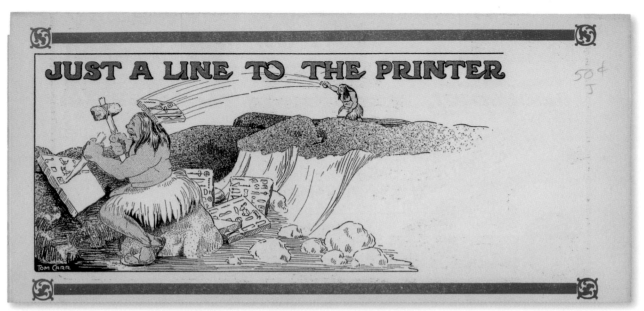

A folder from Carr Engraving Company of St. Paul displayed a number of company logos and name plates that they created for media advertising, circa 1915. Courtesy of the Minnesota Historical Society (Museum collections).

On the back of a puzzle, Louis Dow placed his own advertisement for novelties and "goodwill advertising." The Dow firm opened in 1900. Courtesy of Glenn Wiessner.

Other printers advertised their specialties in different ways. Louis F. Dow's message stressed novelties. On the reverse side was a puzzle. The Abbott Printing Company did legal printing and gave its union "bug" a prominent place. Carr Engraving specialized in logos and company nameplates. These are all displayed in a folder whose cover showed a caveman hammering symbols into a clay tablet.

As printers and publishers went their separate ways, sometimes both continued to use the word *press* in their names. A look at the title page of a book will reveal the publisher such as the University of Minnesota Press, while the printer may be noted, such as Lund Press or North Central Publishing, may be noted on the following page.

The development of the computer would also change many aspects of both the printer's and publisher's work. Today an author often submits a manuscript to the publisher electronically. After editing is completed, the electronic file goes to the printer. Graphic artists who design book covers and jackets and the professionals who plan the layout of books and magazines all use computers. This has also made it possible for individuals to self-publish books using their home computers and for copy shops to produce the books. Firms have recently entered this field to offer what is known as the print-on-demand book.

The computer also plays its part in producing many forms of ephemera seen in this book. Invitations, programs, funeral notices, and newsletters that might once have been taken to the job printer

WHO MADE EPHEMERA?

go directly from home computer to copy shop. For those willing to receive such communications on their computers rather than by mail, notices and invitations come by e-mail. There, in the computer owner's e-mail in-box, they must be sorted from the many commercial messages that have been received. These commercial messages have long been known, unfortunately, by the name of Hormel's canned meat, Spam.

In addition to changes in type and design, today's ephemera is often printed on vinyl rather than paper. Peel-off decals for car windows, bumper stickers, and political stickers (used instead of buttons) are now rather common, as are vinyl shopping bags.

Typefaces

Every early printer needed a variety of type specimens for his work. Printing salesmen would use books with their firms' type specimens shown in the different fonts available, followed by assortments of decorative borders and other ornaments. As Alastair Johnston pointed out in his delightful study of printing sample books, *Alphabets to Order* (2000), printers tired of using only the alphabet to show off the typefaces. Instead they used fragments of poetry and prose, sometimes making critical comments in these examples. A sample book used by McGill-Warner salesmen contains these brief statements, ostensibly showing off types and font sizes:

Famous Books are based on facts (Antique, 30pt)

Zanzibar's merchants are (Caslon light, 36 pt)
In the future will there be $? (Swing bold)
Puddles Never Have been Wetter, nor Chuck Holes (Sans Serif bold)[24]

A very new typeface recently won a contest devised by the University of Minnesota Design Institute. Called Twin, this "morphing" typeface is intended to change according to the weather. Twin has three typographic traits: formal with serifs, informal with rounded letters, and weird with a variety of unusually shaped letters. How the typeface appears depends not, as it would have a century or more ago, on the nimble fingers of the printer, but instead on the weather. Cold weather will bring the formal letters while nice and warm temperatures (in the Twin Cities) bring rounded shapes. Twin was created by Erik van Blokland and Just van Rossum of Letterror, a Dutch design firm, and can be seen at the Design Institute's Web site (design.umn.edu).[25]

Frederick Goudy, the famous type designer who once worked in Minneapolis, wrote that for printing, the typeface used must be appropriate. "The printing of a mere advertisement or a simple narrative should no more be given the form or treatment of an epic poem or dignified essay than a farmhouse should be built to look like a city mansion, or a cottage be given the air and character of an ornate villa."[26] Goudy, whose *Typologia* used a typeface which he designed for the University of California, might have been amused that the University of Minnesota selected a typeface affected by weather, which so concerns Minnesotans, and he probably would have been astonished at the concept of a morphing typeface.

The Advertising Agency and Art Training

A current telephone directory of Minneapolis and St. Paul businesses lists six pages of advertising agencies. Some create advertisements, while others specialize in direct mail, Internet advertising, outdoor advertising (billboards), and promotional materials. Printed paper advertising, like so much of the ephemera in this book, is now created by hundreds of practitioners whose specialties did not exist before relatively recent times. Nationally, Juliann Sivulka writes, the first advertising agent was Volney Palmer, who opened his business in Philadelphia in 1843.[27] It would be fifty years before a similar firm operated in St. Paul, opened by an entrepreneur named William L. Banning Jr.

Early advertising often consisted of a block of type set off by decorative fonts in columns of the local newspapers. A business that needed more space—to promote land sales or boat trips, for example—might obtain a partial news sheet, or broadside. In either case the message was created by the client with the assistance of the printer. The first advertising agents soon realized that they could profitably serve as middlemen, buying the newspaper space, subdividing it into smaller blocks, and then creating the texts to fill the spaces.

When the Banning firm moved its offices in 1896, it notified clients by postcard of its ability to place advertising in any newspaper or periodical, anywhere.[28] Until the 1890s, when Minnesota firms needed trade cards, posters, or calendars in color, they would order their supplies from printing houses elsewhere in the country. At that time, when newspapers and job printers did not print in color, the chromolithographic process gave a few specialized printing houses the option of preparing color-rich advertising handouts. Early illustrations were often taken from a printer's stock imagery, at least until lithography became widespread. Then a lithographed view of the firm's place of business could be used in a newspaper advertisement, as letterhead stationery, on invoices, or as a page in a city directory.

William L. Banning Jr. ran St. Paul's first advertising agency on Wabasha street, until 1896. The blue word IDEAS superimposed across the façade of their premises and a small blue printing press logo suggests the firm's ability to prepare advertising materials for use by newspapers and magazines. Courtesy of Fred Foley.

Later advertising agencies would coordinate print, radio, point-of-sale, and television advertising for their clients. Notable Minnesota advertising agencies such as Campbell Mithun; Fallon Worldwide; and Miller Meester Advertising, all began operations during the twentieth century. Campbell Mithun, founded in 1933, noted in a fiftieth anniversary pamphlet that three of its original clients, Land O' Lakes, Northwest Airlines, and Andersen Windows, remained their accounts.[29]

One of the earliest Minneapolis advertising agencies was that of Mac Martin, founded in 1904. Although the founders of many agencies were known for their skills as writers, Martin's strength was as an artist. Martin's firm, known as Erwin, Wasey & Company after 1931, prepared newspaper and magazine advertising for such companies as the Eagle Roller Mill of New Ulm and its Daniel Webster flour, the J. R. Watkins Company of Winona, the Cream of Wheat Company, and the Federal School of Commercial Designing.[30]

Mac Martin's advertising agency, and other early agencies, had staff artists, but before these firms were organized most commercial artists were em-

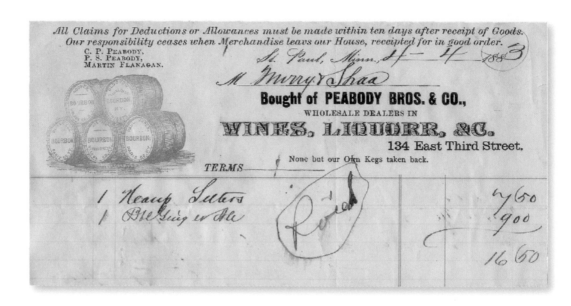

Printers worldwide face criticism for failure to proofread their products carefully enough. This 1883 invoice has two spelling errors. *Courtesy of the authors.*

ployed by printers. One local printer, the Bureau of Engraving, established in 1898 in Minneapolis, discovered that artists it trained were often hired away by other printers. Accordingly, the Bureau of Engraving decided to make artist training available for a fee, thus creating a unique, new profit center. What was first known as the Federal School of Commercial Designing opened in 1914. (It became known as Art Instruction Schools after 1941.) An undated sixty-two-page booklet entitled *Your Future* explained the purpose of the Federal School and its organization and told the success stories of several graduates and teachers.[31]

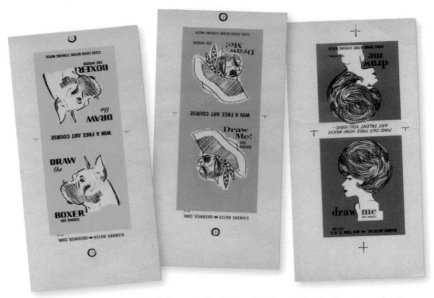

Prototypes for the "Draw Me!" matchbooks. Courtesy of Art Instruction Schools.

The Federal School's advertising offered prizes to those who copied a drawing. These line drawings could be of a woman's head, the profile face of a cute animal with a friendly name, a clown, or a pirate. Steve Unverzagt, current director of marketing, said that which drawing was selected depended on the magazine or newspaper used. The most familiar "Draw Me" girls appeared in women's magazines. The animals were used in wildlife or outdoor publications, and the pirate found his way into comic books. Those who sent in the "Draw Me" coupons were eligible for prizes and scholarships.

The Federal School also used matchbooks to carry this message, but for less than a decade. For ephemera collectors, these matchbooks are highly collectible Minnesota printed paper items. The "Draw Me" girls, whose hair styles changed with the times, the animals, GIs in helmets, cars, and animals all appeared on the front panels of matchbooks. The coupon was printed inside. It is claimed that more than three million of these "Draw Me" invitations on different-colored matchbooks were prepared by the Diamond Match Company through the 1960s.

"Draw Me! Try for a Free Art Course," read the text. Winners would learn through submitting work by mail that would be returned with the critiques of the faculty. Students who enrolled in the course were expected to take two years to complete their lessons. The art school had no campus. It was, instead, an early and successful example of distance learning.[32] The faculty included C. L. "Bart" Bartholomew (the *Minneapolis Journal*'s cartoonist), Edward Brewer (known for his Cream of Wheat and Winchester Arms Company advertising illustrations), Frederick D. Calhoun, and Mac Martin. Brewer wrote a small booklet, *Composing an Advertising Illustration* (1918), for the school, according to Patricia C. Johnson, who discussed the artist's career in an article.[33] Calhoun received his training at the University of Minnesota, the Minneapolis School of Fine Arts (MSFA), and the Art Students League. He exhibited his work as a painter and worked as a commercial artist for both Mac Martin's firm and the Bureau of Engraving. For over twenty-five years he taught at the MSFA (now the

WHO MADE EPHEMERA?

Minneapolis College of Art and Design, or MCAD). Mac Martin taught the Federal School course on booklet and catalogue construction.[34] In addition to his agency work and teaching, he was involved in founding professional groups such as the Advertising Forum.

Many of the men and women who undertook the challenge of "Draw Me" became commercial artists, hired by printers and companies such as Brown & Bigelow and Red Wing Pottery. Artists included Neysa McMein (creator of the first Betty Crocker image in 1936), cartoonists (such as Charles Schulz), or wildlife specialists such as Les Kouba or David Maass. For Arnold Friberg, whose portraits of red-jacked Canadian Mounties graced years of Northwest Paper Company calendars, art training via the Federal School's program began at the early age of fourteen.[35]

Your Future emphasized that art training could lead to jobs with commercial art studios; advertising agencies; book, newspaper, and magazine publishers; and lithographers. "This is truly an age of pictures," the unknown author of *Your Future* wrote, noting that the future of advertising in all of these aspects was assured. It was a field with equal opportunities for women.[36] Women would do fashion illustrations for newspapers and magazines and design greeting cards. The only woman mentioned in *Your Future* was Neysa McMein, but women active in Twin Cities commercial art at that time included Mary Moulton Cheney and Alice Hugy.

For specialized advertising involving product labeling and package design, two Minnesota firms used the talents of Chicago's Leo Burnett. The first was the Minnesota Valley Canning Company of LeSueur. That company had developed a giant as a trademark for their large-sized peas, but the first drawings of him for print advertising showed a fierce and quite grim character better suited for Grimm's Fairy Tales. Leo Burnett, then working for Erwin Wasey & Company, made the Giant stand tall and gave him a healthy, happier face. Seven years later Burnett opened his own agency and the Jolly Green Giant became his continuing responsibility. The canning company became known as the Green Giant Company in 1950 and is now a part of General Mills.

Poppin' Fresh, the Pillsbury Doughboy, was another creation of the Burnett agency, imagined by creative director Rudy Perz in 1965. The Doughboy, like the Jolly Green Giant, was part of television commercials, happily giggling when his tummy was poked. Both brand icons were also available as toys, continuing the tradition of marketing to children and families which was begun by flour millers in the nineteenth century.

In 1999 *Advertising Age* selected its ten top advertising images for the twentieth century. The Marlboro Man headed the list, with the Jolly Green Giant (in third place), Betty Crocker (as the fourth), and the Pillsbury Doughboy (as the sixth).[37] Due to the merger of General Mills with the Pillsbury Company, all three of these celebrated Minnesota brand icons are now part of the same company.[38]

CHAPTER TWO

Ex Libris

WHILE BOOKS THEMSELVES ARE NOT PART of the world of ephemera, a bookseller's mark, a bookplate, a bookbinder's mark, a bookmark, or even the publisher's prospectus certainly are. Marks and plates document the history of a book throughout its ownership, as it passes from publisher to bookseller, to bookbinder, and then to book collector or library. Bookplates have long been collected. Their collectors have national organizations and publications. Those interested in the books themselves find colleagues in the Manuscript Society of Minnesota, the Ampersand Club, and the various Friends groups who support public, academic, and private libraries throughout the state.

The Book Prospectus

Book publishers use the prospectus as one means of promotion. In a typical prospectus the contents of the book, its premise, and its value to readers are all stated. The author's credentials and praise for his previous works are usually noted. The prospectus is often the place to showcase prepublication comments or endorsements, now commonly called blurbs, by scholars or authorities in the field. The early prospectus, whether sent by mail or made available in the bookstore, customarily offered a special price to induce an advance purchase. In a typical prospectus books were touted as entertaining, interesting, original, and cheap, something that could be "Read at Home, On the Steamboat, Or in the Car," as Edward D. Neill's *Dakotah Land and Dakotah Life* was described.

Some early Minnesota guidebooks for "immigrants, invalids, capitalists and businessmen" sought advertisements to help pay the costs of publication. For J. W. McClung's *Minnesota as It Is* (1868), advertisers were offered prospectus space at rates from five to thirty dollars per page.

A prospectus circulated in advance of publication might also affect other books being completed. In the introduction to his 1876 history of St. Paul, J. Fletcher Williams wrote that he had spent ten years compiling information for what was intended

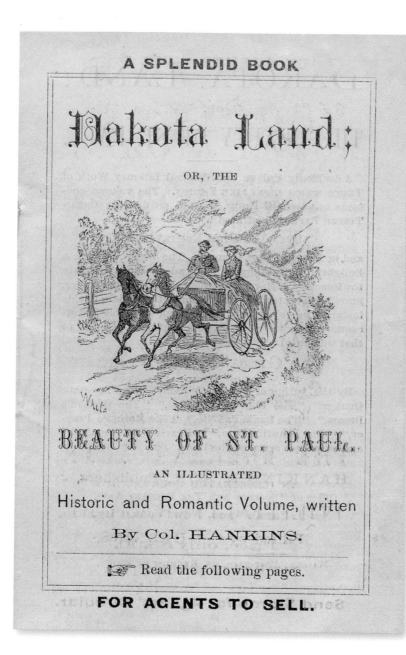

A SPLENDID BOOK

Dakota Land;

OR, THE

BEAUTY OF ST. PAUL.

AN ILLUSTRATED

Historic and Romantic Volume, written

By Col. HANKINS.

☞ Read the following pages.

FOR AGENTS TO SELL.

A prospectus for a 460-page book about St. Paul, with over 100 illustrations and a map. Dakota Land was published in New York in 1868. Courtesy of Patrick Coleman.

to be a pamphlet but became a book. He planned to include more biographies of early settlers, but decided to omit them since a "Historical Atlas" had superseded his work, "and quite recently the city has been flooded with the circulars of publishers from abroad, proposing to issue more works of that kind. In the face of such schemes, any legitimate work, purely in the interest of history, and *not* for profit, has but little chance of success, and I was compelled to forego much of what I had hoped to secure."[39]

For any book on Minnesota history published during his lifetime, approving words from Theodore Blegen, the dean of Minnesota historians, were a necessity for a publisher's prospectus. Other reviewers in the past century whose encomiums would encourage the sale of a book included local critics such as James Gray or John T. Sherman.

Booksellers' Marks

Booksellers' marks are advertising stickers. One of the tiniest versions of printed ephemera, they typically include the name of the selling firm, its address, and occasionally further identifying information. Booksellers used their marks as advertising on books, sheet music, maps, printing, and stationery. Normally the booksellers' marks were applied to the book's endpapers.

Since the middle 1700s, booksellers' marks have been a customary form of printed advertising in the bookstore world. Tiny, less than two inches generally, and found in die cut circles, rectangles, or even in the shape of miniature books, many booksellers' marks come in vivid colors. Booksellers' marks are occasionally printed on foil or even embossed or rubber-stamped. A Minneapolis bookseller, Larry Dingman, lists twenty-seven different marks from eight different Minnesota cities in his seminal book.[40] Today such marks have nearly vanished, replaced either by computer-generated stickers or generic bookmarks bearing a store's name and logo.

Bookbinders' Marks

Bookbinders' marks, mostly from the earliest days of Minnesota statehood, are elusive and rare. Few bookbinders who specialize in the restoration of old and rare books are active today. One, however, is the Campbell-Logan Bindery, run by three generations of the same family. Located in the Minneapolis warehouse district, "it's one of the few commercial binderies in the nation that still do things the old-fashioned way."[41]

Minnesota's booksellers placed these small advertising stickers in the books they sold, whether new or used. Courtesy of Larry Dingman.

Early printers offered bookbinding services as well. This mark for the Press Printing Company is found in a volume dated 1860. Courtesy of Rob Rulon-Miller.

Bookmarks and Other Giveaways

Printed bookmarks are offered by most bookstores today to their customers. These strips of thin cardboard may note a shop's address or business hours and areas of specialization. In addition, bookmarks often contain a logo, a book-related design, or an appropriate literary quotation.

Bookmarks are also used by libraries to indicate their rules or hours and by publishers to market their new book titles. Earlier bookmarks often have a ribbon or bit of yarn attached to make it easier to locate the bookmark, and the place of the reader in the book. Libraries, book fairs, and publishers find bookmarks to be useful devices to promote their goals.

An unusual die-cut bookmark advertised the Rasmussen Practical Business School of St. Paul. Courtesy of the Minnesota Historical Society (Cleora Wheeler Papers).

(ABOVE, LEFT):

Imagination soars like a Red Balloon held by the enchanted reader. This logo was designed by Warren Hanson in 1984. Courtesy of Patrick Coleman.

(ABOVE, RIGHT):

Reading by Candlelight. Gringolet (the name came from a horse in a medieval romance) was part of the St. Anthony Main development from 1979 to 1991. Courtesy of Patrick Coleman.

Stone's Bookstore in Duluth issued this small catalogue for its book and magazine customers in the fall of 1934. New books, dozens of magazines, and books not yet published could be delivered in jig time. Courtesy of the authors.

Many booksellers have printed catalogues listing their wares. Dealers in rare books may even issue a special catalogue for an important collection, much as Rulon-Miller Books of St. Paul did in 1992 when the Elmer and Eleanor Andersen collection of specialized Minnesota titles was sold. The catalogue was titled *A Minnesota Adventure*. In the 1930s Mabel Ulrich sent a flyer called "Bookstore Trivia" to her customers. It listed new titles, art displayed in her gallery, and authors who had been invited to lecture at her stores in Minneapolis, St. Paul, Duluth, and Rochester. Most booksellers today continue the practice of Mrs. Ulrich. A typical newsletter lists meetings of store-sponsored reading groups, author events and book signings, and features new titles. Such a newsletter is usually available in the store itself and on a Web site.[42]

Bookplates

The bookplate is said to be over 500 years old, originating in Germany before finding favor in France, Holland, and England. Then, as now, bookplates indicate pride of ownership, either by a library or an individual collector. They can also denote gifts by collectors or groups to libraries. According to Maurice Rickards, the earliest English bookplates appeared at Cambridge College in the late 1500s to record the gift of books to its library. From these, the concept of a personal label or bookplate spread to private collectors for whom the design was often based upon the owner's coat of arms.[43] While American bookplates might also use heraldic motifs, most are less genealogical. A favorite landscape or attributes of a hobby, a library showing bookshelves, a person reading beside the fireplace, a wise owl, an Aladdin's lamp, or the book itself, all appear on nineteenth- and twentieth-century bookplates. These small examples of fine printing emphasize both the collection and the book collector.

Bookplates may be designed for engraving, lithography, or woodblock printing. Many artists who are skilled illustrators have designed bookplates, and some have specialized in this miniature art form, as did Cleora Clark Wheeler (1883–1980) of St. Paul. Miss Wheeler completed her first bookplate for the St. Paul YWCA in 1908 and the last, for F. T. Weyerhaeuser of Cloquet, nearly 50 years later. She prepared bookplates for members of Kappa Kappa Gamma, a sorority that she joined at the University of Minnesota, as well as for the libraries of many of her St. Paul neighbors.[44] One of her bookplates, a scene of Lake Nebagamon for Phillip Weyerhaeuser, whose family spent summers there, won a first prize at the Minnesota State Fair in 1913. Few bookplates address the perils of the borrowed book as succinctly as did one bookplate in the Cleora Wheeler Collection at the University of Minnesota

(FAR LEFT):

Ora Brownfield Laughlin's interests appear on the bookplate designed for her by Mary Moulton Cheney. A woman reads in her garden, and birds perch and fly overhead while her dog watches peacefully. Courtesy of the Minnesota Historical Society (Mary Moulton Cheney papers).

(LEFT):

For banker Samuel Arthur Harris, the artist selected an open book, a lamp, and oak leaves to fill the quatrefoil. Courtesy of the Minnesota Historical Society (Mary Moulton Cheney papers).

library; across the top of the bookplate were the words "Return It, Dammit!" Of her own bookplate, a winter scene of birch trees along Minnehaha Creek, Miss Wheeler once wrote that "birch trees are native to Minnesota. So am I. These footprints in the snow are only transitory, but while they last they add beauty to the landscape. My life may be as transitory as they, but if the trail I blaze adds some beauty to the world through which it leads, I shall be content."[45]

Miss Wheeler called herself a "designer-illuminator," not a printer. Often her designs were cut into metal plates for printing by others. She very carefully documented her work and noted that she would be willing to affix the ordered bookplates onto the flyleaf of each client's books—five thousand times in the case of Frank B. Kellogg's library. Kellogg was the only Minnesotan to serve as Secretary of State of the United States, from 1925 to 1929.

Minneapolis artist and teacher Mary Moulton Cheney (1871–1957) began designing bookplates by 1899. She later sold them at the Artcraft Shop: At the Sign of the Bay Tree. Miss Cheney's first studio was in the old Boston Block in downtown Minneapolis. In 1904 she was one of the founders of the Handicraft Guild, which occupied its own building on Tenth Street until 1918, when its curriculum was merged into the University of Minnesota's Department of Art Education.[46] Cheney's bookplates were designed in the simple curves of Arts and Crafts style.

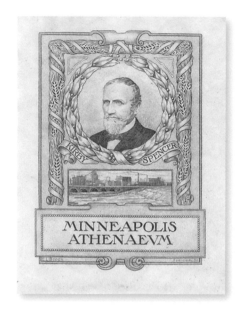

Dr. Kirby Spencer, a Minneapolis dentist, bequeathed his estate to the Minneapolis Athenaeum to purchase books. The bookplate was designed by artist Emma Brock. Courtesy of Cleora Wheeler Papers, Special Collections and Rare Books, University of Minnesota Libraries.

In 1927 the New Century Club, a St. Paul women's group, held a competition to select a bookplate to insert in books they gave to the library. George Resler won the job. Courtesy of Cleora Wheeler Papers, Special Collections and Rare Books, University of Minnesota Libraries.

Oscar Taylor Blackburn (1869–1956), an engraver and watch repairman by training, designed and engraved intricate bookplates for over forty years. Blackburn's work was displayed in a small catalogue prepared by Leonard Wells, longtime manager of the important book department in Powers' department store in Minneapolis.[47] The cost for these bookplates was $3.50 per hundred in black and $4.50 per hundred in brown.

A list of all Minnesota artists who have designed bookplates would be a long one. Those were Lowell Bobletter, S. Chatwood Burton, children's book illustrator Emma Brock, George Resler, George Rehse, and Jane McCarthy, the well-known designer of books for the University of Minnesota Press.

Usually a single bookplate remains on the flyleaf of a treasured tome. But sometimes multiple bookplates are preserved in a single volume, marking stages in a book's travels, like the ownership marks on a Japanese scroll. A book from one of the many editions of *Nouvelle Découverte*, the travel tales of Father Louis Hennepin, was published in Amsterdam in 1698.[48] Inside the front cover is a bookplate, a truly incredible heraldic genealogy of five related Dutch noble families. Sometime later on the book entered the collection of a bishop, whose bookplate was also inserted. Continuing its journey, probably through the hands of other book dealers and collectors, none of whom added further marks or plates, it was acquired by J. Christian Bay of the John Crerar Library in Chicago. Its next voyage, in 1943, was north, back to the location of Father Hennepin's stories. Mr. Bay gave the book to John T. Flanagan, then an assistant professor of English at the University of Minnesota, who cherished it throughout his life.[49]

Artist Clement Haupers designed this bookplate for his friend Patrick Coleman. Courtesy of the authors.

Keepsakes or Souvenirs

Among the most coveted bits of ephemera are keepsakes, which were frequently produced in small quantities and given to those who attend a special event.[50] Non-paper examples of ephemera are the bobble-head figures and homer hankies given to those who attended certain games of the Minnesota Twins or St. Paul Saints baseball teams.

These marketing gimmicks proved so popular that lines of hopeful recipients formed hours before game time in order to get their small Kirby Puckett or Harmon Killebrew figures.[51] One collector noted that each bobble head came with a paper certificate of authenticity, similar to those offered with another once-popular toy, the Cabbage Patch doll, or the birth certificates for Beanie Babies.

Printed keepsakes have proved to be equally popular with collectors. These keepsakes are sel-

One of the most cherished children's books is Margaret Wise Brown's Goodnight Moon, *which was illustrated by Clement Hurd. The Kerlan Award was given posthumously to Ms. Brown and her many illustrators on May 15, 1984. Courtesy of the authors.*

dom invitations but may serve as expanded programs. The support group for the University of Minnesota's Children's Literature Research Collections (CLRC), usually referred to as the Kerlan

Logo of the Ampersand Club, Minneapolis. Courtesy of the authors.

Friends, has honored a children's book author or illustrator annually since 1975. Each year's keepsake provides a short biography of the honoree, a bibliography of the artist's or writer's work, and illustrations or manuscripts from the CLRC collections.[52] The keepsakes are presented at meetings where the honorees speak.

Across the country a number of clubs have been founded to celebrate printing, book design, and books. New York's Grolier Club and the Caxton Club of Chicago are well-established groups of this nature. The Ampersand Club began in the Twin Cities with an invitation sent in 1930 to men interested in "all phases of fine printing and book collecting," by Frank Walter, then University of Minnesota librarian, and Arnett Leslie, president of the Leslie Paper Company. Sixteen men became

charter members of the Unnamed Book Club as a result of that invitation. Christopher Morley, on a Minneapolis visit in 1935, suggested the name Ampersand, which was duly adopted as the club's name. An elegant logo featuring a slim litterateur leaning on the club's symbol was designed in July 1940 by C. A. Weston. The club reprinted a speech made by Morley at the fiftieth anniversary dinner of the Minneapolis Public Library in 1939. The resulting book, *Friends Romans …* (1940), was the club's first publication.

In 1980 Rutherford Aris presented an essay on the history of the ampersand itself at a club meeting.[53] The essay included this limerick:

He thought he saw an Ampersand
That stretched for miles and miles
He looked again and saw it was
A club of bibliofiles.
"At least it's better far," he said,
Than "Bombay Bicycles."

The Bombay Bicycles had been suggested previously as a name for the unnamed book club.

Ampersand members receive keepsakes including programs, broadsides, and occasional short publications, all related to books and the art of printing. Members who are printers have often produced these unique examples of their art. Two of the club's early members, printer Emerson C. Wulling and bookseller and collector J. Harold Kittleson, have been honored in club keepsakes. Wulling wrote a history of the club in 1965 and often printed other keepsakes at his Sumac Press.[54] When Jane McCarthy retired from the University of Minnesota Press in 1971, the group honored her for her career and her designs of award-winning book jackets. Ms. McCarthy was an honored yet honorary member of the Ampersand Club since women were not admitted to full membership until a few years later.[55]

One of the more unusual episodes in British printing history involved the freezing of the Thames River in London. An intrepid printer brought a printing press out onto the ice to demonstrate his skills. In emulation of that deed, in January 1997 printers of the Ampersand Club

worked in subzero weather in two icehouses on the frozen surface of White Bear Lake to produce the keepsake *On the Rocks*.

Honoring another date of yore, Dennis Ruud and Wilbur Schilling, Ampersand Club members, printed as a broadside Oscar Wilde's essay "The Beauties of Bookbinding," for the founding meeting of the Oscar Wilde Society of North America in March 2002.

Fine Press

As a change from their usual work, some printers venture into the world of fine press printing. Short runs of specially selected texts give them the opportunity to use handmade papers, unique fonts, and special bindings in books not intended for commercial bookstore sales.

Alfred Muellerleile, of North Central Printing, began a series of Christmas books in 1947. Press runs were usually limited to fewer

Printed on the ice of White Bear Lake, Minnesota, 1997

On the Rocks *was printed in an icehouse on the frozen surface of White Bear Lake, on January 12, 1997. The day was clear, the temperature was minus twenty degrees. The text is a wordlist found in the library of food writer M. F. K. Fisher.* Courtesy of the authors.

hail blessed flower!

the spicers and tille thekers pageants
from the york cycle of mystery plays

Title page from Hail Blessed Flower, *the 1973 Christmas book of the North Central Publishing Company. 1,250 copies were printed. Courtesy of the authors.*

than one thousand copies, and the copies were given away. Carols, holiday poems, and religious topics were typically selected. In 1952 Frank Kacmarcik began designing these Christmas books. The thirty-fifth book, *In the Day of the Nativity,* published in 1981, was the last to be produced.[56] After Muellerleile died, in 1985, his papers and a collection of the North Central Christmas books were bequeathed to the library of the College of St. Catherine in St. Paul.

The Minnesota Center for Book Arts offers classes in papermaking, printing, book design, and bookbinding. An exhibition schedule and occasional lectures on book history are part of its offerings. Each year since 1988 the Center has selected a unique text to become its Winter Book. Handmade papers and bindings, and carefully chosen type are used to create standard-size and chapbook editions. The 2003 book is entitled *Winter Reader 2003–2004,* and uses texts by Louise Erdrich.

Many other papermakers, book designers, and bookbinders make their homes in Minnesota. In recognition of their work the Minnesota Center for the Book awards a prize in its annual book awards competition to a fine press book.

CHAPTER THREE

Through the Mails

"AND HE SENT LETTERS UNTO ALL THE JEWS, to the hundred twenty and seven provinces of the kingdom."[57] This Biblical reference may be the first historical description of sending letters. For numerous centuries thereafter letters have remained the principal means of communication for kings and clerics, and more recently, for ordinary people.

In Europe during the late Middle Ages, paper became cheaper and more readily available for letters. The message was written on what has become known as the letter sheet. The sheet was folded, addressed, sealed with wax, and entrusted to a messenger. While the various postal systems grew in succeeding centuries, the basic form for the message remained the folded letter sheet. In the United States, beautiful and elaborate printed letter sheets were in use by the 1840s as letter wrappers, often for political campaign advertising. However, both in Europe and in the United States, it cost more to use an additional page as a letter wrapper because postal rates were based on the number of sheets mailed rather than the weight.

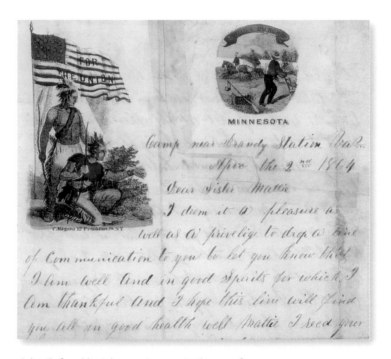

A detail of a soldier's letter written on April 2, 1864, from a camp near Brandy Station, Virginia. The stationery was headlined with a Magnus patriotic image and the Minnesota state seal. Courtesy of Floyd Risvold.

Using a lettersheet with an 1859 view of St. Paul, Edward Cutler wrote to a friend in Brookline, Massachusetts. His family lived in a house marked with a dot, he said, not far from the city end of the bridge. He believed St. Paul was prettier than his family had expected, but he missed the kind of ice hockey played back home on Jamaica Pond. The building with the cupola was the state house, the large square structure with a flag flying was the International Hotel, and most of downtown had wooden sidewalks. Courtesy of Floyd Risvold.

Published by Munger Brothers 1859.

ST PAUL. MINN.

December 14th 1863.

Grocer M. M. Goodwin ordered his envelopes from a Philadelphia firm. The letter was mailed in 1856 from St. Anthony. Courtesy of Floyd Risvold.

Advertising Envelopes

Hand-folded envelopes for letters first came into use in the 1700s in Europe. Envelopes in the United States were initially produced and sold by stationers or bookstores. A tin pattern or template was used to create the desired envelope shape from piled sheets of paper. The blanks were then folded by hand into envelopes and the side flaps sealed. The top flap was left ungummed, to be closed later with sealing wax or gummed seals. When U. S. postal rates were reduced in March 1845 to five cents per half ounce for 300 miles, and ten cents for more than 300 miles, the use of envelopes became widespread. By the 1850s the use in the United States of automatic envelope folding machines resulted in envelopes becoming far less expensive, and this in turn caused a major growth in mail carried by the post office.

The first envelope with a printed illustration was probably the so-called Mulready Envelope. Introduced in England in 1840, this postage prepaid, one-penny envelope featured the figure of Britannia seated upon the British lion, sending winged messengers to far-flung parts of her Empire.[58] The use of the printed envelope in the United States first occurred in the 1850s when envelopes were printed with presidential campaign illustrations and slogans. A decade later, during the Civil War, envelopes were printed with patriotic illustrations and messages extolling either the Confederate or Union cause. On occasion, the designs on these envelopes were hand colored.

FOUR FACTS

We are THE ONE and ONLY FIRM manufacturing the Patent Adjustable Double Slip Socket Limb.

We are THE ONE and ONLY FIRM giving a Financial Guarantee NOT to CHAFE the STUMP.

We are THE ONE and ONLY FIRM employing a force of skilled workmen wearing Artificial Legs.

We took more orders for Artificial Legs at the World's Fair, the California Mid-Winter International Exposition and the Atlanta Exposition than all other exhibitors together.

"I'm Wearing a Single Socket Leg. It's killing me."

"Why don't you get a Double Slip Socket Leg and enjoy life like I do?"

Advertisements were also printed on the reverse side of envelopes. The Winkley Artificial Limb Company of Minneapolis was one of a group of specialized companies that made the Twin Cities a major center of artificial limb manufacturing. This envelope was postmarked January 23, 1896. Courtesy of Tom Reiersgord.

In addition to the political or patriotic envelope, advertising envelopes, or covers (collectors call envelopes covers), appeared in the United States prior to the Civil War. These envelopes used illustrations similar to, but smaller than, those on letterheads or billheads. Beginning as woodcuts, then imprinted by stone and metal embossings, they evolved into lithographed works of art in one or more colors. As the nineteenth century progressed, illustrated covers, and their enclosed letterhead stationery, were more and more used as one of the principal forms of advertising for products and services.

A 2005 Solar y Llach (Barcelona, Spain) postal history sale catalogue included what was said to be the earliest use of an albumin-processed photograph mounted on the front of a Minnesota advertising cover. The cover was postmarked January 19, 1870, and was sent from Minneapolis to St. Charles, Illinois. It bore that old faithful image, Minnehaha Falls. Illustrated advertising covers customarily

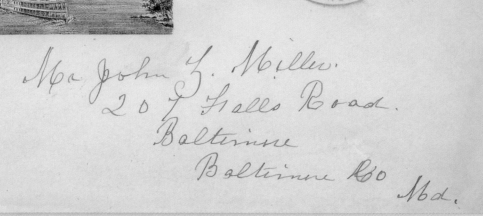

Hotel Lafayette

Minnetonka Beach, Minnesota

Mr. John L. Miller.
207 Falls Road.
Baltimore
Baltimore Co
Md.

The Lafayette Hotel at Minnetonka Beach was built between 1881 and 1883 by the St. Paul, Minneapolis and Manitoba Railroad as a retreat for railroad officials and guests. It was destroyed by fire on October 4, 1897, just 35 days after this advertising envelope was postmarked. Courtesy of Tom Reiersgord.

If not called for in 10 days, Return to
WEST PUBLISHING CO.,
ST. PAUL, MINN.

c239

A Combination of Books and Book Holder Giving the Brief-Maker Complete Command of the Case Law.

AN INGENIOUS NOVELTY.

M J HAWKINS
RIDGEWAY, N C

The West Publishing Company, one of the world's largest publishers of law books, now markets a computerized legal research system, a library of case law. This 1894 envelope shows an earlier, ingenious method of researching the law. Courtesy of Tom Reiersgord.

The green ox cart stamp honors the centennial of Minnesota becoming a territory. As the map within the cachet shows, the territorial boundaries were larger than those used to delimit statehood nine years later. Courtesy of the authors.

depicted buildings—hotels, restaurants, banks, or factories—that were home to every sort of retail or wholesale business, large and small. Logos and symbols, along with images of the company's principal products, often covered the entire envelope. As cities and towns promoted civic celebrations, their correspondence was likewise mailed in appropriately illustrated envelopes.[59] Nineteenth century job printers producing lithographed advertising covers for their customers often noted their name or initials beneath the image.

Cacheted Envelopes

The illustrated advertising cover showing a building is seldom seen in today's mail as companies now imprint their envelopes with other messages. Still, other imprinted envelopes continue the tradition. A design printed on an envelope to celebrate an event such as the first day of issue of a postage stamp, the opening of airmail services, or a new post office is called a cachet. While the design on the advertising envelope sometimes covered both sides of the envelope, any cachet is normally restricted to the left side of the envelope's front side. To a philatelist, a first day cover is an envelope to which a postage stamp has been affixed and cancelled on its initial day of issue. These envelopes can be hand decorated, printed in the hundreds or thousands by national first day cover companies, or even produced by local collector groups. A list of postage stamps dealing with Minnesota subjects, personages, and places has been previously compiled by the author.[60] That list begins with two postage stamps commemorating the hundredth anniversary of the arrival in New York City of the first group of Norwegian immigrants to the United States. These two- and five-cent postage stamps had their first day of issue sale on May 18, 1925, in St. Paul, Minneapolis, Benson, and Northfield, Minnesota. For this event a Minnesota stamp dealer, E. J. Weschcke, prepared and sold what have been characterized as among the earliest known cacheted first day covers.

George Seibert's Great Western Band and Orchestra participated in many of St. Paul's nineteenth-century events and parades. In this letter of June 12, 1893, he hoped that James J. Hill would sponsor an open-air concert in Summit Square, which would give "pleasure refreshing and refining to the masses." The lithography was done by Seibert Brothers Litho of St. Paul. Courtesy of James J. Hill Library (Hill papers).

The Hotel Ryan opened in 1885 in time to serve as headquarters for the first St. Paul Winter Carnival, which was held early the following year. The first year's ice palace appears on the right and the Hotel Ryan (demolished in 1962) is shown on the left of this envelope. Courtesy of the James J. Hill Library (Hill papers).

Other cacheted envelopes include those commemorating first airplane flights. An example is the so-called Route 9 of American Contract Airmail, whose inaugural flight occurred June 7, 1926, between Chicago and Minneapolis. Still other examples of cacheted envelopes celebrate airport dedications (e.g., St. Cloud, May 23, 1929; Coleraine, July 4, 1929; Worthington, August 23, 1930; and Minneapolis, September 19, 1930, to name a few). Finally, a goodwill flying tour by Charles A. Lind-

bergh was celebrated with cacheted envelopes from Little Falls. That tour (August 25–29, 1927) included a visit by the famed aviator to his hometown. These and other airmail ephemera are listed in a 1933 catalogue.[61]

Business Stationery

Fancily lithographed letterhead stationery was extremely popular between the 1880s and the 1920s. Its development and period of usage closely mirroring that of the advertising envelope. The letterhead design could be adapted for use on invoices, bills of sale, envelopes, and memoranda.

For most nineteenth-century entrepreneurs the lithographic display on their stationery had the same advertising importance as the present-day Web site. The majority of the designs depicted an office building or manufacturing premises. The structure usually loomed larger than life, with tiny pedestrians, carriages, or automobiles passing in front. Often the building stood alone, without its neighboring buildings, as if to focus attention on it. Such stationery was obviously a marketing tool. Only later would the entrepreneur's products or logo be utilized instead.

From a review of their microscopically small signatures or initials, either beneath or incorporated into the design, a handful of Minneapolis and St. Paul lithographers appear to have prepared the majority of Minnesota letterheads during this period of time.[62] Other letterheads, usually simpler in appearance, were produced by job printers in out-state Minnesota. A number of additional, perhaps finer, lithographed letterheads were made in Chicago, Milwaukee, Buffalo, and St. Louis. Even more exquisite and fancy letterhead sheets were photoengraved, many in New York City, by the largest security printer of the times, the American Bank Note Company. Of the hundreds of letterheads that we have examined, only a single example carried the union "bug."

Logos and text from letterhead stationery were also routinely used on business cards and memo pads.

Postcards

The grand vistas of the agricultural, fisheries, and woman's buildings, and other magnificent palaces at the 1893 World's Columbian Exposition in Chicago, appeared on a brand new souvenir for sale at that fair: the postcard. The cards were an immediate success, launching new ways to communicate and advertise.[63] They also became a new collectible for family albums. Printed by the American Lithographic Company of New York, and sold at the fair by Charles W. Goldsmith, the Chicago cards showed how attractive a souvenir a view card could be. The only problem was the format, which collectors refer to as the undivided back. Post office regulations at that time required that only the address appear on the back side. Messages were restricted to the picture side and thus had to be squeezed into any available blank space, sometimes obscuring the view itself.

In 1907 postal regulations permitted the back side of the card to be divided, allowing both the address and a message to appear there; this relieved the frustration of the writer who needed more words to recount his experience. Postcard manufacturers printed cards for every subsequent fair,

national or international. These temporary exposition cities were well documented and soon, too, were other cities both far and wide. Photographic cards (known as "real photo" cards by collectors) and lithographic cards were guidebooks to a town's treasures. Main streets, churches, courthouses, city halls, parks and gardens, and outdoor sculpture became subjects for the postcard photographer. These tourist views were quickly followed by true advertising postcards. Owners of restaurants, hotels, resorts, and gas stations all found the 3½ by 5½ inch card a valuable marketing tool. Along with the matchbook, the postcard would, for most of the twentieth century, be prominently displayed on the counter next to the cash register in many retail establishments.

The earliest view postcards were produced in Europe by German or English companies. American printers followed their lead. After 1900, Minnesota postcards were printed by, among others, Detroit Publishing Company, V. O. Hammon Publishing Company, The Albertype Company of New York, E. C. Kropp Company of Milwaukee and, especially, Curt Teich of Chicago. Other local firms, such as

Night scenes make exciting postcard views, and the brightly lighted Donaldson's Glass Block, a department store in downtown Minneapolis, was no exception. Opened in 1888 it had colored lights around its four floors and outlining its dome. Later in its life the Glass Block was covered with metal sheeting. It was finally destroyed in a massive downtown fire in 1982. This is V. O. Hammon card, No. 284, postmarked in 1906. Courtesy of the authors.

Brown & Bigelow, Louis Dow, and Northwest Paper, printed postcards using the same images that appeared on their blotters, calendars, and playing cards. Like matchbooks and trade cards, generic images for national products could be issued on a postcard bearing a local retailer's address.

During the golden age of the postcard, deemed by deltiologists to be from 1893 to 1918, photographs of American small town scenes were often sent to Germany for printing. American postcard publishers hired their own photographers to cover the larger cities. Curt Teich, whose firm became the largest American publisher of view postcards, began by taking his own photographs. According to the oft-told tale, Teich took a train west from Chicago in 1907. At every stop he would get off, visit possible clients such as hotels, restaurants, department stores, and offer to print postcards of their establishments for $1.00 per 1,000 cards. He returned from the trip with $30,000 in orders.[64]

At that time, according to a later sales director for the Curt Teich firm, each postcard began with a black and white photograph. Unsightly objects such as telephone wires, trash cans, or signs would

In the records of the Curt Teich postcard firm of Chicago, this statue of George Washington was shown on their first postcard for the city of Rochester. A local variety store ordered the cards. Vandals later knocked down the statue as well as its companion figure, Abraham Lincoln. The site became known as Statuary Park in memory of the two presidents. Courtesy of the authors.

Statue of George Washington, presented to the City of Rochester, by the Mayo Family, Nov. 30, 1910.

all be removed by retouching. On a tissue overlay the customer would indicate the desired colors and the text needed.[65] Thus the customer was able to show his business as if it were newly built, in fine weather, on a traffic free street, "postcard perfect," as the old saying went!

Although Teich began making postcards in the "real photo" era, Teich cards are best known for their textured look: the linen variety published in the 1930s and 1940s. The Curt Teich Company printed 6,500 different postcard views linked to 170 different Minnesota communities. Archives of the company, in business from 1898 to 1974, are housed in the Lake County Museum in Wauconda, Illinois. A smaller collection of V. O. Hammon postcards can also be viewed at this museum.

View cards were one sort of tourist advertising, usually focused on either the built or the natural environment. Other promotional postcards were those showing Native American life. Patricia Albers and William R. James analyzed over 300 postcards showing Minnesota's Ojibwe people.[66] While some early photographic postcards were accurate depictions, later postcards offered stereotypes promoting Native American culture as it had come to be expected. The garb of the Plains often became the dress for Native Americans in other regions of the country. These cards were often sold in northern Minnesota, near Native American communities, sometimes by those portrayed on the cards like the well-known Ojibwe man called John Smith.

Another type of promotional postcard featured annual events. The ice palaces of St. Paul's Winter Carnival, the summer sports of Minneapolis' Aquatennial,

Like Joel Whitney, the master of the cartes de visite, photographers for the V. O. Hammon postcard firm were fascinated by Minnehaha Falls. Their very first postcard was a view of the falls, and there would be many more cards with similar views in later years. Courtesy of Clark Hansen.

"WHERE THE FALLS OF MINNEHAHA FLASH AND GLEAM AMONG THE OAK-TREES, LAUGH AND LEAP INTO THE VALLEY"

No. 1. V. O. Hammon Pub. Co., Minneapolis and Chicago

John Smith, aged 128 at the time his photograph was taken, appears on more Minnesota postcards than any other Native American person. This real photo portrait was taken by a local photographer in Cass Lake. Courtesy of the authors.

and parades at every town festival are all recorded on such cards. They were a perfect way to promote the event as well as to serve as a souvenir.

Product advertising probably represents the largest category of postcards, since it includes everything from the factory, to the retail establishment where the product was sold, to the object itself. For example, the Sleepy Eye Flour Mills issued postcards with scenes of the mill as well as episodes of Native American life. Postcards for Hamm's beer include the brewery and its happy-go-lucky Bear cavorting in northern Minnesota lakes. Postcards may show a unique product such as William Marvy's barber poles. For a restaurant, the postcard view might be the elegant façade or the pristine vista of white-covered tables awaiting hungry gourmets, while a hotel's cards could show bedrooms, dining rooms, or a spacious lobby and shops.

While the advertising postcard needed to show the business or product in perfect condition, the exaggerated or tall-tale postcard became a popular exception. For example, tourists who visited Garvin, Minnesota, were

Creameries, often farmer-owned cooperatives, opened throughout Minnesota as railroads made it possible to ship butter from rural areas to larger towns. Butter makers competed for prizes at both county fairs and trade expositions. Courtesy of the authors.

sure to catch enormous fish because, as the text on a real photo card read, that's "how we do things in Garvin."

Postcard collecting has long been organized into clubs whose members schedule meetings and exhibitions at the Minnesota State Fair. In Minnesota, the Twin City Postcard Club has regular meetings, shows, and exhibitions. In the vast postcard literature, writers have examined postcards focusing on publishing houses, artists, or subject matter. View cards often illustrate historical texts, and advertising cards supplement business history.

For some, Maurice Rickard wrote, covers and postcards represent specialist fields and are not really ephemera. Others, however disagree: the fact that an item is widely collected by specialists does not by definition disqualify it as ephemera. No matter which side of the argument a collector subscribes to, specialized collecting aids those who collect ephemera by topic. Philatelic clubs, catalogues, and a vast multilingual literature provide a wealth of information for collectors. Dealers regularly segregate their holdings by theme, geographic location, and even by artist (especially for postcards). Thus, it is far easier to find Minnesota-related covers and postcards than to find most other types of Minnesota-related ephemera.

CHAPTER FOUR

For Boxes, Bottles, Barrels, Bags, and Cans

IT IS CLEAR THAT BOTH THE TEXT ON A LABEL and its design are meant to persuade customers to purchase the product. An early advertising label will at a minimum contain the company name and address, its trademark or logo, and some indication of the contents of the package. To these could be added various appropriate design elements, such as the sprigs of hops and barley on beer labels or the portrait of the company founder.

But as time passed, other outside requirements began to affect the content of an advertising label and challenge its designers. There were, first of all, additions to text that appear because of federal or state governmental initiative. Included in this category are notices or warnings on alcoholic beverages and tobacco products, ranging from the early, briefest statements to the more recent dire predictions of danger to health and well-being. The body of such required messages changed over time and can help to date the advertising label. More recently, various Pure Food and Drug laws and comparable legislation have required notices that provide comprehensive statements of content and dietary information. The most recently required information has been the result of new federal standards for organic produce.

There are also wordings or symbols not required by law but used voluntarily by the maker of a product to protect the ownership of a trademark or logo. These include © (copyright), ® (registered), or ™ (trademark) symbols. Further, there are often symbols that appear as a result of contractual arrangements, such as the so-called union bug or symbol to indicate that the contents of the package, or the label itself, were produced in a union shop. In addition, there are those modern intrusions upon the design of the product label advertising: the ubiquitous bar codes. These codes enable retailers with optical scanning equipment on their cash registers to account for the purchase of the item and control their product inventories. Even more recently there have been added symbols urged by public activists to indicate conformity with community ecological demands, such as the recycling symbol and, on

The oval seal of Good Housekeeping magazine has symbolized their approval of the quality of a product since 1909. Courtesy of Watkins, Inc.

beer and soft drink labels, the state cash refunds that may be obtained by returning cans or bottles.

Good Housekeeping magazine began selecting products for quality in 1909. The chosen goods could use the special seal on packaging, and the magazine would vouch for them.

Finally, there are symbols with religious connotation. The capital *U* enclosed in a circle, for example, indicates that the contents have been prepared in accordance with the kosher requirements of the Union of Orthodox Jewish Communities. More than fifty other kosher certifying entities have symbols that are placed on manufactured food containers.[67]

Beer and Wine Advertising

At the end of the Civil War, when some of Minnesota's oldest brewing companies were founded, beer was delivered to taverns or hotels in kegs or barrels with the brewer's name burned into the wood. Labels were not needed.

When pasteurization made the bottling of beer possible (around the 1870s), the first bottles were sometimes made of stoneware but more often

From 1850 until his death in 1887, John Orth brewed beer in Minneapolis. An immigrant from Alsace, Orth was the city's first brewer. His labels were printed by Johnson, Smith & Harrison of Minneapolis. Courtesy of the Minnesota Historical Society (Museum collections).

Christopher Stahlmann's Cave Brewery was at Fort and Oneida Streets in St. Paul from 1855 to 1897. New ownership took over at that time, and three years later Jacob Schmidt purchased the property. The label was lithographed by Wittemann Bros. of New York City prior to 1884. Courtesy of the Minnesota Historical Society (Museum collections).

The brothers Fleckenstein, Ernst and Gottfried, opened a brewery in Faribault in 1857. After they ended their partnership fifteen years later, Ernst built a new plant, which lasted until 1964. Natural rock caves were used for storing the lager and were considered a promotional plus. Courtesy of the authors.

were made from glass with the brewer's name embossed on the body of the bottle. Labels were printed in a single color with the basic information, usually the company's name and location, framed by stock border designs. Local printers such as Brown and Treacy in St. Paul or Johnson, Smith & Harrison in Minneapolis put their company names along the lower edge of the labels.

As breweries expanded and added bottling plants, the labels applied by the brewery workers grew more elaborate. Most labels were square or rectangular with the brewery name written, often in script, diagonally from lower left to upper right. Oval labels used by the Shakopee and Drewry breweries were an unusual choice of shape. Sprays of hops or barley added interest to multicolored designs. For the latter designs Minnesota brewers sought the expertise of specialized lithographers in Chicago or Milwaukee.

Logos soon appeared on labels and some labels became pictorial. Elves (perhaps the same Black Forest denizens said to make Volkswagens), brewery workers, harvest scenes, and tavern interiors now helped to market the beer. Because lager beer needs to rest during its brewing process, early brewers used caves (where elves were supposed to dwell) to store the resting barrels. Thus, "cave beer" was considered to have a marketing

John Orth's brewery became part of the Minneapolis Brewing Company in 1890. While brewing companies often used the names of their founders, using the portrait of the founder on a label is quite unusual. Courtesy of Bob Kay.

Elves taste the brew on the Old Kind label. Vignettes show traditional scenes of harvesting hops and barley. The listing of alcoholic content and number of ounces was required on labels by 1912. Courtesy of Bob Kay.

(THIS PAGE, CLOCKWISE):

Glencoe Brewing Company's plant, first built in 1901, appears in full production mode on its die-cut labels. Uncle Sam was a brand name introduced in 1907. This company was in business from 1901 until 1918. Courtesy of Bob Kay.

Hubert Nyssen's Shakopee lager boasted elegant typefaces on their oval labels, dated in the late 1880s. Courtesy of Bob Kay.

The Drewry brewery was a St. Paul neighbor of Theodore Hamm's operation. Oval labels with colorful lithography were typical in the 1890s. Courtesy of Bob Kay.

tures perhaps not worthy of the engraver or lithographer's art. Only toward the end of the nineteenth century did the beer barons invest in new castle-like breweries, certainly appropriate for use on labels and letterheads. On twenty-first century labels, old brewery buildings convey a sense of tradition and nostalgia, so these edifices now loom behind old beer wagons and buggies on labels.

Elements seldom, if ever, seen on Minnesota beer labels are images of Gambrinus, the jovial king of beer; scenes of water in the form of waterfalls, rivers, or lakes (despite Minnesota's 10,000 lakes nickname); brewery owner portraits (such as John Orth's); and proud garlands of medals. Brewers in other cities entered the beer competitions at world and national expositions. Those who won, such as Pabst, would then advertise the fact on labels by using the medal itself in the design, much as Minnesota flour millers and pickle makers did.[68] Minnesota

advantage. Labels such as those of Yoerg (St. Paul), Peter Bub (Winona), Old Kind (Appleton), Ernst Fleckenstein (Faribault), and August Schell (New Ulm) show such peaceful storage scenes.

Although French wine *étiquettes* (labels) usually show vineyards and chateaux, beer labels with factory scenes are not common. The earliest brewery buildings were plain, nondescript struc-

David Bailly produced the first wines from his vineyard south of Hastings in 1977. The hardy Maréchal Foch grape is often used by Canadian and American vintners. The French World War I general visited Minnesota in 1921, posing for his portrait sculpted in ice. Courtesy of the authors.

brewers evidently did not think the competitions were worth the effort, so they had no medals to illustrate.

State and federal regulations made changes in label design necessary, and these changes often help collectors date labels.[69] After 1906, notice of the Pure Food and Drug Act had to be included. In 1912 brewers were required to indicate the volume of beer in a bottle (in ounces) and its alcoholic content. Then in 1919 came Prohibition. Many Minnesota breweries closed, but those that remained open needed labels for their malt tonics, near beer, or soft drinks.

After Prohibition was repealed in 1933, labels had to mention that taxes had been paid. This IRTP, or Internal Revenue Tax Paid, statement remained on labels until 1950. Brewery addresses

An Indian chief in full Plains headdress was a frequent subject for labels on products such as baking powder, tobacco, and beer. This label for Chief beer can be dated to between 1933 and 1936, based upon the use of the U-permit notice. Courtesy of Bob Jackson.

CONTENTS 12 FLUID OZ.
BREWED & BOTTLED BY DULUTH BREWING & MALTING CO. DULUTH, MINN.

on labels became more precise with the addition of zip codes after 1963 and, more recently, brewery Web sites were also added. The UPC bar codes and bottle redemption or refund information appeared

Brewery workers capture the sense of authenticity and tradition in this label for the Duluth Brewing Company's longtime brand. Karlsbräu was named after owner Carl Meiske. This label was used from the repeal of Prohibition until the brewery closed in 1966. Courtesy of the authors.

by the 1970s. Latest to appear was the government health warning statement required after 1989.

Some brewery labels remained the same over time. Others were redesigned to follow marketing campaigns. Hamm's, for example, chose a simplified crown and pine tree label design in the 1960s. The modernized style replaced an older design that used a script signature and logo. Labels chosen by breweries of the 1980s and 1990s vary from the stylized hops and barley of Summit (St. Paul) to the realistic birds and animals of James Page (Minneapolis) and Schell's (New Ulm).

Paper coasters (and later, pressed paper or cardboard coasters, called "mats" in Europe) became available in the United States after 1900. They were one way to promote a brewery and its products in bars. Coasters could be printed on both sides. They are usually round, although square versions have been noted. They measure at least 3½ inches in diameter or 4 inches square so that a can, bottle, or glass can be set on the coaster with room to spare.

Catchy words around the border of coasters can be an important point-of-sale promotion. One example reads, "You're welcome to set your glass down here—provided it's filled with Schmidt's fine beer."[70] Gluek's brewery in Minneapolis used words on its coasters to promote a jingle writing contest: "Are you a Poet?"[71]

Collectors have sought out coasters mostly produced between 1945 and 1960 for two dozen Minnesota breweries. Recently they've added small breweries and brewpubs to the list. Assigning a date to a coaster is often difficult, with the exception of those produced by the Hamm's brewery. Hamm's coaster images often matched other advertising campaign designs for which a launch date can be ascertained.

Pocket-size sports schedules were another new advertising format. Functioning as mini-calendars, they listed home and away games for Minnesota's professional sport teams, including baseball's Twins and Saints, football's Vikings, hockey's North Stars and the Wild, and basketball's Timberwolves. Radio and television stations that broadcast games, and corporate sponsors of those broadcasts, paid for the schedules, which were then given to fans at the games. Pocket-size sports schedules were usually folded, and most measure 3 inches high. Sports schedules appeared by the 1960s, and are still both issued and collected.

Bumper stickers were part of the campaign that the Minnesota Brewing Company launched for its Pig's Eye pilsner in 1992.[72] The brewery even suggested Pig's Eye Parrant as a presidential candidate on the stickers and on billboards. Shortly thereafter the Brewery hired a first-ever spokesman for their beer; they felt their political acumen was sharp when that spokesman, Jesse Ventura, became Minnesota's Governor in 1998.[73]

While Minnesota's vineyards are neither as numerous or as venerable as those of California or New York State, Minnesota can count eleven wineries within its borders. The Alexis Bailly Vineyard, south of Hastings, begun in 1977, is the oldest.

Others include the Carlos Creek Winery (near Alexandria), Scenic Valley Winery (Lanesboro), Minnesota Wild (McGregor), Forestedge (Bemidji), Luedke (near Princeton), Morgan Creek (New Ulm), WineHaven (Chisago City), Northern Vineyards (Stillwater), and Saint Croix Vineyards (Stillwater).[74]

Minnesota winemakers use locally grown grapes as well as fruit such as raspberries (Saint Croix Vineyards) and rhubarb (WineHaven). Labels show grape leaves, the entrance to the wine cellar (Alexis Bailly), and a series of drawings for wines named after Minnesota wildflowers such as Yellow Moccasin, Columbine, Lady Slipper, and Prairie Rose (Northern Vineyards). One of the most unusual labels features a torn top edge (Saint Croix Vineyards). Wine labels carry the usual information concerning variety, producer, amount of alcohol, and the government warning label required since 1990.

Collectors of beer labels and coasters may belong to several national breweriana groups (the National Association of Breweriana Advertising, known as N.A.B.A., and the American Breweriana Association) who focus on beer advertising. Those interested in memorabilia from one St. Paul brewery find fellow collectors in the Hamm's Sky Blue Waters Club. All of these groups hold meetings and publish magazines or newsletters.

Rosé wine label of the Saint Croix Vineyards, with its intentionally serrated top and its serene Renaissance maiden. Courtesy of the authors.

Cigar Advertising

When the protagonist in English poet laureate Rudyard Kipling's famous poem "The Betrothed" chose a good cigar instead of his wife Maggie, most smokers in Minnesota during the 1890s would have agreed.[75] Statistics contained in the report of the Collector of Internal Revenue indicate that in the year 1895 there were 550 cigar factories in Minnesota.

SAINT CROIX VINEYARDS

These factories utilized 842,561 pounds of tobacco to produce 39,077,501 cigars.[76] Minnesota cigar manufacturers processed cigar-binder leaf tobacco that was then widely grown in southeast Minnesota and much of Wisconsin.[77] St. Paul had sixteen cigar manufacturing entities in 1876, while Minneapolis had thirty-three similar concerns in 1888.[78] Before the end of the nineteenth century, national brands in the cigar industry were virtually nonexistent. The industry was highly localized, with most of a company's production "going no further than a man could walk in a day."[79]

During the first third of the nineteenth century, cigars were essentially sold in bundles. Cedar boxes were soon prepared for the more expensive Havana cigars, while the use of colorful lithographed labels began in the late 1830s. Brand identification quickly became important, and cigar bands were introduced by a Dutchman, Gus-

tave Bock, by the middle of that century. The other reason customarily given for the use of cigar bands was to keep unsightly nicotine stains off the fingers of lady smokers. Superior quality cigar labels and bands, with meticulous workmanship, were lithographed in Germany, the United States, and Cuba.[80] By the early 1900s, however, only a small number

Louis Hill, president of the Northern Pacific Railroad, revived the dormant St. Paul Winter Carnival in 1916. He felt the city should once more enjoy the fun of winter sports, an ice palace, and the thrills of snowy parades and pageantry. Joining the 1916 carnival parade were marching units, which included the Hook 'Em Cow Club of South St. Paul. This club's drum corps, horse patrol, and marching unit were a part of carnival activities for many years to come. This cigar box label used by Bahnerman & List of St. Paul was copyrighted in 1921 by J. C. Verheeg. Courtesy of the authors.

FOR BOXES, BOTTLES, BARRELS, BAGS, AND CANS

of cigar manufacturers actually designed and printed their own labels and bands. Instead, generic, or stock, label designs were offered by traveling salesmen to the smaller cigar manufacturers. The same designs were quite often found on the cigars of unrelated manufacturers. By the third decade of the twentieth century, the consolidation of national brands and fierce price competition among cigar manufacturers caused a marked decline in printing quality of cigar labels and bands.

One important Minnesota firm, the J. W. Pauly Manufacturing Company, began business in 1887 in Minneapolis. As time passed, it became one of the largest and most successful manufacturers and distributors of cigars in Minnesota. The company had a number of its own labels and brands, but it

N. Nelson used the Quadriga to emphasize that his cigars were made in Minnesota, and not made by some national trust. Courtesy of the Minnesota Historical Society (Museum collections).

FOR BOXES, BOTTLES, BARRELS, BAGS, AND CANS

also prepared colorful cigar packaging materials for other local manufacturers, tobacco distributors, and retailers.[81] Under the leadership of its founder, J. W. Pauly, who was president for nearly 50 years, the company had a long record of furthering trade unionism in the tobacco industry.

For a box of cigars, a stock set of packaging materials would include the inner lid label, the outer lid label, the closure label, the guarantee label, and the edging strip. Also available was a printed or embossed paper to cover the top layer of cigars. The inner lid label was the canvas upon which the most artistic point of sale advertising was placed. More expensive cigars had bands with similar designs. Turn-of-the-century price quotations from Michigan and New York printers for both outer lid label and inner lid label with stock designs ranged between $25.00 and $35.00 per thousand pieces. A cigar band with a stock design from a German printer at roughly the same date was $1.20 per thousand pieces.

Another Minneapolis manufacturer and distributor, Winecke & Doerr, utilized a handsomely illustrated catalogue that offered imported, domestic, and house brand cigars and tobacco products on a wholesale basis. Its 1908 catalogue offered imported Hoyo de Monterey Havana cigars at $323 per thousand, in boxes of 25, while the Perfectos of H. Upman were $180.00 per thousand, also in boxes of twenty-five.[82]

Nineteenth-century competition was fierce among tobacco processors. One ploy worth mentioning preceded the absurd moneymaking antics of the present-day United States Postal Service by more than a century. It involved cooperation in 1884 between the Post Office and the Durham Tobacco Company: The Minneapolis letter carriers would pick up empty smoking tobacco bags and send them to the company to be counted. A $5,000.00 prize was offered to the person who sent in the most empty tobacco bags.

Cigar label art featured beautiful ladies festooned with roses, Cuban scenes, and portraits of famous men, historical events, and important buildings. But occasionally others helped to market cigars. The Yellow Kid, the first successful American comic strip character, was featured in two New York City newspapers between 1895 and 1898. Drawn by artist R. F. Outcault, the character wore a bright yellow nightshirt. The comic strip was widely read, primarily by adults. The Yellow Kid was soon merchandising every conceivable product, from soap to whiskey to cigars.

Cigar band collecting was a major hobby in the United States from approximately 1900 until World War I. Cigar label collecting became an important hobby in the late 1970s, perhaps due to the intricate beauty of these chromolithographs. Antiques dealers and department stores featured them in their home furnishings displays. Fortune 500 Companies, including Minnesota Mining and Manufacturing (3M), even gave framed label panels as executive gifts.[83] A number of public institutions maintain collections of cigar art, including the Cleveland

Box label for Theisen Bros. cigars. Courtesy of the Minnesota Historical Society (Museum collections).

FOR BOXES, BOTTLES, BARRELS, BAGS, AND CANS

Public Library, the Chicago Historical Society, and the Smithsonian Institution in Washington, D. C.

Most point-of-sale advertising came from the box in which cigars were displayed. Trade card advertising was by and large too expensive for such relatively inexpensive merchandise. But giveaways caught the eyes of the cigar smoker in a highly competitive market. These items included small calendars, playing cards, sewing notions, pocket cigar carriers, blotters, and postcards.

For those interested in viewing additional cigar box advertisements, the filings made pursuant to Minnesota's first trademark registration law would be of interest.[84] We note at least twenty-five full-color trademark renditions in three extra-large folio volumes prepared by the office of the Secretary of State, which are now in the archives of the Minnesota Historical Society.[85] The more significant marks include lithographic renditions of nineteenth century Minnesota political figures (Senator C. K. Davis, Governor

This point-of-sale advertising for the Seal of Minnesota cigars offered by Kuhles & Stock of St. Paul was printed by Brown & Bigelow. Courtesy of Mike Schwimmer.

S. R. Van Sant, and Civil War captain Josias R. King), the mass hanging of the sixty-two Native Americans convicted of participating in the 1862 Dakota Conflict, and the "Mudcura Sanitarium" of Shakopee. The manufacturers filing these trademarks were located in Austin, Chaska, Duluth, Graceville, Minneapolis, Shakopee, and St. Paul.

Flour Advertising

Minnesota's flour mills have long been major advertisers, utilizing every format from the earliest printed examples to the most modern. At first, flour advertising was aimed at wholesale markets. Mill lithographs show large buildings with tiny wagons, steamboats, or trains arriving to transport the thousands of barrels of flour to local and worldwide destinations. The barrels themselves, with their stenciled labels, frequently appear in these advertisements.

By the 1880s flour millers were directing their advertising copy to homemakers. The text on a trade card from the St. Paul Roller Mill Company, titled "An Open Letter" began by urging "Dear Madam" to use their Orange Blossom flour because it

The figure of Liberty, sporting her Phrygian cap and dangling her Gold Medal Flour emblem, watches from her pedestal as ships unload flour to waiting trains. The title of this folded trade card, The World is Ours, indicates the readiness of Washburn, Crosby Co. to export flour everywhere. The reverse side of the card has a recipe for bread and an offer to obtain the company's cookbook. Courtesy of Fred Foley.

FOR BOXES, BOTTLES, BARRELS, BAGS, AND CANS

would encourage "home industries" and thus build up the city. Orange Blossom flour, wrote the mill's manager, was being used by the Ryan, Merchants, and Windsor hotels of St. Paul, as well as by the city's leading bakeries.

In 1885 Kingsland Smith, manager of the St. Paul Roller Mill Company, introduced another promotional effort for Orange Blossom flour, a cookbook. Like some of the children's books offered by other flour mills, *The Orange Blossom Cook Book* contained a story, facts about flour milling, and recipes, which Smith felt were sorely needed.[86]

A rubber band placed on the cardboard toy could be tightened to mimic a bee's buzzing. This novelty was given out by Ceresota flour. Courtesy of Fred Foley.

Hanging tags for stores, made from cardboard, were another colorful way to advertise flour. The fine whiteness of Barber's flour is emphasized by its name, the color, and the grains falling from the child's hands. Courtesy of Fred Foley.

Northwestern Consolidated Milling of Minneapolis chose a small boy (named Ceresota) as their trademark. Ceresota, the son of the harvest goddess Ceres, was sold or given away as an image on blotters, calendars, playing cards, and even as a doll. This trade card, lithographed by the Monasch firm, shows Ceresota in trademark pose. Courtesy of the authors.

Other advertisements targeted the family by offering toys, dolls, and coloring books. In *The Adventures of Ceresota* or *Mother Hubbard and the Fairies*, finding the best flour triggers the plot. Ceresota, the Northwestern Consolidated Milling Company's trademark, was dressed in overalls, a large hat, and boots. In describing his attire, the booklet author noted, "In addition to these he had some bread and a knife / Which he carried about him the rest of his life." Thus, the idea of the chef, the knife, and a loaf of bread as used by other flour millers is continued in the concept of Ceresota.

In contrast to the historic and fairy tale names is the racist imagery depicted in the Duluth Imperial lithograph. Black bakers and chefs are not uncommon in flour milling and cereal advertising dating from the 1890s. Aunt Jemima made her appearance at the 1893 Chicago world's fair, and Rastus, the Cream of Wheat chef, was introduced at about the same time. The pose of the Cream of Wheat chef, with a ladle slung over one shoulder while he holds a bowl of cereal in the other, was based on a stock image of a black baker.[87] Flour millers in Minnesota used that image of a baker, with his bread knife and loaf of bread, on their letterheads and envelopes.

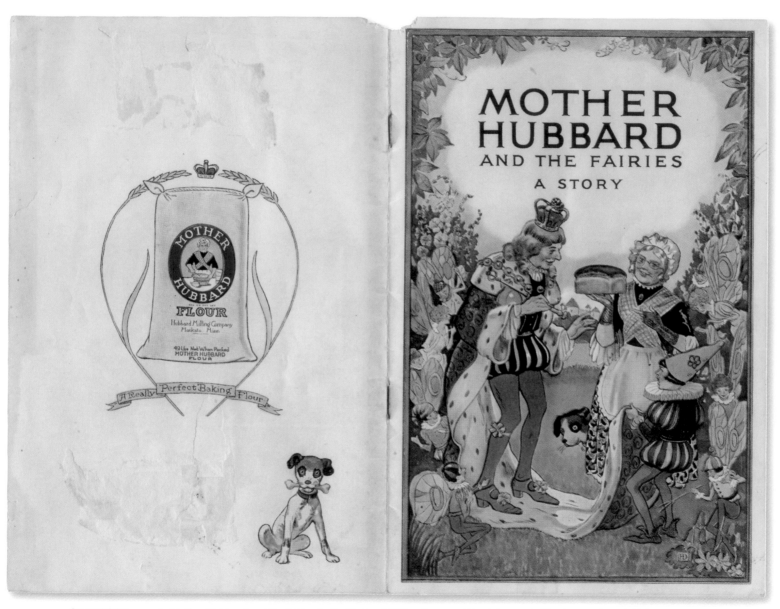

George W. Davey wrote Mother Hubbard and the Fairies for the Hubbard Milling Company. The plot presented by the story is twofold: her dog has no bone and the King of Fairyland lacks good bread. With the help of fairy friends, Mother Hubbard locates spring wheat, the King is satisfied, and the dog is rewarded. This full-color booklet was published in 1927. Courtesy of Fred Foley.

OLD SLEEPY EYE

IN 5 DAYS RETURN TO

Sleepy Eye Flour Mills Company

FLOUR EXCHANGE BLDG.

Minneapolis, Minn.

BEN-HUR FLOUR

"MADE IN MINNEAPOLIS"

"HIGH QUALITY WINS."

Sleepy Eye flour was ground in the town of the same name, but used a Minneapolis address for its prestige. While the mill was quite small, its owners invested heavily in advertising. Collectors treasure many items with Chief Sleepy Eye's image. Courtesy of Fred Foley.

Whether a chariot race or a comparison of flour for bread or pastry, quality wins, argued the Royal Milling Company of Minneapolis. Recipes are found on the reverse of this small sheet, lithographed by the Monasch firm. Courtesy of Bob Jackson.

Poster for a new brand from a Duluth flour mill. Like the rest of the nation, advertisers in Minnesota occasionally used racist imagery. A black chef was one of the company's principal logos. Lithographed by Henry Seibert & Bro. Co. of New York. Courtesy of Fred Foley.

Flour mill advertising includes barrel-top signage, posters, postcards, trade cards, letterhead stationery, blotters, cookbooks, and point-of-sale materials.

The Minnesota Historical Society's Mill City Museum, built within the ruins of the Washburn-Crosby A Mill on the Minneapolis banks of the Mississippi River, displays many items of flour mill advertising.[88] Another rich display of flour ephemera may be found in a St. Paul restaurant; the Copper Dome Pancake House and Restaurant is decorated with Fred Foley's collection of flour milling artifacts.

A recent television commercial showed a precocious tyke bearing a bowl of cereal for "his daddy's cholesterol." His sleepy mother asks whether he has been reading the cereal box again, and the answer is a nod. Reading the cereal box has been a common practice at American breakfast tables since the 1930s. Cereal box backs were perfect spaces for games, jokes, riddles, and toys to be cut out once the box was empty. Cereal boxes often contained prizes and coupons to order gifts dear to a child's heart.

In 1934 General Mills began placing drawings of athletes on boxes of Wheaties cereal, the "Breakfast of Champions." This slogan was created by Minneapolis advertising executive Knox Reeves.[89] Their

first champion was the fictional Jack Armstrong from the company-sponsored radio program. After that, athletes in nearly every individual and team sport were featured. Baseball players have appeared the most often. Among the Minnesota-connected stars featured on Wheaties boxes are baseball's Dave Winfield and Kirby Puckett (2001), University of Minnesota Gopher football player Bronko Nagurski (1937), and the "Miracle on Ice" United States men's gold medal ice hockey team (1997). In 1997 a set of five special-edition Wheaties boxes featured football stars painted by Minnesota artist LeRoy Neiman.

Liniment, Brooms, Onions, and Other Products

Still other posters and labels for Minnesota companies emphasize awards, prosperous factory buildings, and satisfied consumers (especially of the porcine sort). Marion Savage's International Stock Food company manufactured and sold its products from the old Minneapolis Exposition building for over thirty years. This poster, emphasizing the international awards won by their animal feed, was probably displayed at the Company's Minnesota State Fair booth. The M. A. Gedney onion label includes its two world's fair gold medals as well as a small vignette of Minnehaha Falls. The Smith broom label, on the other hand, is a factory scene in the Art Moderne style of the 1920s.

In the 1930s a researcher for the Minnesota W.P.A. Guidebook wrote that three bottles of Watkins'

The International Stock Food Company, owned by Marion Savage, had its headquarters in the huge Minneapolis Industrial Exposition building from 1903 until 1935. This poster, advertising animal feed, was lithographed by the company. Courtesy of the Minnesota State Fair History Museum.

liniment were used every minute.[90] Liniment, good for man or beast, was the first product made and sold by Joseph R. Watkins. He acquired the formula from Dr. Richard Ward of Cincinnati and began making his heal-all product at his home in Plainview, twenty-five miles from Winona, in 1868. The liniment was offered in a bottle with a "trial mark" molded into the glass. A customer who was unsatisfied with the liniment and who had

The M. A. Gedney Company's Holland onion label was submitted for state trademark registration. The onions had won medals at both the 1876 Centennial and 1893 Columbian World's Fairs. Courtesy of the Minnesota Historical Society (Secretary of State papers).

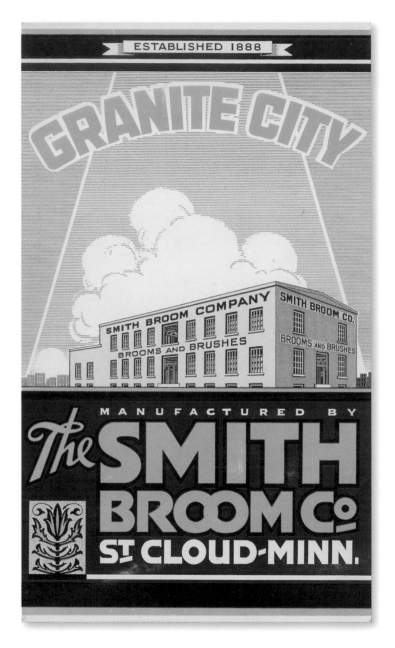

used it to the trial mark level could return the remainder for a refund. Watkins' concept of satisfaction guaranteed or money returned would be copied by numerous other manufacturers and retailers. By 1885 the J. R. Watkins Medical Company had moved to Winona.

Watkins originally sold his liniment and his gradually expanded line of products, including vanilla, pepper, and cinnamon, by visiting nearby towns and farms in his buggy. Early labels for his bottled products carried his picture and signature.

Printing was done in the Watkins print shop. Labels, package inserts, and, beginning in 1901, the famous *Watkins Almanac* were all produced by staff printers. The *Almanac* carried weather predictions, horoscopes, and recipes as well as a checklist of Watkins' products. The W.P.A. researcher wrote that "farmers, housewives, and others refer to it as a standard guide for treatment of minor ailments and for its valuable information on other subjects."[91]

Illustrations in an early edition of the *Watkins Almanac, Home Doctor and Cookbook* (1911) were cuts supplied by the Capper Engraving Company of Topeka, Kansas. That year the *Almanac* was mailed

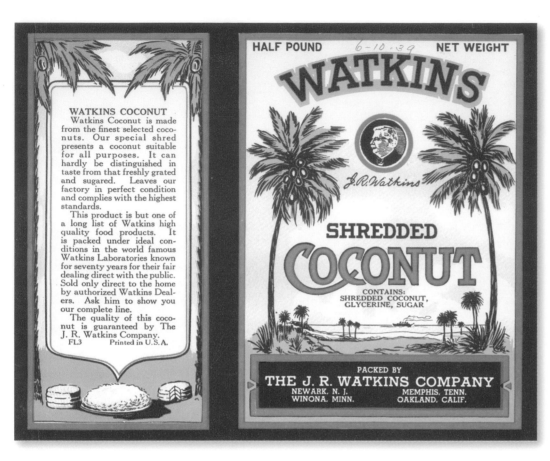

WATKINS COCONUT
Watkins Coconut is made from the finest selected coconuts. Our special shred presents a coconut suitable for all purposes. It can hardly be distinguished in taste from that freshly grated and sugared. Leaves our factory in perfect condition and complies with the highest standards.

This product is but one of a long list of Watkins high quality food products. It is packed under ideal conditions in the world famous Watkins Laboratories known for seventy years for their fair dealing direct with the public. Sold only direct to the home by authorized Watkins Dealers. Ask him to show you our complete line.

The quality of this coconut is guaranteed by The J. R. Watkins Company.

FL3   Printed in U.S.A.

HALF POUND   6-10-39   NET WEIGHT

WATKINS

J. R. Watkins

SHREDDED

COCONUT

CONTAINS:
SHREDDED COCONUT,
GLYCERINE, SUGAR

PACKED BY
THE J. R. WATKINS COMPANY
NEWARK, N. J.   MEMPHIS, TENN.
WINONA, MINN.   OAKLAND, CALIF.

This 1939 label for Watkins coconut bears the familiar profile of the company founder, flanked by palm trees and an ocean view. Courtesy of Watkins, Inc.

to two million farm homes. According to Jim Welch of the Watkins art department, the first artist hired to design labels, *Almanac* covers, and print advertising was Tubby Beynon. Hired in 1928, Beynon spent forty-two years at Watkins.[92]

Calendars with the Watkins name, a specialty item often printed by Brown & Bigelow, made their appearance in 1930. The *Almanac*, calendars, and many examples of Watkins packaging and labels are exhibited in the company's Heritage Museum, which opened in 1993. Jerry Whetstone,

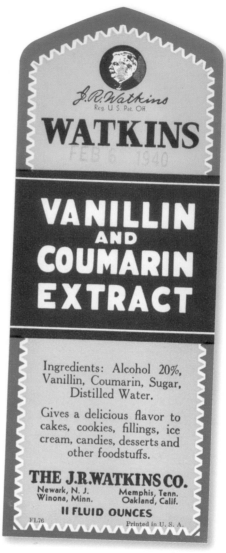

J. R. Watkins
Reg. U. S. Pat. Off.

WATKINS

FEB 6 1940

VANILLIN
AND
COUMARIN
EXTRACT

Ingredients: Alcohol 20%, Vanillin, Coumarin, Sugar, Distilled Water.

Gives a delicious flavor to cakes, cookies, fillings, ice cream, candies, desserts and other foodstuffs.

THE J.R. WATKINS CO.
Newark, N. J.   Memphis, Tenn.
Winona, Minn.   Oakland, Calif.

II FLUID OUNCES

FL76   Printed in U. S. A.

One of the most popular products of the Watkins company was its vanilla extract. This label is circa 1928. Courtesy of Watkins, Inc.

Various Minnesota fruit and vegetable labels with PLU codes are shown. Courtesy of the authors.

a Watkins premium support manager at that time, organized the exhibits in what had been the company's print shop until 1988.[93] The opening of the museum coincided with the company's 125th anniversary.[94] The J.R. Watkins Company, now named simply Watkins, has been owned by Minneapolis investor Irwin Jacobs since 1978. Many former employees and others belong to the Watkins collectors' group.

The Price Look-up Number

One of the newest, tiniest, and most universal labels is the price look-up (PLU) sticker, or P-seal.[95] Smaller than a quarter, multicolored, and printed on an adhesive material, PLU labels are stuck on individual fruits and vegetables. They carry a basic four-digit number that identifies the type of fruit (a Gala apple, for example, rather than a Golden delicious apple), which can be preceded by a number 9 (for organic fruit) or a number 8 (for genetically engineered produce).

PLUs began as a convenient way for supermarkets to identify fruits and vegetables. Bananas were the first items to be so marked, with United Fruit Company's Chiquita dancing cheerfully on their tiny stickers. Other banana growers soon followed the practice. By 1980 collectors of stamps and seals observed the variety of PLUs that existed and a new hobby was born. Banana seals are still said to be the most numerous. Minnesota growers use PLUs for apples and tomatoes. Minnesota apples were first grown in orchards near Winona, so a small steamboat recalling that city's river heritage is often printed on PLUs identifying certain apples, such as Gala (4134) and Cortland (4106). Another sticker uses PLU 4058 for the Minnesota-grown Haralson apples.

Unique PLU numbers for all fruit and vegetable varieties are assigned by the Produce Electronic Identification Board. To date, more than 2,000 numbers have been used. Most of the small sticky labels are printed by Sinclair International of Norwich, England. Virtually all of the labels are round or oval; recently small tabs have been added to make them easier to remove.

CHAPTER FIVE

Merchant Giveaways

OST MERCHANTS IN THE RETAIL WORLD historically have used various forms of ephemera. Some were giveaways to establish customer loyalty, such as trade cards, fans, toys, art calendars, poster stamps, blotters, matchbooks, and postcards. Other forms of retail ephemera involve packaging on which a store's name appears: bags, boxes, and stickers. Trading stamps also have functioned as giveaways that encourage return customer visits. (They are included in a discussion of scrip and coupons in chapter 9). Signs for auctions and garage sales represent the last stage in the life of many consumer objects, when the buyer or customer in turn becomes a vendor. Finally, signs and posters are used for many business purposes.

Art Calendars

The Minnesota art calendar was born when a salesman from Iowa arrived in St. Paul in the early 1890s. Herbert H. Bigelow had sold art calendars for the Thomas Murphy Company of Red Oak, Iowa, until he decided to begin his own business. Hiram Brown,

a partner in the Brown, Treacy & Company printing firm of St. Paul, agreed to help finance the operation. Brown & Bigelow was quickly on its way.

Like other early printers of art calendars, Brown & Bigelow used stock images at the beginning.[96] A portrait of George Washington appeared on the first calendar it ever printed, which was for the Schleh Brothers Coal Company of St. Paul. Until 1899, Brown & Bigelow calendars featured either plain black-and-white or duotone (two color) pictures. Their favorite calendar subjects then consisted of little girls picking daisies on dangerous cliff tops with angels hovering about them ready to take them out of harm's way if they came too close to the edge. The four-color printing process was introduced about 1899. That year essentially marked the beginning of the era of beauty and color in art calendars.[97]

Later Brown & Bigelow calendars featured work by many artists of both local and national repute. Thus a bank, department store, garage, or any of the many other customers for what the firm called

SERIES THREE ★ ★ ★

PIN-UPS

FAITHFUL REPRODUCTIONS
OF ORIGINAL PAINTINGS

12 GORGEOUS GLAMOUR GIRLS

ELVGREN

Each print is securely bound, yet
will tear out with a nice clean
edge for Pin-Up or framing.

•

Easily mailed to any part of the
world for 3c postage (3rd class).
Must be mailed under 12c postage (1st Class) to Army men in
foreign countries. Convenient
self-mailer attached to back
cover.

A LIVE WIRE

OTHER SERIES TO FOLLOW • WATCH FOR THEM!

Cover of a World War II set of pin-up girls by Gil Elvgren. Produced by the Louis F. Dow company. Courtesy of Paul Schoenecker.

Caught in the Draft

OCTOBER • 1946

ELVGREN

A typical Gil Elvgren beauty keeps her hat on while her skirt lifts. The 1946 calendar was produced by the Louis F. Dow company. Courtesy of Paul Schoenecker.

Remembrance Advertising could choose from the vignettes of Norman Rockwell, the misty landscapes of Maxfield Parrish, the comic monkeys of Lawson Wood, the poker-playing dogs of Cassius Marcellus Coolidge, or the pin-ups drawn by several specialists in that genre. Calendars, matchbooks, place mats,

A 1916 woodblock calendar designed by Mary Moulton Cheney. Curious birds printed in soft colors frame the pad of monthly pages. Courtesy of the Ramsey County Historical Society.

postcards, playing cards, and blotters were later available with the same Brown & Bigelow artwork.

The first offices for Brown & Bigelow were located on Third Street (now Kellogg Boulevard). In 1914 a large plant was opened in the Midway district of St. Paul on University Avenue. By the 1960s Brown & Bigelow was one of the largest calendar printing firms in the country, competing with several other firms begun by alumni of the Thomas Murphy Company.[98] Eventually the company moved to the West Side and a new headquarters on Plato Boulevard.

The Shedd-Brown Company was another Minnesota calendar printer. It began business in Red Wing in 1904, relocated in Minneapolis from 1909 until 1949, and then moved to Eau Claire, Wisconsin. During the 1940s Jensen Printing of Minneapolis issued an annual series of calendars featuring Minnesota scenes painted by Edward Brewer. This St. Paul artist is best known for the many magazine advertisements he designed for the Cream of Wheat Company, featuring Rastus, the smiling chef. For the Jensen calendars he painted Red River oxcarts, the Minnesota State Fair, and the Spiral Bridge at Hastings, Minnesota, among other subjects.[99]

Louis F. Dow founded his printing firm in St. Paul in 1900. His first order was five thousand postcards for the Griggs-Cooper firm. Later his Goodwill Advertising would include calendars.[100] There were many Dow artists over the next five decades, including a father-son pair named Hintermeister. But one star artist was a St. Paul man whose specialty was cute but sexy pinups. Gil Elvgren established his style while at Dow from 1937 to 1944, but was soon offered more money by Brown & Bigelow, where he joined Zoe Mozert and Rolf Armstrong as masters of the pin-up.

In the early years of calendar printing, one image had to suffice. A small pad of monthly calendar pages was affixed beneath the artwork. Space was left for "Compliments of …" followed by the name and address of the calendar sponsor. Calendars would be hung on the wall by ribbons, hooks, or cords, features that often required additional assembly by the printers. Calendars were available in many standard sizes for home or office use, as small pocket calendars for housewives, as larger wall models for farmers, and in a very large, jumbo size for railroad stations, where travelers could gaze at a calendar featuring the Blackfeet Indians painted by Winold Reiss.

Calendars came in many shapes and sizes as they still do. A small hanging wall calendar was designed by artist Mary Moulton Cheney with hand-tinted birds looking on from its frame. A Finnish-language calendar reflects labor difficulties in Minnesota's Iron Range. And an intricate die-cut, many-sectioned calendar was a Hamm's brewery giveaway. Many different Hamm's calendars were supplied over the years, including

Bells and violets decorate a die-cut calendar produced for the Theo Hamm Brewing Company in 1898. Lavender ribbons held the calendar sections together. Courtesy of the Ramsey County Historical Society.

Priscilla was often shown in advertisements for the New England Furniture Company of Minneapolis. The winsome lass was drawn by Alice Hugy, one of the first commercial artists in St. Paul. Courtesy of the authors.

Patrick Towle began selling his blended cane and maple syrup, available at first in a log cabin-shaped tin, in 1887. This lithographed blotter shows both the original container and the maple syrup's source. Courtesy of Glen Wiessner.

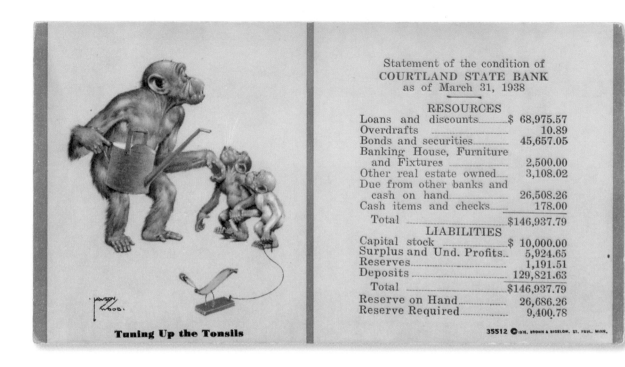

Statement of the condition of
COURTLAND STATE BANK
as of March 31, 1938

RESOURCES

Loans and discounts	$ 68,975.57
Overdrafts	10.89
Bonds and securities	45,657.05
Banking House, Furniture and Fixtures	2,500.00
Other real estate owned	3,108.02
Due from other banks and cash on hand	26,508.26
Cash items and checks	178.00
Total	$146,937.79

LIABILITIES

Capital stock	$ 10,000.00
Surplus and Und. Profits	5,924.65
Reserves	1,191.51
Deposits	129,821.63
Total	$146,937.79
Reserve on Hand	26,686.26
Reserve Required	9,400.78

35512 © 1934, BROWN & BIGELOW, ST. PAUL, MINN.

Tuning Up the Tonsils

English artist Lawson Wood's chimps brighten all sorts of advertising produced by Brown & Bigelow. Tuning up the Tonsils appeared on a blotter for a bank near New Ulm. Courtesy of the authors.

huge portraits of beautiful ladies for tavern walls and small folding calendar cards available in pre-Prohibition days.

The work of many Minnesota artists has appeared on calendars.[101] Other wildlife artists followed the successful careers of Les Kouba and Roger Preuss. After the 1960s, wildlife painters were joined by wildlife photographers such as Les, Nadine, and Craig Blacklock, whose work appeared on the calendars of Voyageur Press of Stillwater.

Original artwork for calendars, now of great interest to collectors, may remain with printers. But if the corporate client specified and commissioned the work of certain artists, then their paintings usually stayed with that company. Thus the Win-old Reiss paintings for the Great Northern Railway calendars are owned by that railroad's successor company. The Les Kouba paintings done for the Red Wing Shoe Company hang in their corporate offices. What is now called the Potlatch Collection of Royal Canadian Mounted Police Illustrations was originally commissioned for the Northwest Paper Company of Cloquet. This company, later known as the Potlatch Corporation, gave most of the original artworks to the Tweed Museum of Art in Duluth in 1981.[102]

Blotters

Once a common form of advertising and a useful tool on every desk, the blotter is now extinct. Every writer who used ink with a quill point, a metal nub, or a fountain pen needed a way to dry his words. Air and sand were regularly employed until absorbent paper was perfected in about 1830. Blotters came in several sizes and even in large desk-sized sheets.[103]

Blotters did not serve as advertising vehicles until another grade of paper was affixed on top. When that was done, the medium for the message was in place. Until the advent of the ballpoint pen made blotting ink unnecessary, companies large and small used blotters for advertising images and even for small calendars.

Trade Cards

While trade cards advertising goods or services were printed in America as early as the eighteenth century, the chromolithograph versions distributed between 1875 and 1900 are the best known today. Robert Jay notes that "no other medium

Earl Moran's pin-ups, which were quite popular during World War II, often appear on Brown & Bigelow advertising specialties. Inflation Control (1942) offered a calendar on this blotter. Courtesy of the authors.

The Arbuckle Coffee Company issued a set of fifty trade cards, one for each state and territory. Each card gave a brief history on one side and had appropriate advertising images on the other. Minnesota's card included a view of Minnehaha Falls. Courtesy of Clark Hansen.

could reach so many households and no other one was saved and cherished by the consumers themselves. At the height of its popularity in the 1880s, the trade card was truly the most ubiquitous form of advertising in America."[104]

Each of the basic colors of a chromolithograph was applied using a separate stone. Louis Prang of Boston was considered to be one of the pioneering printers of fine trade cards. Flowers, especially roses, were his favorite subjects.

Primarily produced by lithographers in Boston (such as J. H. Bufford), New York, Philadelphia, and Chicago, advertising trade cards were designed to merge advertising messages with interesting images. The cards were intended to be saved as reminders of goods or services. According to Luna Lambert Levinson, Boston lithographers of show cards (the much larger variation of a trade card), produced images including factory views, exhibition endorsements (medals won in competition), feminine images (derived from mythology), animal images, product illustrations, humorous designs, and testimonials.[105] Cards were given away at fairs (beginning with the 1876 world's fair at Philadelphia), tucked into product containers (known to collectors as insert cards), and offered to customers in stores. Albums were produced to collect and display what soon became the subject of a collecting frenzy.

Stock trade cards in sizes from 1½ by 2½ inches to 6 by 10 inches, or even larger, were printed and sold. Both manufacturers and retailers used them,

Skating ladies adorn this oversize trade card of Altman & Company, clothiers of Minneapolis. Courtesy of Paul Schoenecker.

Compliments of
ALTMAN & COMPANY, CLOTHIERS.
31 & 33 WASHINGTON AVENUE SOUTH, MINNEAPOLIS.

Printers could supply stock trade cards, which a business would then have overprinted with its name, address, or message. The Boston One-Price Store in Winona used such a card, which bore the name of George Hayes and the date of 1881. Courtesy of the authors.

imprinting their own names, addresses, and messages on the reverse side. One series of stock images, showing an accident-prone farmer, his plow, and his pigs, was engraved by J. H. Bufford of Boston. Numbered 468, and bearing a copyright date of 1887, the series was used by St. Paul Book & Stationery Company.[106] On the image side a diamond-shaped sign advertised Matchless Ink & Mucilage, while the entire reverse side gives the

company's name and address (127 East 3rd Street, St. Paul).

The earliest trade cards are found printed only in black and white. Most were square or rectangular, but die cuts are known, especially product-related shapes such as a high, button-shoe shape for a shoe store or a top hat for a hat maker. A die cut artist's palette was used for historic bird's-eye views of cities, perhaps to suggest that it was an "artistic" appreciation of the city, not a realistic one, as was usually the case.

Sellers of stoves, shoes, patent medicines, soaps, thread, sewing machines, flour, and canned or packaged grocery items of many kinds used

Long before it launched the Got Milk? print advertising campaign, the National Dairy Council office in St. Paul distributed this friendly cow. On the back a milk bottle is labeled "use more milk" while other figures stress milk's aid to good health. Courtesy of Paul Schoenecker.

Ground linseed cake makes cattle as fit as this beast for market. Trade card from the St. Paul Linseed Works. Courtesy of Glen Wiessner.

This trade card suggests that the easiest way to reach J. G. Schmidt's boat works was to take the train. At the store on Como Avenue, shells, gigs, barges, and canoes were to be seen. Courtesy of Glen Wiessner.

trade cards. And long before the Golden Arches of McDonald's carried signs with the ever-changing number of hamburgers sold, the Washburn-Crosby Company of Minneapolis was proudly announcing on its trade cards the number of barrels of flour it milled each day.

Despite the popularity of trade cards, their heyday was not to be long lasting. Manufacturers and retail businesses found they could reach even more potential customers through magazine or newspaper advertising. By 1900 the mass production of stock trade cards was over, although the printing for individual clients continued for a short time.

Matchbooks

One local collector got his start in phillumenology during the early 1940s, in old Memorial Stadium on the University of Minnesota campus. After each football game he would wander through the rows of seats, picking up used matchbooks for his collection. Matchcovers (the cardboard folders placed over the rows of matches) have been used since the late 1890s to promote every aspect of American life. For more than four decades of the past century, they were the most popular form of advertising known to consumers. They have also been the object of strong collecting interest since the various world's fairs of the 1930s.

While fire was essential to the caveman and to all who followed, the first sulfur-tipped matches weren't invented until 1827. The first matchbook was created in 1889. The inventor, Joshua Pusey,

St. Jacob's Oil certainly conquers pain, according to Lyons & Ticknor, druggists of St. Paul. Courtesy of Paul Schoenecker.

was one of the founders of the Diamond Match Company, a large conglomerate that has had a major manufacturing facility in Cloquet, Minnesota, since 1905.[107] The earliest known commercial advertising on matchcovers was created in 1895 for patrons of the Mendelson Opera Company. Other early patrons of matchcover advertising were the Pabst Brewery of Milwaukee (Blue Ribbon beer), the William Wrigley Company of Chicago (chewing gum), and the Duke Tobacco companies (tobacco products). During the 1970s, when matchbook production was at its height, it is estimated that approximately 600 billion lights (one match is called a light) were manufactured.

Before examining Minnesota's place in the field of phillumenology (the given name for this hobby, as derived from the Latin for "lovers of light"), the terminology of matchcover production and collecting needs to be briefly examined. The entire object is a matchbook (although in Britain the word is reversed: bookmatch); its wrapper is the matchcover. These terms are often interchanged. The striking surface, or striker, for the matchcover was in the earliest days on the front side (a front striker), but for safety reasons was later moved to the rear (a rear striker) to prevent the user from burning himself. Collectors usually remove, or

Inside the matchcover of the Hotel Leamington in Minneapolis is a "feature," colorful printing on the matches themselves. Courtesy of Rachel and Chuck Salloway.

HÔTEL LEAMINGTON

3rd Ave. 10th and 11th Streets

Minneapolis' Finest, 700 Luxuriously Furnished Rooms and Suites.

- **Beautiful Mayfair Restaurant**
- **Popular Coffee Shop**
- **Famous Sunday Smörgåsbord**
- **Smart New Cocktail Lounge**
- **Two Parking Lots Adjoining**

ASK THE HOSTESS ABOUT OUR
BANQUET AND PARTY ROOMS
CRYSTAL BALL ROOM
LANTERN TERRACE
DUBONNET ROOM
ROSE ROOM
JADE ROOM
LA PETITE SALLE
CAPE COD ROOM
MARIGOLD SUITE
FRENCH SUITE

GIANT FEATURE MATCH BOOKS
LION MATCH Co., Inc. CHICAGO, ILL.

shuck, the matches for safety reasons, unless the matches themselves are stapled or bear printing; these are known as features. Contours are uniquely shaped matchcovers. The size of matchbooks is based upon the number of combs, or rows, or the number of matches, 20 to 30 being the usual num-

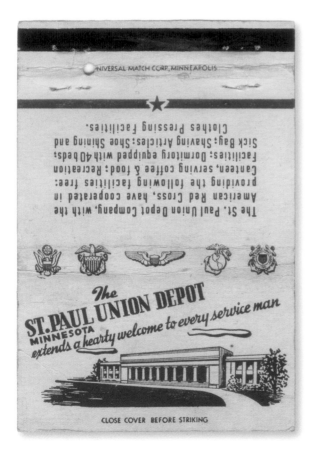

Municipal activities are illustrated in this matchcover from the St. Paul Union Depot. Courtesy of Rachel and Chuck Salloway.

Patriotic matchcovers from World War II were quite common. Courtesy of Rachel and Chuck Salloway.

Fraternal groups, such as the Military Order of the Cootie, would distribute free matchbooks to their members. Courtesy of Rachel and Chuck Salloway.

(THIS PAGE, FROM LEFT TO RIGHT):

Testing one's art abilities could lead to lessons-by-mail from the Art Instruction Schools, advised the inside of this matchcover. Courtesy of Rachel and Chuck Salloway.

A matchcover from the Hotel Lowry in St. Paul. Courtesy of Rachel and Chuck Salloway.

The most common matchcovers were those from hotels, restaurants, and movie theatres, such as the Alvin Burlesque theatre in Minneapolis. Courtesy of Rachel and Chuck Salloway.

ber. Midgets have 14 matches and measure 11/16 by 1½ inches, while there are various larger sizes known as giants.

Advertisers in Minnesota have utilized matchcovers for the promotion of countless varieties of products, trades, businesses, and organizations, and even for political campaigns. Only one company located in Minnesota is known for sure to have solicited, manufactured, and printed advertising on matchcovers. That was the Gopher Match Company. Possibly the E. B. Crabtree Co. of Minneapolis did so as well. The imprints of other Minnesota companies in their capacity as promoters, advertising agencies, or printers are found from time to time on matchcovers.[108] The imprint of the H. A. Olson Specialty Co. of St. Paul, for example, is noted on several early matchcovers. It is most likely that these companies solicited advertising for matchcovers in one capacity or another, but had them manufactured and printed by others.

Other national matchcover manufacturers had representatives or salesmen located in Minnesota to take orders.[109] Some of these manufacturers would place their logo or service mark and ordering information on the inside of matchcovers that apparently were supplied without cost to civic groups.

What choices did a prospective advertiser have? In its simplest and most economical form, he could have his business information rubber-stamped on the rear of a stock design matchcover. Then there were generic designs into which the information for a local merchant could be printed. Finally, there were matchcovers specially designed for the advertiser, in one-, two-, or even four-color format. There are collectors who classify their collections simply by color. Most collectors, however, sort them by image or category, or geographic location.

Matchcovers were normally lithographed in sheets of forty (two rows of twenty) on very poor-quality paper stock. Due to the need to produce the matchbooks in great bulk and at the lowest possible competitive prices, the printing quality is often quite rough, with the results sometimes poorly aligned and unclear. These elements affect the collectibility of matchcovers.

Within the hobby it is generally agreed that the rarest and most valuable matchcover features a Minnesota subject. That matchcover was one commemorating Charles Lindbergh's 1927 transatlantic solo flight. Only two are known to exist; both are in private collections.

Matchcovers are collected by museums and other large institutions. The Franklin Institute in Philadelphia, the Ford Museum in Dearborn, Michigan, and the Smithsonian Institution in Washington, D.C., have exhibited them in the past. The lobby of the offices of the Diamond Match Company in Cloquet, Minnesota, has an exhibit on the history of matches. Nationally, collectors have banded together in forty-two different clubs to talk about and trade their matchcovers. The largest, with 1,100 members, is the Rathcamp Match Society, located in Vandalia, Ohio. Another large regional organization for collectors is the Sierra-Diablo club in California. In Minnesota, collectors meet bimonthly in the Great Lakes Match Club. That club, with over 50 members, has undertaken a number of interesting civic and promotional activities, including supplying the governor's mansion in St. Paul with imprinted matchbooks. In 2005 the club members loaned items from their collections to a summertime exhibit at the William F. Eisner Museum of Design and Advertising in Milwaukee, Wisconsin. The exhibition's title was the familiar five-word phrase, "Close Cover Before Striking Match." Several local collectors have in excess of 50,000 matchcovers in their collections, while the record number for an American collection is said to be 280,000.[110]

What is the future of matchbooks and phillumenology? Both public policy and new technology caused a major slump in matchcover production during the last third of the twentieth century. As fewer people smoke and smoking is banned from offices, restaurants, and retail establishments, matches for the smoker are no longer an attractive giveaway. Those who still smoke may have already switched to using inexpensive, disposable cigarette lighters. However, there are two factors that seem to be harbingers of a somewhat rosy future for the matchbook: its cost and its appeal. First, it is arguably clear that from the standpoint of the matchbook manufacturer, "the strength in match sales lies in its inexpensive advertising power."[111] Matchbooks also offer snob appeal hard to achieve with most other paper collectibles. Lighting one's cigarette with a matchbook from the White House, an elite club, or an expensive restaurant implies a visit or perhaps membership. While some businesses no longer give away matchbooks, preferring instead tiny scratch books or postcards, matchbooks remain on counters, to the delight of collectors.[112] As the local president of the Minnesota collectors' group, Mark Quilling, said, "We live, breathe, and die matchbooks!"

Sheet of Munsingwear paper dolls with clothing, distributed to retail customers by Duluth Glass Block Store, Inc. Courtesy of Paul Schoenecker.

Paper Dolls and Other Toys

In 1914 the Northwestern Knitting Company of Minneapolis estimated that every tenth person in the United States who wore a union suit was wearing one bearing the Munsingwear brand name. For an underwear manufacturer to insist on using its own brand name rather than a retailer's name on its clothing was unusual at that date. But this was the company's program, and it was highly successful.

According to its first salesman, E. J. Couper, the company treated its retail outlets as dealer-agents and assisted them with unusual advertising.[113] There were newspaper and magazine advertisements supplied, as well as calendars, fans, and two items to appeal to the youngest Munsingwear customers: doll underwear and paper dolls.

Eight paper dolls and their clothing appeared in a small booklet, *The Munsingwear Family Cut-Outs*. The set included grandparents, parents, older brother and sister, and younger sister and brother. Advertising manager William B. Morris submitted printer's proofs of the dolls, or cut-outs, to the company's supervisory board in 1918.[114] He planned to order two million of the individual dolls, probably from Harrison and Smith, the firm long responsible

for Munsingwear's printing. Another cut-out was a single sheet bearing Miss Molly Munsing, her wardrobe, and her undershirts, and was imprinted with both the Munsingwear logo and its slogan, "Beyond Compare." Miss Molly's sheet was also imprinted with a store's address and logo at the top.

How a firm distributed paper dolls depended on the product being advertised. As Lagretta Metzger Bajorek notes in her book on advertising paper dolls, some dolls could be inserted in a product's container while other dolls were obtained by mailing back a coupon with stamps or coins in payment.[115] Nationally, beginning in the 1880s, companies selling sewing machines, thread, notions, and coffee and tea used paper dolls in their advertising. In Minnesota, in addition to Munsingwear, flour millers chose paper dolls for their promotions. Both the Pillsbury and Washburn-Crosby companies

Lithographed and die-cut teeter-totter distributed by the New York Tea Company of St. Paul. Courtesy of Glenn Wiessner.

The New York Tea Co.
377 Wabasha Street,
Near Post Office.
St. Paul, Minn.

Eight updated rhymes appear in Mother Goose Now-A-Days, *a children's paint book from 1906. Bo Peep, for example, has lost her sheep, but won't abuse her Foot Schulze shoes "by hitting the trail behind them." Each verse appears as a color lithograph with the same drawing ready to paint opposite it. Lithographed by the Mac Martin Company. Courtesy of Glenn Wiessner.*

placed their paper dolls inside flour sacks. Pillsbury's dolls were adult women, some from foreign lands, each standing next to a barrel of flour on an easel base. The Victorian lady wore a petticoat made of Pillsbury flour sacks. For the Washburn-Crosby set of sixteen head and shoulder dolls (four each of Mommies, girls, boys, and babies), the advertising was printed on the back of each doll. The identical set of sixteen dolls was used by other companies, including McLaugh-

lin Coffee Company of Chicago, a major user of paper dolls as advertising.

Coloring books were a popular giveaway at many retail stores. Before the invention of wax crayons, small pads of watercolors and tiny brushes were provided with the books. Often the illustrations were printed twice, with the outline on one page and the color placement on the facing page so that children would know what shades to use. Millers, shoemakers, and clothing manufacturers used these booklets to attract customers' children.

Fans

While the folding fan, with its spokes of wood or ivory, was part of a fashionable woman's accessories in the nineteenth century, simpler folding and flat fans continue to be a useful giveaway to both sexes. They appear, logically, in hot weather so printed fans are often given away at summertime events such as fairs. A recent Pan-Asian fair at Lake Phalen distributed fans as did gubernatorial candidate Tim Penny at the Minnesota State Fair (see chapter 9).

A ham-shaped fan promoted Hormel's meats, while an unusually talented frog appears on a fan for a buggy-maker who perhaps imagined fair ladies needing fans as they rode through the countryside. What seems at first glance to be a fan is actually what one printer called a "favor." Attached to the fan is a honey-combed paper that becomes a turkey when the two sticks are spread apart.

The front side of this small 1909 booklet, entitled What's Wrong, contains puzzle pictures for children with crayons to color. The reverse side, which contains the name of a Minneapolis pharmacy, advertises headache remedies. Courtesy of the authors.

Fans have been a popular giveaway. The musical frog, strumming on his toadstool while he considers a flying tidbit, was distributed by St. Paul carriage maker Mast, Buford & Burwell. Courtesy of Rob Rulon-Miller.

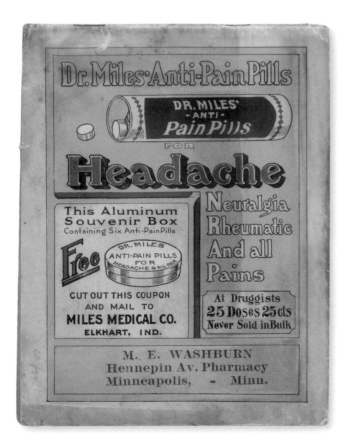

In Minnesota's exclusive shops and fine department stores, the clerks of yore would lovingly wrap the purchase in tissue paper and seal the contents with a distinctive adhesive label. Or, that label,

(THIS PAGE, FROM LEFT TO RIGHT):

A ham-shaped fan is an early souvenir for Minnesota's famed meatpacking firm, Geo. A. Hormel of Austin. Hormel opened in 1891, specializing in pork products. Courtesy of Glenn Wiessner.

This favor, which opens up into a crepe paper turkey, was distributed by the Minnesota Linseed Oil Paint Company, circa 1920. In 1970 the company merged with Valspar Corporation. Collection of the authors.

Tiny gummed package labels, often printed on heavy gold or silver foil paper, are used to hold together sheets of tissue paper inside a box. These labels from Twin Cities jewelry stores were used to fasten tissue paper wrappings in 1956. Courtesy of the authors.

often in brilliant silver or gold to emphasize luxury, would be prominently placed on the shopper's parcel to identify the source of the merchandise. A simple logo or store name was printed on an adhesive-backed or self-stick paper, often embossed, and the result then die cut into various shapes. Used most often during the middle decades of the previous century, these labels were produced for upscale department stores, jewelry stores, shoe stores, and candy stores. The authors are not aware of any previous effort to study or catalog these labels.

Company Logos

Prominently displayed on retail packaging of all kinds is the corporate or business logo. It may be a stylized signature (The Dayton Company), or a sans-serif block letter (3M), or an image. One formerly well-known logo can still be seen in bronze on the corner of a Nicollet Mall building in downtown Minneapolis. It is the seated lady, known as Inspiration, used by the Young-Quinlan Company from 1927 until that specialty clothing store closed in 1985.[116]

Elizabeth Quinlan and Fred Young launched what was the second women's clothing store in the country in 1894. After Young's death in 1911, Miss Quinlan became sole proprietor and in 1926 opened an expanded store at Nicollet Avenue and Ninth Street. The following year, on a European trip, she sought out a designer for a store logo.

Armand Albert Rateau (1882–1938) was a leading Art Deco designer of furniture and interiors in Paris.

His work for couturière Jeanne Lanvin was well known, especially his graceful woman and child for Arpége, Lanvin's perfume. For Young-Quinlan his concept was a sophisticated odalisque, which Miss Quinlan liked but at first rejected because, said she, "She's nude." The artist quickly added a beaded necklace. So Inspiration became the Young-Quinlan lady. This lady, dangling a lorgnette in one hand as she reclines against a background of flowers, appeared on packaging and dress labels, and remains on the bronze plaque, a reminder of a fashion pioneer.

In 1944 Young-Quinlan published nine full-page human interest newspaper advertisements to mark the fiftieth anniversary of the store. The seventh featured Inspiration, the store's logo created by Parisian artist Armand Albert Rateau. He was asked to create "a beautiful, cold, ageless woman who would live as long as beauty lived." And he did. Courtesy of the 901 Nicollet Company.

(THIS PAGE,
FROM LEFT TO
RIGHT):

The dramatic scene of fire wagons and firemen with their hoses trained on a blaze makes the need for fire insurance obvious. Courtesy of Paul Hemple.

An Art Nouveau maiden sniffs a rose from the Holm & Olson florists in St. Paul. Courtesy of Paul Hemple.

Harvey Blodgett opened a separate lithographic business after leaving his previous employer, Brown, Treacy & Sperry. Courtesy of Paul Hemple.

Poster Stamps

Poster stamps are neither posters nor stamps, but are related to both. Printed in sheets that were then gummed and perforated, poster stamps were an early form of collectible advertising. They were distributed by the millions, cost next to nothing, and reached a very wide audience of prospective buyers. An early description noted that "poster stamps present in miniature all that the largest bill-boards portray, and accomplish all that is required of an efficient poster.... Affixed to the advertiser's packages, letters, invoices, circulars, catalogues, price lists, etc., they import a pleasing tone of individuality and embody a persistency of advertising and are valued by many collectors. Poster stamps have scored a hit and people WANT THEM."[117]

Poster stamps were also used to promote world's fairs and expositions, international sporting events, and charitable organizations. In their golden age, starting in the late 1890s, there were more poster stamp collectors than postage stamp collectors. There were said to be over 1,000 poster stamp clubs in the United States alone, and there were poster stamp exhibitions and dealers.[118] Just as trade cards had been previously preserved by collectors, albums were extensively available to house the poster stamps.

Lithographers in most major cities could print poster stamps. In St. Paul, the Pioneer Company; Brown, Treacy & Sperry Company, the Harvey Blodgett Company, and Brown & Bigelow were among the nationally known printers of poster

stamps. Occasionally the designs were unique. One series of Indian portraits was printed for the Great Northern Railway. Another large set was part of that railroad's "See America First" campaign, but was used by the Schuneman and Evans department store in St. Paul. Both sets were printed by Brown & Bigelow.

Stock designs offered a blank area in which to insert the message of an advertiser. The Volland Poster Stamp Company of Chicago made many holiday poster stamps of this type. Paul Frederick Volland founded his company in Chicago in 1908. His specialties were calendars, greeting cards, and poster stamps, that is, until an illustrator named Johnny Gruelle brought him a book idea in 1916. Gruelle's creation, the ever-smiling rag doll Rag-gedy Ann, was the subject of the first of Volland's many books for children. The Volland Company eventually merged with the Gerlach-Berklow calendar printers of Joliet, Illinois.

The Shopping Bag

For customers in every shop, from small boutique to giant supermarket, the cashier's question, Paper or plastic? is routinely posed. While some grocery stores require customers to bag their own purchases, virtually every retail establishment provides them with the box or bag to do so. In fact, current Cub Foods bags are printed with graphics showing customers how to place their groceries in the bags. That was not the case before St. Paul inventor Walter Deubener had his idea in 1918.

(THIS PAGE, FROM LEFT TO RIGHT):

A grocer discusses one of the products of food wholesaler Griggs, Cooper & Co. Courtesy of Paul Hemple.

Crescent Creamery's butter appears on a poster stamp. Other creamery products in the poster stamp set included ice cream and milk in bottles. Courtesy of Paul Hemple.

Brown & Bigelow's impressive headquarters was a landmark on University Avenue from 1914 to 1980. Courtesy of Paul Hemple.

Volland poster stamps left a space for a business to overprint its name. This holiday candle design dates from 1914. Courtesy of Paul Hemple.

Mrs. Walter Deubener carries groceries in the newly invented shopping bag, circa 1921. Courtesy of the Minnesota Historical Society (Walter H. Deubener Papers).

Deubener and his wife, Lydia, managed a small grocery section in a Kresge department store in downtown St. Paul. They had often observed that how much their customers purchased depended on what they could easily carry away. If, thought Deubener, customers used paper shopping bags they might buy more, since "a customer's purchases were limited by her arms rather than her pocketbook."[119]

Taking a brown paper bag, Deubener pierced holes in it with an ice pick and inserted twine through the holes. The twine passed under the bag and formed a double handle at the top of the bag. Mrs. Deubener cut illustrations from magazines, affixing them to the bags as decoration. The Deubeners sold their first twenty-five handmade bags quickly. Within a year they had launched a business, obtained patents, opened a factory, and sold their first million paper bags. The business remained in St. Paul until 1928. A more central location and the support of an eastern firm resulted in

a move to Indianapolis. Two years later Deubener sold his Company for one million dollars.[120]

The simple bag Deubener designed, using Kraft Mosinee paper with twine supports, was soon available throughout the country. The company's 1928 catalogue offered a basic bag that measured 16 by 18 inches. Illustrations for the bags came from Brown & Bigelow's stock of calendar lithographs, and the catalog itself was printed by the Brown-Blodgett Company of St. Paul.[121]

The Deubener bags were first sold directly to the customer. "A dime for a Deubener—everywhere" was the slogan. Soon stores and businesses of all kinds were ordering bags imprinted with their own logos to either sell or give to customers. Producing a paper shopping bag involved many hand assembly steps. When flexographic printing techniques were used, fabrication became faster and cheaper.[122] By the 1930s color printing technology for bags was available although still quite expensive. Wartime shortages meant that the true design explosion for bags had to wait until almost the 1960s.[123] Stores such as Dayton's in Minneapolis that had used a simple signature logo on their Deubener bags in 1940 could now include shopping bags as part of their holiday advertising.

In 1954 Bloomingdale's may have been the first department store to feature a special shopping bag. The Bloomingdale bag was a part of its New York City Christmas promotions. What was once unique was soon copied by stores throughout the country. The Christmas bag joined window

The Deubener grip cord handle shopping bags could be imprinted with a logo such as Miss Minneapolis or display an art print from Brown & Bigelow's stock, according to the Deubener company's 1928 catalogue. Courtesy of the Minnesota Historical Society (Walter H. Deubener Papers).

THE ARCHITECTURE OF REASSURANCE
DESIGNING THE DISNEY THEME PARKS

Walker Art Center
October 26, 1997,
through
January 18, 1998

displays and in-store promotions as part of regular holiday retail excitement. The Dayton's 1966 Dickensian bag was linked to a special display on the eighth floor of the Minneapolis store. From then on, a Christmas display with a related bag would be an expected annual event, just as the spring flower show, planned with the assistance of the Bachman's floral company, would be.

Dayton's, known since 2001 as Marshall Field's and since 2006 as Macy's, worked with both the Walker Art Center and the Minneapolis Institute of Arts on several art bag projects. Support for local museums was easily emphasized through the "walking billboard" of a shopping bag. Artists were commissioned to design large-sized paper shopping bags to be sold in conjunction with exhibitions. Each bag would be available as part of a museum promotion at Dayton's stores as well as in the museums' gift shops. Minneapolis newspaper columnist Barbara Flanagan wrote of one bag, "Where else can you buy a collector's item for 30 cents?"[124]

Shopping bag produced by Target, Mervyn's, and Dayton's for the Architecture of Reassurance: Designing the Disney Theme Parks exhibit at the Walker Art Center (1997–1998). Courtesy of the authors.

DAYTON'S

The Twelve Days
of Christmas
shopping bag
for the 1999
Dayton's holiday
show. Courtesy
of the authors.

DROP YOUR
SOCKS

CITY PAGES   CARIBOU COFFEE   KS95·FM

The Walker Art Center series began in 1980 with a canvas tote bag for the show "Picasso—From the Musée Picasso." The bag bore Pablo Picasso's signature. Unfortunately, the Paris museum did not approve the use of the artist's signature, so that bag, although advertised as being available, was quickly withdrawn. Artists were commissioned to produce unique designs for subsequent art bags. For the opening of new Walker Art Center print galleries in 1984 and a show of Tyler Graphic work, Frank Stella produced a print from which a bag was designed. The underlying lithograph is now in the museum's permanent collection. David Hockney's colorful *Punch and Judy* appeared on a bag celebrating both the museum and the 1985 British Festival of Minnesota. For the "Tokyo: Form and Spirit" show in 1986,

Shopping bag for shops in the Calhoun Square mall, Minneapolis. Courtesy of the authors.

Japanese graphic artist Eiko Ishioka designed the bag. In 1988 a design by Roy Lichtenstein celebrated both Dayton's annual flower show and the opening of the Minneapolis Sculpture Garden across the street from the Walker Art Center. Dayton's graphic design department contracted out the printing of most Walker Art Center bags with the exception of one based on a frame for Yoko Ono's film *No. 4*. This image was used for the "In the Spirit of Fluxus" show in 1993; the bag was produced by Distributed Art Publishers of New York.

In addition to the Dayton's–Walker Art Center bags, the store's design department created holiday and in-store label bags. Among them were some featuring its Santa Bear stuffed toy and a 1985 bag showing Willard Scott, the television weatherman, dressed as Santa in a photograph by Annie Leibovitz. A bag promoting its Boundary Waters label was a sold-out success. Designed by graphic artist and University of Minnesota professor Patrick Redmond in 1988, it appealed to shoppers who appreciated its outdoors symbolism. According to Redmond, it was also the first Dayton's bag to include a credit line for the artist.

Not all shopping bags are designed for use by only one store. Holiday or special event promotion in a shopping center may result in a bag that all stores in a mall will use. A holiday sales promotion for the Calhoun Square mall in Minneapolis used a design featuring a clothed penguin and the admonition that customers would drop their socks as they encountered bargains.[125]

Graphic design scholars have become interested in shopping bag history, but any list of shopping bag exhibitions and collections is so far quite limited. Exhibitions include the Cooper-Hewitt's "The Shopping Bag: Portable Graphic Art" in 1978, the University of Minnesota Goldstein Gallery's "Shopping Bag Design" in 1992, the Newark Public Library's "Shopping Bags Go Worldwide" in 2000, and the Hennepin County History Museum's "Wrap It Up: Holiday Bags, Boxes and Ephemera from the Nicollet Mall" in 1995. One of the larger national collections is that of the Department of Environmental Design at the University of California-Davis, with 10,000 examples to date.[126]

Signage

From broadsides to billboards and Burma-Shave poems, signs with letters and sometimes pictures are an inescapable part of the advertising world. Whether printed or painted they are captured more often in photographs than collections. Signs, in fact, like bumper stickers, often suffer destruction removed from places where they were displayed.

Beginning each spring, found in full bloom at every intersection, are the printed or hand-lettered Sale signs. By Labor Day and certainly before Halloween or the first snowfall, such signs vanish. By then families have sorted through their excess belongings, rid their homes of "nearly new" or "gently used" treasures, and the weather has grown cold. Sale signs usually give the reason for the sale (estate sale or moving sale), the inclusive identity of the sellers (single or multi-family, neighborhood); its location (garage, block, yard, or even cul-de-sac); and hours (typically weekends).

An estate sale may be conducted by a dealer, and the term suggests merchandise of value or simply reasonably old stuff. Estate sales may be advertised in newspapers, just as their equivalent, the farm auction, usually was. Moving sale, estate sale, and farm auction signs imply that these particular events will not happen again. Other sales often take place annually and even grow to become townwide events, such as the annual summer sale of antiques in Orinoco, a small town north of Rochester.

Estate sales are often held throughout a house (which will usually be for sale as well). Occasionally such a sale may be only a beginning. Two St. Paul women, Billie Young and Mary Wilson, decided to hold an attic sale of Mexican folk art since, as Billie Young wrote, "sales and bazaars were what women did." Friends and neighbors came in droves, so the two repeated their success with a second sale. These sales led to a new venture, a shop selling Mexican crafts on St. Paul's Grand Avenue. Their Old Mexico Shop lasted for twenty-two years (1972–1994) and was certainly one of the factors that led other entrepreneurs to launch stores and restaurants along what has now become one of the city's premier shopping streets.[127]

Auction poster for a farm sale in Alexandria, 1933. Courtesy of the Minnesota Historical Society.

Lake Shore FARM

For the next ten days I will offer the fine

217-acre Farm

of E. F. Needham, lying on the south side of Lake Darling and close to Alexandria.

Fine buildings: Barn 30x70, with large silo; 5-room house; granary and hog house; large machine shed; and nice summer cottage on lake.

This farm has ½ mile of very desirable lake shore frontage; 160 acres in field and balance in pasture and timber; all fenced.

This place will be offered at the low price of $34.00 per acre.

See or address
W. K. BARNES, Alexandria, Minn.

Dated December 18, 1933.

AUCTION!

The undersigned will sell at public auction at his residence in Wasioja, on

Saturday, Oct. 22,

at 11 o'clock A. M., the following described property, to-wit: One span of matched mares, six years old; one brood mare 11 years old, one mare 4 years old, one yearling colt and one colt 5 months old, two or three cows, one yearling steer, one shoat, six swarms of bees, one double wagon, one single buggy, one set double harness, two single harnesses, one pair of bob sleds, one Marsh Harvester, one seeder, one drag, one straw cutter, and Household Furniture, consisting cook and parlor stoves, bureau, tables, bedsteads, chairs, etc., etc.

TERMS---All sums less than $15, cash. All sums over $15 and less than $100, one year's time. All sums over $100, two years' time will be given on an approved note or security with annual interest at the rate of twelve per cent. per annum.

W. C. SHEPARD.

WASIOJA, OCT. 13, 1870.

MINNESOTA HISTORICAL SOCIETY
Pamphlet Collection.

While sale signs may be purchased ready-made, many are homemade, painted on scraps of wood, cardboard, or corrugated box material. Sale signs in the city may be nailed to fences or telephone poles. In the suburbs many signs are freestanding, stuck into the grass at street corners. Most are small, sometimes ridiculously so. One bright pink sign, on very short sticks, was seen at an intersection. Measuring 5 by 8 inches, it was too small to read until the corner was reached. Then it was possible to decipher the message in spidery letters written with a ballpoint pen, "Huge Sale Today!"

The term *garage sale* usually indicates the location: inside or in front of a garage. On at least one occasion, however, it meant "contents." After following numerous garage sale signs on the

Auction poster from Wasioja, 1870. For the seller, W. C. Shepard, his animals were the attraction, not the furniture. Courtesy of the Minnesota Historical Society (Pamphlet collection).

outskirts of a small country town, we reached the location only to discover that for sale were old gas pumps, signs, and all the tools actually used in a filling station about to close forever.

The whole phenomenon of garage sales seems to have begun in the 1970s. Treasures and discards that once went automatically into Goodwill bins, Vietnam Veteran or Salvation Army trucks, or to the neighborhood church, hospital guild, or rummage sale, now are sold at home.

Farm auctions are usually advertised in local newspapers and with 8½ by 11 inch posters, tacked on bulletin boards or telephone poles. Auctions are usually daylong affairs with lunch served by women from church guilds. During the 1950s and 1960s, a familiar presence at farm sales in Chisago County was Dennis Magnuson, collector and auctioneer. As Gareth Hiebert wrote, Magnuson collected implements, machinery, tractor seats, Victrolas and other things that would show what country life had been like. He exhibited it all at his Yesterfarm of Memories Museum near Center City.[128]

Political signs for candidates are also seasonal. They appear often in front yards before the primary elections in September and remain until after the general election in early November. Candidates for every office, from local to national, obtain signs with their names (only the surname if they are especially well-known) and the office they seek. Red, white, and blue are the usual colors for political yard signs, with the lettering often identical to that on the candidate's buttons and bumper stick-

ers. Recent exceptions were the orange signs of Tim Penny, a candidate for governor in 2002, and the green signs with exclamation points of the late Senator Paul Wellstone. Many municipalities regulate placement of these signs. Campaigns vie for sign locations visible from a distance, with the result that drivers become aware of signs for candidates screaming their message from opposing intersection corners. Other yards become political sign gardens, with messages supporting candidates for every office imaginable.

Political signs of protest have been part of demonstrations and parades for most of Minnesota's history. Some support a cause, others argue fervently against it. Often marchers (and their signs) pass in front of the capitol in hopes that legislators, the governor, and television cameras will witness their protest. Prior to the invasion of Iraq in March 2003, pro- and anti-war protesters stood on many Twin Cities bridges, holding their signs so that drivers below could see them. Other protesters used the Stillwater bridge on Sundays to demonstrate their support or opposition to the Iraq conflict.

And then there are what one reporter termed "signs of grief." Families, friends, even some who never knew victims of highway accidents, place flowers, crosses, teddy bears, and signs near the accident sites. In Minnesota such roadside memorials are illegal, and the Minnesota Department of Transportation will eventually remove them.[129]

After Senator Wellstone was killed in an airplane crash in northern Minnesota in October

2002, a giant temporary memorial was created at his campaign headquarters in St. Paul. His green bumper stickers were a bright counterpoint to flowers, photographs, and printed and hand-written signs on the walls of the building and the adjoining parking lot fence. Messages in English joined notes in Spanish and in the various languages of Southeast Asia. A red Silent Witness figure stood amidst the display to honor Sheila Wellstone, who also died in the crash, for her work with victims of domestic abuse.[130]

Recently there has been interest expressed and even a book published about a new aspect of loss: signs asking for the return of lost pets.[131] These printed, typed, or handwritten signs are tacked to telephone poles and grocery store bulletin boards and placed in veterinarians' offices. A photograph, the

Following the death of Senator Wellstone in an airplane crash in October, 2002, handwritten notes, flowers, and Wellstone campaign posters were quickly attached to the walls of his campaign headquarters on University Avenue in St. Paul. Photograph courtesy of the authors.

pet's name and description, the owner's telephone number, and perhaps the mention of a reward complete the sign.

Posters

Posters, bills, flyers, and billboards differ in size but are part of a long-standing tradition in public communication. These are signs that announce events and try to persuade the consumer, the voter, and the ticket buyer through their graphics and messages. And they are everywhere, even when their presence is distinctly unwanted. "Post No Bills," may be the warning on a wall that its owner hopes will remain pristine. NIMBY (not in my backyard) is the argument made by opponents of billboards. "Billboard correctors" take their spray paints and marking pens to change the meaning and the messages on billboards. Those who do post their signs are asked firmly to remove them from telephone poles, although such requests are rarely observed.

The size of these signs has usually been governed by what a press could conveniently print. With the earliest broadsides, the job printers could expand vertically but not horizontally unless additional sheets were assembled. Early broadsides might use stock drawings or woodcuts and every font and decorative ornament the print shop possessed.

Flyers, on the other hand, are often found in the paper size available on a copy machine (usually 8½ by 11 inches or 11 by 14 inches). Originally, flyers were typewritten with added hand-drawn graphics.

The flyer was then copied for hand distribution and posting on bulletin boards, kiosks, and telephone poles. They could be copied on colored paper as well as on white. Due to their small size, flyers are intended to be read at close range. Thus, their design and wording can be more complex than that of the largest example: the billboard.

A flyer in the 1800s was known as a handbill, or a poster small enough to be distributed by hand. It was printed, but seldom had much in the way of imagery. Posters would carry that aspect to a new dimension. The ubiquity of the word *handbill*, however, suggests other terms such as the bill of fare and the bill of lading. All of these were printed forms that listed items. A billposter took a stack of bills to affix to a wall whose use had perhaps been leased. Alastair Johnston used a painting of just such a billposter at work in London in the 1830s for the dust jacket of his book, *Alphabets to Order*.[132] The brick wall on which the billposter is gluing his advertisement for a performance of *Otello* is already covered with notices for ship sailings, lectures, candidates for office, and other theatrical events. Behind him on the ground lie bills, perhaps fallen from the wall, while in a bag slung across his back are the bills he had yet to post. Although the painting shows a London scene, billposters were doing the very same work in America. In their timeline of graphic design in America, Ellen Lipton and J. Abbott Miller note that by the end of the Civil War firms of billposters existed as well as unions for their employees. Much later came other firms that built the billboards, maintained them, and leased the space to those with posters to display.

Larger presses made larger handbills possible, and the introduction of lithography brought color to the printed bill, now more often called a "poster." For many scholars, the golden age of the poster began in the 1890s. Lipton and Miller wrote that a new kind of advertising, "the artistic poster," had emerged in America at that time.[133] The work of French artists such as Jules Chéret and Toulouse Lautrec provided inspiration for American posters. The first American art poster was designed by Louis Rhead for the Century Publishing Company. They wanted posters for windows of bookstores that sold their books.[134]

One golden age customer for the poster printer was the traveling circus. The source for many circus posters was the Cincinnati printers: the Enquirer, Strobridge Lithographing, and Donaldson Lithographing (which moved across the Ohio River to Newport, Kentucky in 1902).

Circuses concentrated most of their advertising budget in their posters. As each circus worked out its schedule, management also planned the

A poster for the 1890 season of the Minneapolis Exposition combined two favorite subjects: a pretty girl and the American flag. The printing was done by the Strobridge Lithographic Company of Chicago. Courtesy of Rob Rulon-Miller.

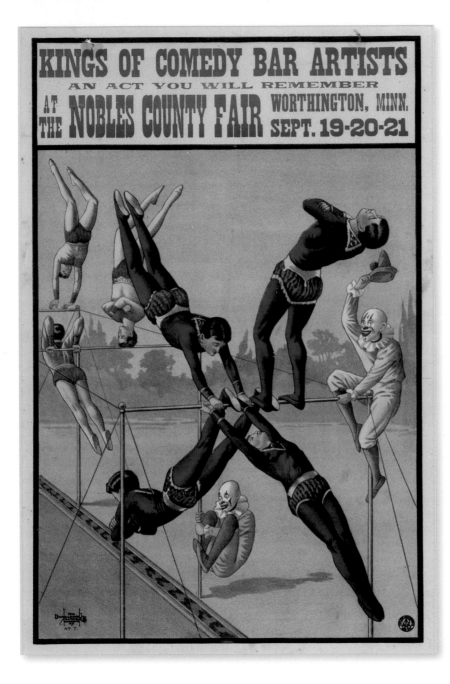

number of posters needed for each of its stops. Circuses ordered either stock posters, or specialty designs featuring a headline act.

A stock poster would have a strip added at the top or bottom giving the circus name, location, and performance dates. Circus employees serving as billposters posted posters outside, on city walls or barns, while the lithographers delivered posters to stores for window placement. The circus crew was known as the advance, as their wagons or, later, railroad cars, were the ahead-of-time arrivals.[135] Many circus posters measured a basic 28 by 42 inches, but larger combinations are known.

One circus poster, printed by the Calvert Litho Company of New York in 1891 had a most unusual source. Former Civil War general Lew Wallace published his novel about ancient Rome in 1880. The famous chariot race won by Wallace's hero, Ben Hur, excited readers, artists, and circus promoters. A Hungarian artist named Alexander Von Wagner painted the scene in the Hippodrome, which inspired circus owners to build Ben Hur rides and spectacles. The chariot race became a very popular fairground scene as well as the brand name of a Minnesota flour (see chapter 4).[136]

The circuses came to Minnesota on steamboats and by train to perform at county fairs and

Clowns and trapeze artists headlined a traveling circus at the Nobles County Fair in the early 1900s. The poster was No. 7 in a series produced by the Donaldson Lithography Company of Newport, Kentucky. Courtesy of Rob Rulon-Miller.

in indoor auditoriums. Traveling circuses tradition-
ally performed outdoors until 1906, when a fraternal organization in Detroit, Michigan, had the idea
of staging a winter indoor circus to raise funds for
charity. The members of the Detroit Shrine Temple
launched this concept, which was quickly adopted
elsewhere. Zuhrah Shrine Temple in Minneapolis
hosted the first such event in Minnesota in 1918.
The Rhoda Royal Circus performed, raising funds
for World War I relief efforts. The Zuhrah Temple
has continued to host the Shrine Circus ever since,
with the events taking place at the old Minneapolis
Armory, the old Auditorium, and finally the Target
Center.

One Minnesota lithographic printer is known to
collectors of circus posters. Neil Cockerline, paper
conservator and poster collector, noted that the
Standard Litho name exists on some Minnesota
circus posters. Cyrus Sherman and Roy R. Boorman
were officers in that St. Paul firm, located at 76 East
Fifth Street in 1904, and later in the 300 block of Rice
Street. There the firm identified itself as "Poster
Printers and Lithographers."

American railroads also commissioned posters,
just as their counterparts in Europe and in the mass
transportation systems such as the London Underground did.[137] While Minnesota's railroads all used
broadsides and small posters to present schedules
and fares to the traveling public, most of the best-
known poster artists received commissions after
1900. One well-known poster used by the Northern
Pacific Railroad showed its famous North Coast

A poster, sponsored by the Saint Paul and Duluth Railroad, advertises the thirty-seventh Minnesota State Fair (in 1896). The poster was produced by L. N. Scott, who was better known for his theatrical promotions. Courtesy of Mike Hajicek.

Limited passenger train passing through Bozeman Pass in Montana. Gustav Krollmann, a muralist and art teacher in Minneapolis, did that painting in 1929. The Krollmann painting and Thomas Moran's *The Grand Canyon of the Yellowstone* (1893–1901) were often used in Northern Pacific advertising.

As Kirby Lambert pointed out, "until automobile travel boomed after World War I, railroads held a virtual monopoly on western tourism and consequently were without rival in their ability to promote western parks in the years preceding the war." The Northern Pacific allied itself with Yellowstone, the Southern Pacific celebrated Yosemite, the Santa Fe claimed the Grand Canyon, and the Great Northern promoted Glacier. Each railroad hired artists and photographers to record the natural wonders past which their trains could transport tourists. Paintings were reproduced on posters and calendars to be displayed on station walls.

Louis W. Hill, Sr., president of the Great Northern, enthusiastically adopted the slogan See America First to promote travel to Glacier National Park. Those who viewed Great Northern travel publicity saw the western landscapes, but even more often saw the striking portraits of the Blackfeet Indians from that region, painted by Elsa Jemne and Winold Reiss. The paintings of both artists appeared on posters, calendars, menus, and railroad promotional literature after the mid 1920s.

Art posters may have passed their golden age, but posters themselves never did vanish. During both World Wars posters were a prime means of communication used by the federal government. The University of Minnesota, the Minneapolis Public Library, and the Minnesota Historical Society all have large collections of these posters, some of which have been scanned and appear on the Internet.[138]

Many other posters were designed and printed by Works Progress Administration artists during the WPA's lifespan, from 1935 to 1943. WPA artists designed posters for health and education programs, theatrical productions, outdoor recreation, and the National Park Service.[139]

In his essay for the *Graphic Design in America* catalogue, David Kunzle discusses the political poster. He notes that while the anti–Vietnam War posters ended with the close of that conflict in 1975, other poster artists took up themes of racism, women's rights, and gay liberation, as well as causes involving labor and the environment.[140] Two firms began producing and distributing political posters: the Syracuse Cultural Workers and the Northland Poster Collective of Minneapolis.[141] The NPC was founded by Ricardo Levins Morales in 1979. It has worked with labor unions and organizations such as WAMM (Women Against Military Madness), supplying posters, picket signs, T-shirts, and buttons, all with appropriate imagery and messages. Some of its posters have been designed by Morales himself, others by Janna Schneider.

Once it became possible to print larger handbills or assemble numerous poster sheets, the billboard appeared on the scene. John W. Merten, in discussing the history of the Strobridge firm, notes that the first large outdoor poster, sixteen sheets wide, appeared in Cincinnati's Fountain Square in 1878. The subject was Eliza crossing the ice, from *Uncle Tom's Cabin*.[142] The firm's largest poster was done for the W. W. Coles circus, and was printed on 100 sheets measuring, when assembled, 15 feet high by 100 feet long.[143]

By 1912, the number of separate sheets used on an outdoor billboard was standardized at twenty-four. More recently the number was expanded to thirty sheets. Where a billboard stands has often been a source of contention as it can quite effectively block a view. Along interstate highways, built with money from federal coffers, billboards must be set back certain distances from the right of way. While this prohibition did remove large signs from the immediate view of the drivers and passengers, it predictably resulted in the even larger signs that are now erected beyond the forbidden zone, as is the case on I35 north of the Twin Cities. Billboard space is rented, often by the month. Advertisers include local and national firms as well as those sponsoring events.

To conclude the discussion of posters, it is tempting to suggest that the invention of one Minnesota company relates both to the act of installing a poster ("posting") and the use of a gummed strip to make it stay in place. 3M's Post-It notes, first available in yellow, are papers to be applied to another surface and then written upon. They are mini, blank, do-it-yourself posters, in effect, and a very successful product.

CHAPTER SIX

Eat, Drink, and Be Merry

S HEET MUSIC, MENUS, PROGRAMS, AND INVITA-
tions are all related to celebrations, whether
personal, private, or commercial. Many are unique,
one-time events, rather than occasions that find a
place in the yearly calendar.

The Message Is the Music

Before Edison invented the phonograph and
records became the easiest way to listen to music
at home, sheet music made new songs popular.[144]
Across the country old standards, new hit melo-
dies, songs written for events, causes, and commercial campaigns all made their way into sheet music
folders. Sheet music covers often bore engravings
and then lithographs created by printers both in
the East and in Minnesota.[145] Covers of these folders often credited the singing star who popularized
the song, which everybody could now play on the
piano at home to the delight of friends and family.

Breweries commissioned sheet music as early as
1903, when "Under the Anheuser Bush" appeared.[146]
Many other forgettable beer songs followed, includ-

ing "Zum Zum Zum" for the Minneapolis Brewing
Company in 1914. Breweries later offered small
booklets of songs connected with beer and *gemüt-
lichkeit*, such as "There Is a Tavern in the Town" and
"Beer Barrel Polka."

Flour mill advertisers were musically inspired as
well, according to Kate Roberts. From General Mills
came a ditty in 1915 called "Eventually. Why Not
Now?" which told of a young man from the (y)east
who sought his fortune in Minnesota.[147] The title,
of course, used the company's slogan.

But greater than the commercial connection was
the influence of events on sheet music. Composers
sought every way possible to salute the joys of winter in songs written for the Saint Paul Winter Carnival. A portfolio of wintry ballads was published in
1886, marches appeared for the revived carnivals of
1916 and 1917, and new songs were written for 1937
as well.[148]

The Minnesota State Fair inspired at least one
composer, and a 1909 competition brought forth
a number of lively tributes to the University of

Often mentioned in Minnesota music collections is the 1919 tune "From the Land of the Sky Blue Waters." The melody was an Omaha Indian air collected by Alice C. Fletcher. It was orchestrated by Charles Wakefield Cadman with words from a poem by Nelle Richmond Eberhart. The song has been linked to the noted Hamm's beer jingle. Courtesy of the authors.

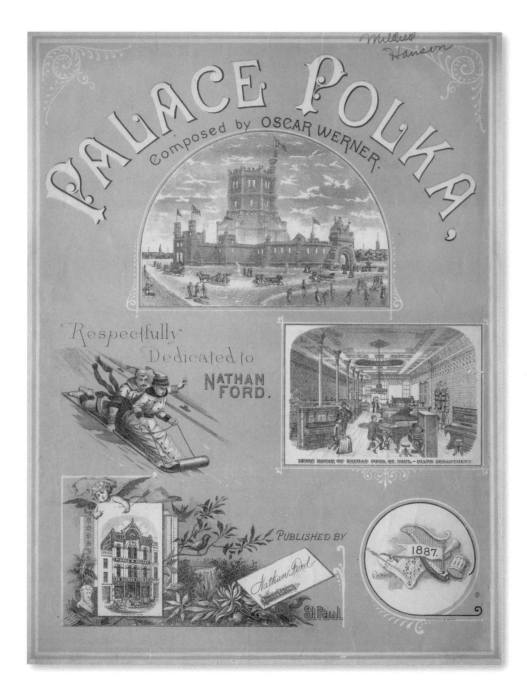

For the second St. Paul Winter Carnival in 1887 Oscar Werner composed his "Palace Polka." That year's ice palace is shown on the sheet music, which was dedicated to Nathan Ford. Ford's music store at 92–94 East Third Street is illustrated both inside and out. Lithographed by Berlandi and Bott. Courtesy of Glenn Wiessner.

In 1909 the Minneapolis Tribune sponsored a contest for a new school pep song for the University of Minnesota. Floyd Hutsell's words and music won first prize and $100.00. His "Rouser" with its line, "Minnesota Hats Off to Thee," has been sung on campus ever since. Courtesy of the authors.

Minnesota. Floyd Hutsell's effort was the winner in the contest for a rouser, or pep song.

Charles Lindbergh's historic trans-Atlantic flight inspired many songwriters. "Lucky Lindy" was probably the best known song of this repertoire, and apparently it was the one the pilot especially disliked.[149] He resented the implication that luck was more important than skill in his successful flight.

By the 1950s sheet music had lost its consumer market. Rock 'n roll, with its emphasis on guitars and amplification, made songs played on the piano seem old-fashioned. New music could be heard on LPs and, later, on CDs. Knowledgeable advertisers had already headed in a different direction. Even though consumers no longer purchased sheet music, jingles such as those for Hamm's televised cartoon "From the Land of Sky Blue Waters," and the "Cream of Wheat is so Good to Eat" melody that introduced the radio children's program *Let's Pretend* continued the commercial concept formerly found in the printed pages of sheet music.

Sheet music has become a collecting interest, both public and private. The Minnesota Historical Society holds a collection of over 200 state-related songs. Indiana and Duke Universities also have large holdings of sheet music. But the ultimate collection is at the Library of Congress, which possesses copies of all music submitted for copyright protection, a collection that is being digitized for display on its Web site.[150]

The Bill of Fare

Writing about the events of 1846 in St. Paul, J. Fletcher Williams noted the city's growing attraction for visitors and the severe lack of amenities for them. He said that "St. Paul has now become quite a 'point' on the river." He noted further that:

> There were only three or four points on the Upper Mississippi, above Prairie du Chien, where boats ever touched, and only one where they landed with any regularity. St. Paul might be classed in the latter list. Considerable goods were now received here by the five or six traders who carried on business in the village, and there was some passenger business to and fro. Strangers, travelers, and tourists, generally—sometimes an adventurous trader, from below, seeking for a location—would occasionally land, to 'look around' a little. There was no tavern to go to, and Henry Jackson, whose hospitality was a distinguishing trait, usually invited them to his house, where they were entertained free of charge.

Williams noted that the generous Mr. Jackson was also a justice of the peace, merchant, saloonkeeper, and unofficial postmaster.[151]

The Pioneer and Democrat Steam Press printed the Winslow House menu for May 10, 1858. On one page the printer managed to include the menu, distances to nearby towns, a wine list, hours, and even scheduled entertainment. Courtesy of the Minnesota Historical Society.

DINNER

ON BOARD

Steamer HENRY AMES.

Monday March 26 1866

SOUP.

Ox Tail a La Windsor

FISH.

Baked Trout With Fine Herbs

BOILED.

Mutton, Caper sauce.   Corned Beef and Cabbage.   Ham.   Tongue

Chicken Egg Sauce

ROAST.

Beef.   Pork.   Pig.   Mutton.   Turkey.   Veal

ENTREES.

Roned Chicken a La Sualus
Braized Shoulder of Lamb a La Santix
Fricandeau of Veal With Green Peas
Beef Steak With Anchovy Toast

REMOVES.

Chicken Pie With Fine Herbs
Baked Pork and Beans

GAME.

Braized Ducks a La Macedoine

Roasted Goose a La Allemande

COLD DISHES.

Head Cheese

RELISHES.

Worcestershire Sauce.   Assorted Sauce.   Currant Jelly.   Horse Radish.
John Bull Sauce.   Reading Sauce.   French Mustard.   Olives.   Cheese.

VEGETABLES OF THE SEASON.

PASTRY AND DESSERT.

PUDDINGS.

Pound Wine Sauce

PIES AND TARTS.

Cranberry Apple
Blackberry and Mince Pie
Jellie Puffs

CAKES.

Ream Claude Lunch Cake
Pound Fruit
Lady Jelly
Sponge Drop and Spice Cake
Gentian Cake With Almonds

CREAMS AND JELLIES.

Orange Jelly a La Anglaise

Brandy and Wine Jellies
Marazchino Bavarian Cream
Peach Charlotte

DESSERT.

Whipt Cream With Strawberries
Brandy Snaps
Pine Apple Meringue
Fasture of Pears
French Macarons

FRUIT AND NUTS.

Raisins.   Apples.   Almonds.   Figs.
Brazil Nuts.   Filberts.   Pecans.

COFFEE.   **TEA.**

A St. Louis printer supplied this menu for the Merchants and Peoples Packet steamboat Henry Ames for March 26, 1866. Courtesy of the Minnesota Historical Society.

Menu

APRIL 14, 1895.

SOUP

Consomme, Italian

Young Onions   Olives

BOILED

Sugar Cured Ham, Champagne Sauce

Ox Tongue, Sauce Tartar

ROAST

Prime Ribs of Beef, au Jus

Loin of Pork with Apple Sauce

ENTREES

Fricasseed Chicken with Dumplings

Rice Snow Balls, Peaches

Egg a la Swiss

Sardine Salad   Potato Salad

VEGETABLES

Mashed Potatoes   Boiled Potatoes

Creamed Cabbage   Tomatoes

Potato Puffs

RELISHES

Tomato Catsup   Pickles

Worcestershire Sauce   Durkee's Salad Dressing

PASTRY

Baked Indian Pudding, Wine Sauce

Mince Pie   Apple Pie

American Cheese

Lemon Ice Cream   Assorted Cake

Oranges   Bananas

Tea   Coffee   Milk

Grand Central Hotel,

A. CHARBONNEAU, PROP.

ST. PAUL, Easter Sunday, April 14, 1895.

Easter Sunday dinner at the Grand Central Hotel in St. Paul was a full-scale production in 1895. Courtesy of the Ramsey County Historical Society.

TEATER
VISAFTON och BAL

GIFVES AF

Svenska Dramatiska Sällskapet

å

DANIA HALL

Cedar Ave. and 5th St. S.

Söndagen d. 2 Jan.

kl 8 e. m.

Hvarvid uppföres

Tre förälskade
poliskonstaplar

ELNA LILJEQUIST.

Lustspel med sång i en akt af Jo. Jo. Denna berömda svenska pjes med sitt ytterst goda innehåll kommer af sällskapet att uppföras på det mest fulländade vis enär sällskapets yppersta skådespelare och sångare medverka.

Musiken utföres af Prof. Jacobsons Teater-orkester.
Axel Mauritz Sundborg, Mgr.

FÖRKÖPSBILJETTER 35c.
SAMT VID INGÅNGEN 50c.

EFTER FÖRESTÄLLNINGEN STOR BAL.

BILJETTER TILL SALU HOS
LINQUISTS PIANO MAGASIN, Marquette och 9th St. S.
J. O. PETERSONS DRUG STORE, Seven Corners,
P. MELINS MUSIKHANDEL, Seven Corners,
LONERGANS DRUG STORE, 230 20 Ave. N.
A. BAKER, 1109 Wash. Ave. S.

Theatrical events offered in German or Swedish were popular in nineteenth and early twentieth century Minnesota. This program advertised a performance at Dania Hall in Minneapolis. Courtesy of the authors.

As more visitors arrived and immigrants came to settle, the need for more formal hostelries was clear. On land adjacent to Henry Jackson's house, Leonard La Roche, a carpenter, built a sturdy 20 × 28 foot, story-and-a-half cabin of tamarack logs. J. W. Bass leased the cabin in 1847 and named it the St. Paul House. This was an important development for the city. Williams noted that "Mr. Bass kept a right smart tavern in it, too, and old settlers say it helped the town considerable, for no one would want to go to a town that had no good hotel."[152] Bass managed that hotel until 1852. In 1856 E. C. Belote leased it; John J. Shaw and William E. Hunt succeeded Belote. During their tenure, which ended in 1873, a new building replaced the old St. Paul House.

One of the assets of the St. Paul House (later called the Merchant's Hotel) was a restaurant that served breakfast, dinner, and tea and hosted special events. A collection of early menus at the Minnesota Historical Society indicates that hotels were ready to offer a fine dinner and drinking experience in the city as early as the 1850s. From Williams's account and a review of the listings in the

St. Paul city directories, it is clear that diners had no other choice. They could eat either at home or in hotel dining rooms. Saloons and taverns offered meals of a sort, but upscale restaurants did not yet exist.

When Anthony Trollope visited St. Paul in 1862, he found that most of the guests in the city's hotels were actually city residents who boarded rather than trying to keep their own houses in a time of Civil War shortages.[153]

As the Minnesota hospitality industry developed, all sorts of restaurants began to line main streets.[154] Menus, place mats, postcards, and matchbooks became ways to publicize the image of the restaurant. As customs evolved, however, the restaurant matchbook has been replaced by table tents stating that smoking is no longer permitted. Postcards are less frequently seen now than restaurant business cards, which stand in receptacles near the cash register.

The Performing Arts

Early theatre programs, like the halls in which plays were presented, were often fairly simple. A single sheet of paper, typeset in English, German, or Swedish, listed the play's title and

Touring productions brought major plays and great actors, such as John McCullough, to Minneapolis's Academy of Music. Opened in 1872, the Academy lasted just over a decade. It burned down in 1884. Courtesy of the authors.

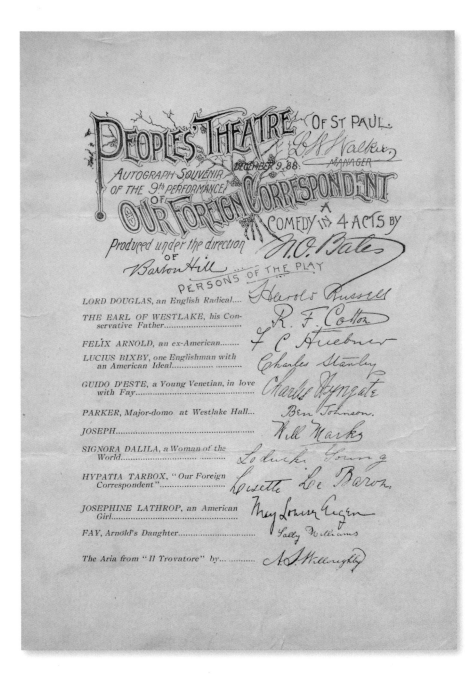

its cast. By the 1880s, when opera houses and grand theatres were the preferred location for both amateur and professional companies, programs became more elaborate. Theatre managers realized that a booklet could present the particulars of a production and announce upcoming theatrical offerings, while leaving ample space for advertising.

Examples of programs from the 1890s and early 1900s show as many as fifteen advertisements surrounding a small box of information about the production. The advertisements themselves provide a fascinating glimpse into society of the time. For the men in the audience, advertisements enticingly offer cars or carriages, cigars, shoes, fine wines, and beer. Women could read about clothing custom-made by local modistes, the laundries that cared for these wardrobes, beauty salons, wigmakers, and business schools (in case milady needed employment skills). For both sexes, hotels and restaurants requested their trade, either before or after the performance, while photographers sought to capture their images.

One unusual advertisement from a Mrs. A. London of Minneapolis suggested that she would be happy to call personally and at the convenience of society ladies to purchase discarded evening gowns, street dresses, and waists (blouses). Then, the advertisement advised, ladies would have

An unusual 1888 program for the People's Theatre of St. Paul came with autographs supplied. Our Foreign Correspondent was written by Will O. Bates, the Pioneer Press drama critic. Courtesy of Clark Hansen.

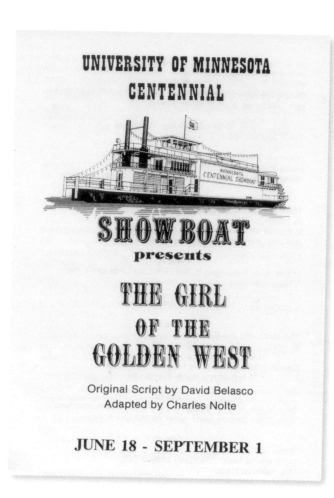

UNIVERSITY OF MINNESOTA
CENTENNIAL

SHOWBOAT

presents

THE GIRL
OF THE
GOLDEN WEST

Original Script by David Belasco
Adapted by Charles Nolte

JUNE 18 - SEPTEMBER 1

The University of Minnesota's Showboat was long moored below the bluffs of the Minneapolis campus. This program for its summer production from 1984 uses the format of a showboat playbill from the nineteenth century. Courtesy of Clark Hansen.

The four St. Paul public high schools (Central, Johnson, Humboldt, and Mechanic Arts) collaborated on a Shakespearean pageant in 1916, the tercentenary of the Bard's birth. Costumes, posters, programs, and postal cards were designed by teachers, while 550 students took acting and musical roles in the production held at the St. Paul Auditorium. Courtesy of Clark Hansen.

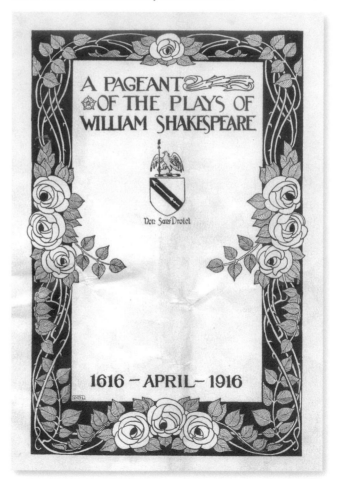

A PAGEANT OF THE PLAYS OF WILLIAM SHAKESPEARE

Non Sans Droict

1616 – APRIL – 1916

their own money for theatre tickets and simply for "spending."

Various printers (including Geesaman & Murphy and the Art Engraving Company) advertised in these programs and were responsible for their production. In an advertisement from 1908, the Bureau of Engraving and Printing cautioned that "The difference between an effective ad and a poor one will

THE JOHNNY PLAYERS

Announce a Stupendous Religious Drama, The

"Great Theatre of the World"

**81 Characters
101 Choristers**

More Impressive Than "EVERYMAN"

ST. JOHN'S UNIVERSITY, Collegeville, Minn.

SUNDAY, MARCH 13, 1932

7:30 in the Evening   Admission 50 cents

Most of the colleges and universities in Minnesota have theatre departments. The Johnny Players of St. John's University, Collegeville, scheduled this impressive production in 1932. Courtesy of the Stearns History Museum.

often be in a cheap half tone or a poor design. A few cents extra for a good plate spread over a long run means the success of your advertising." Not everybody followed this advice.

One name appears on these early programs as manager or lessee of the theatres. Dr. Frank Whiting called Louis Napoleon Scott "Minnesota's dominant theatrical personality" of the period from 1883 until Scott's death in 1929.[155] Scott managed the Metropolitan Opera Houses of Minneapolis and St. Paul, the Lyceum in Duluth, and the Grand in Superior, Wisconsin. Programs from these theatres are filled with revenue-producing advertisements. Scott was involved as well in theatrical productions held during the Saint Paul Winter Carnivals and at the Minnesota State Fair. In 1905 a touring production of *Mother Goose* by J. Hickory Wood and Arthur Collins was staged at the Metropolitan Opera House in St. Paul. The program, with its elegant theatregoers on the cover, was a twenty-page booklet. Following Scott's death, his widow continued as a theatrical producer, offering seasons of touring productions at the Metropolitan Theatre. Programs for these events were smaller, in booklets of sixteen pages. Advertisements were from quarter- to full-page size.

High schools, colleges, and universities had drama departments. Their theatre programs were apt to be simpler and perhaps designed with assistance from campus art departments.

In the second half of the twentieth century, the theatrical program began to grow. Instead of being just a simple list of actors and their roles, short biographies of their careers now appear. The play and its author also rated pages of learned analysis. The change in funding, however, transformed the early program's handful of sheets into a glossy magazine of fifty to sixty pages. Most local theatres, following the birth of the Guthrie in 1963, became nonprofit entities. Foundation support, government grants, donations from the public, and program advertising revenue all supplemented ticket revenue. All those who gave money needed to be listed, so these pages became part of every program as well.

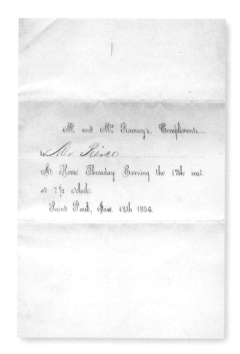

Even in territorial days (1856) social customs called for proper forms, such as this at home card for the governor and his wife. Courtesy of the Hennepin History Museum.

Printing these magazine-like programs became increasingly a specialty. In 1964 a story about Select Publications, founded in Madison, Wisconsin, six years earlier, explained its goal of publishing regional magazines such as *Twin Citian* and programs for the Guthrie Theatre, the Minneapolis Orchestra, and the Minneapolis season of the Metropolitan Opera.[156] By 1968, Group 7 was publishing magazine-format programs for the larger theatres and music organizations. Today the publisher is Skyway Publications. In addition to the weekly newspaper *Skyway News* (now named the *Downtown Journal*), this firm publishes programs for the St. Paul Chamber Orchestra, the Minnesota Orchestra, the Guthrie Theatre, and the Ordway Center.

Twelfth
Masquerade Ball
Mozart Club

Monday, March 2nd, 1908, Mozart Hall

Peter Giesen was a founder of the Mozart Club, for which the family costume business may well have provided costumes and props. Courtesy of the Minnesota Historical Society (Peter J. Giesen Papers).

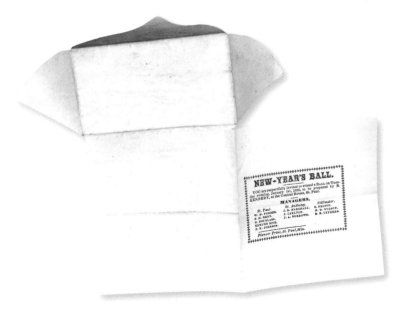

Invitations often call on a printer's ingenuity, as this combination envelope and invitation obviously did. The Central House, on Bench Street in St. Paul, was managed by Robert Kennedy and was often the site for large gatherings during territorial days. J. Fletcher Williams, quoting the Pioneer newspaper, says that nearly one hundred gentlemen, with their ladies, attended this Ball in 1850. Courtesy of Patrick Coleman.

EAT, DRINK, AND BE MERRY

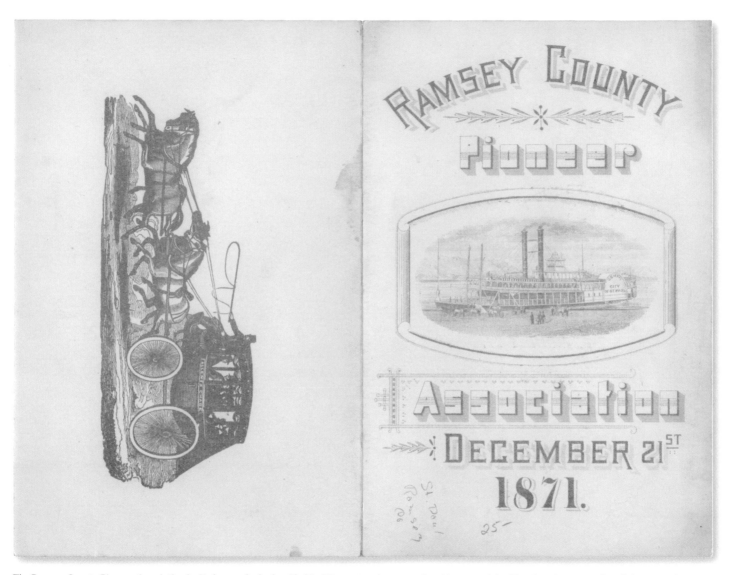

The Ramsey County Pioneer Association invited men who had resided in Minnesota prior to statehood in 1858 to join. The Association was founded in 1871. This menu comes from the thirteenth annual banquet, held at the Merchants Hotel in 1884. Both the steamboat (City of St. Paul) and the Allen & Chase stagecoach, depicted on the cover of the menu, would have been well known to residents of St. Paul in the 1850s. Courtesy of Fred Foley.

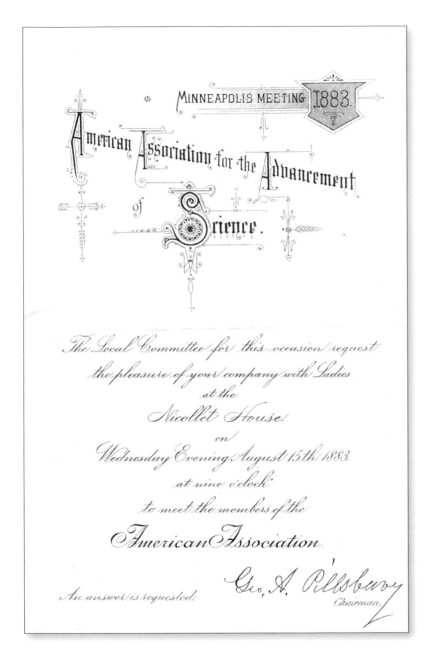

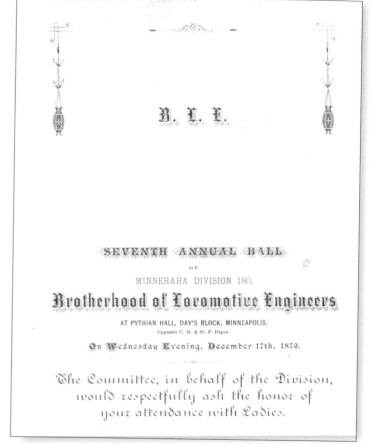

(ABOVE):

Invitation to a ball from the Brotherhood of Locomotive Engineers, 1879. Courtesy of the Hennepin History Museum.

(LEFT):

Invitation to a meeting of the American Association for the Advancement of Science, 1883. Courtesy of the Hennepin History Museum.

EAT, DRINK, AND BE MERRY

LUNCHEON

IN HONOR OF

HIS ROYAL HIGHNESS

PRINCE BERTIL OF SWEDEN

and

THE OFFICIAL SWEDISH PARTY

By

Governor and Mrs. Luther Wallace Youngdahl

The Conservation Building
Minnesota State Fair Grounds

SUNDAY, JUNE TWENTY-SEVEN   -   HIGH NOON

Nineteen Hundred and Forty-Eight

Both Swedish and Norwegian royalty have often visited Minnesota at times of significant events. As a part of the Swedish Pioneer Centennial in 1948, Prince Bertil came to visit. Courtesy of the Minnesota Historical Society (Museum collections).

Unique Events and Celebrations

Society, even pioneer society, soon acquired some of the customs of the older American cities. On New Year's Day, from ten in the morning until four in the afternoon, gentlemen made short visits. A register of callers was kept, with hostesses vying for the most names listed.[157] Printers were quick to supply invitations. From the 1850s onward, clubs were organized, uniting people with similar interests or ethnic backgrounds. Clubs often needed invitations, membership rosters, and event programs.

As noted earlier, milestones in transportation, such as the completion of railroad links and the advent of steamboat tourism (the "Fashionable Tours"), were well celebrated. Likewise, centennials have been noted with parades, pageantry, programs, and ephemera. Minnesota's territorial and statehood centennials in 1949 and 1958 were marked with similar activities and ephemera, including postage

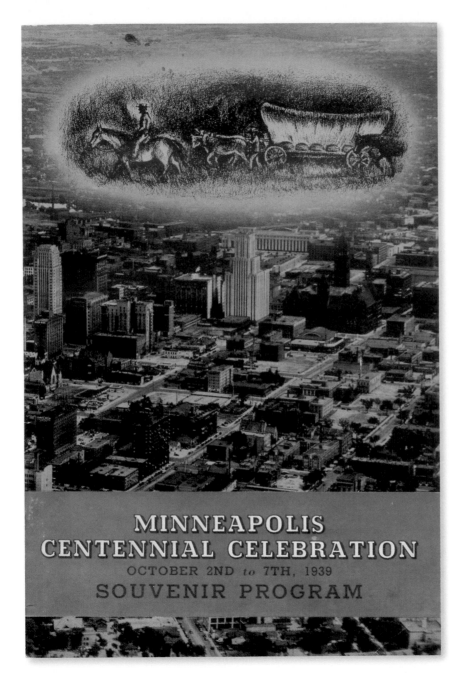

stamps. The centennials of Norwegian and Swedish immigration were equally important moments to celebrate, given the many immigrants from those countries who arrived in Minnesota following the Civil War. Usually the guest list from the European homeland was headed by a member of the appropriate royal family.

Cities and towns have celebrated centennials and sesquicentennials. In 1939 Minneapolis believed that a century's worth of history was worth noting so, for almost a week, there were parades, concerts, stage programs, and art exhibits. In the spring of that year, downtown businessmen had begun talking about starting a summer festival, which they did launch in July 1940.

Like theatre and concert programs, event programs grew fat with articles and four-color advertising. The 1985 *Commemorative Magazine* of the British Festival of Minnesota included 114 pages of articles on links between the British Isles and Minnesota.[158] That festival's

The Minneapolis Civic Council sponsored the Century Celebration in 1939 to commemorate, dramatize, and awaken local pride, according to Major George E. Leech's proclamation. One hundred years after Franklin Steele claimed land for his homestead, Minneapolis had a population of 490,000 people. The celebration featured parades, a pageant, performances of music and dance, and appearances by prominent local athletes. This program summarized city history, provided a map, and gave the weeklong schedule of events. Courtesy of the authors.

EAT, DRINK, AND BE MERRY

AS SHOWN IN THE GREAT WAR PANORAMA BATTLE OF ATLANTA NOW ON EXHIBITION IN MINNEAPOLIS, 5TH ST. NEAR NICOLLET AVE, OPEN ALL DAY, EVENINGS AND SUNDAYS.

Both Minneapolis and St. Paul had circular buildings designed to house panoramas, which were huge paintings of historical or archaeological scenes. William Werner hired fifteen artists to paint The Battle of Atlanta, *a portion of which is shown in this trade card. This panorama was displayed in Minneapolis from June 1886 until March 1888. The Battle of Atlanta panorama may be seen today in Grant Park, Atlanta, Georgia. The card was lithographed by I. Monasch. Courtesy of the Hennepin History Museum.*

royal visitor was Princess Alexandra, who could have viewed British art, heard music from the United Kingdom, and carried her program home in a shopping bag from Dayton's department store, bearing a Punch and Judy image by painter David Hockney.

The siege of Vera Cruz during the Mexican war, remembered by performances in the amphitheatre of the Minneapolis Exposition building, is publicized in this August 1891 trade card. The performances, whose reserved seats cost seventy-five cents, terminated with a "magnificent display of fireworks." Courtesy of the Hennepin History Museum.

Not all forms of early entertainment were plays or concerts. For several years panoramas were so successful that special circular buildings were erected to house these giant paintings. Ancient history, the long course of the Mississippi River, and recent battles from the Mexican and Civil Wars were brought to vivid life on the panorama canvas.

Circuses came to Minnesota by steamboat and later by train. A favorite form of advertising was the circus poster, but an 1858 visiting troupe used printed envelopes to announce a Quadruple Show.

Ice-skating spectaculars, with their mix of beauty, talent, and humor, have attracted Minnesota audiences for many years. In the heyday of the majorette on skates, a pin-up master painted her for a show program.

Conventions and meetings generated their own printed record, from the invitation and ticket to the program and keepsake. Churches, city halls, courthouses, the three Minnesota capitol buildings, and hotels were all substantial urban architecture events which deserved a dedication and thus, a program. Instead of the ceremonial spike hammered into place, a glossy ribbon across the gateway entrance would be ceremonially cut and commemorative ephemera given away.

EAT, DRINK, AND BE MERRY

Circuses large and small wend their way through Minnesota. They appear in parks, auditoriums, and shopping center parking lots. One of the first troupes to come to Minnesota was that of Yankee Robinson. His circus, established in 1854, toured until 1876, when it failed. In 1884 he briefly became an advisor to Ringling Brothers. This cover, postmarked at Minneapolis on January 4, 1858, carries the Yankee Robinson advertisement on the back. Courtesy of Floyd Risvold.

Majorettes were a popular feature of ice skating shows of the late 1930s through the 1940s. The program cover was designed by George Petty, a pin-up master. Courtesy of the Hennepin History Museum.

Auditorium Opening Concert

ST. PAUL SYMPHONY ORCHESTRA

N. B. EMANUEL, CONDUCTOR

TUESDAY EVENING, APRIL 2ND, 1907

8:15 SHARP

SOLOIST: MRS. KATHARINE GORDON FRENCH

Program

MARCH TRIUMPHAL

    "Pomp and Circumstance"   *Sir Edward Elgar*

OVERTURE

    "Leonore" No. 3 . . . *Beethoven*

SONGS

    "Dedication" . . . *Granier*

    "The Cry of the Valkyrie"   *Wagner*

       MRS. FRENCH

SYMPHONIC POEM

    "Les Preludes" . . . . *Liszt*

INVITATION TO THE DANCE   *Weber*

    Concert arrangement by Weingartner

OUVERTURE SOLENNELLE

    "1812" . . . *Tschaikowsky*

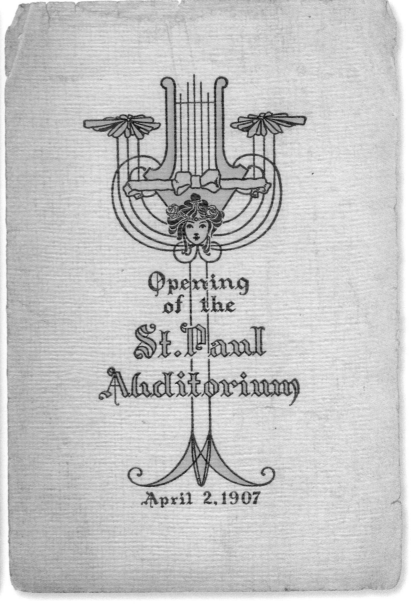

Opening
of the
St. Paul
Auditorium

April 2, 1907

The St. Paul Auditorium, designed by Charles Reed and Allen Stem, was opened with a concert and a grand ball in 1907. Everything from operas to auto shows took place in that venue until 1982, when it was demolished and replaced by the Ordway. This program was printed by the Randall Press. Courtesy of the Ramsey County Historical Society.

    EAT, DRINK, AND BE MERRY

Usually the demise and destruction of a building was noted only in photographs, but the survival and reuse of a building would call for its own printed memorabilia. In 2002 the centennial of a major building took place in downtown St. Paul. Known as the Federal Courts Building when it opened in 1902, the massive structure with its towers and turrets was rumored to be slated for demolition when its government tenants left in 1967. A local citizen's group determined to save the building, and in 1978 a restored and renamed Landmark Center opened its doors. For its centennial, a book, a program, and a "passport" were produced. The passport followed the concept of a traveler's document that needs to be stamped on entering and departing countries. Celebrants were encouraged to visit specified historic St. Paul sites and have their passports stamped.[159]

Other events connected with unique ephemera are often philanthropic in nature: dinners, balls, and receptions sponsored by clubs or volunteer associations to support music, theatre arts, health and welfare, and educational programs. The state's historical museums have collections of these materials, as does the University of Minnesota's Performing Arts Collection in the Elmer Andersen Library.

THE SAINT PAUL

The honour of your presence is requested
at a banquet to be given
by
The Citizens of Saint Paul
to celebrate the opening of
The Hotel Saint Paul
on the evening of Monday, April eighteenth
nineteen hundred and ten
at seven-thirty o'clock
The Saint Paul
Saint Paul, Minnesota

Invitation to a dinner celebrating the opening of the Hotel St. Paul, April 18, 1910. Courtesy of the James J. Hill Library (Hill papers).

GUARANTY LOAN BUILDING

THE BEST OFFICE BUILDING IN THE WORLD.

You are cordially invited to an
Informal Reception to be given by the
Northwestern Guaranty Loan Company,
on the occasion of
the opening of the new
Guaranty Loan Building,
Saturday, May thirty first,
Minneapolis, Minn.

1890.

From two until eleven P. M.

When E. Townsend Mix's Northwestern Guaranty Loan Building opened in 1890, Minneapolis welcomed the spectacular structure with its atrium open from the second floor to the roof. Seventy years later the city no longer felt the Metropolitan (as it was then called) was the "best office building in the world." Despite protests, it was razed in 1961–1962 as a part of the Gateway Urban Renewal project. Courtesy of the Hennepin History Museum.

CHAPTER SEVEN

Holidays and Rites of Passage

Annual Events

WHILE THERE ARE MANY PARADES AND FESTIVALS held to celebrate visits, centennials, and immigration history, the Minnesota festival calendar has certain major recurring events. These begin with the oldest, the Minnesota State Fair, inaugurated in 1854. In *Blue Ribbon*, her history of the State Fair, Karal Ann Marling notes that the fair wandered in its early years. Red Wing, Rochester, Owatonna, Winona, and the Twin Cities were home to the State Fair until 1885, when its final location was fixed in St. Paul.[160] The Minnesota State Fair usually runs for twelve days, ending on Labor Day. Originally more of a harvest festival than it is today, it still includes the competitions for animals and farm produce, although the display of farming equipment on Machinery Hill is long gone. Car races, horse races, concerts, the Midway with its rides and shows, and buildings filled with vendors, products, and programs all guarantee a wealth of State Fair ephemera.

OFFICIAL
RACING
PROGRAM

DAN PATCH
1:55

Price 10 Cents

MINNESOTA STATE FAIR
S. P. NEVINS, Programmer
Cleveland, Ohio

Dan Patch, the great Minnesota race horse, set track records between 1903 and 1908. The time noted in the program was from a 1906 race. Courtesy of the Hennepin History Museum.

OFFICIAL RACE PROGRAM

Wednesday, Sept. 5, 1923

MINNESOTA STATE-FAIR

AND

Northwest Dairy Exposition

HAMLINE
PRICE 10c

Postcards of the State Fair provide views of the Midway, the permanent buildings, and the varied attractions. Firms with State Fair booths sent postcard invitations to their customers. A St. Paul dairy sent such a card in 1910 showing Theodore Roosevelt in Rough Rider garb. The former president was carved in the dairy's butter by Minnesota sculptor John Karl Daniels.

Other typical fair souvenirs are visor hats, fans, toys, cards, and yardsticks. Many of the favored Fair Foods, such as cotton candy, corn-on-the-cob, and ice cream can be eaten while walking. In a play on the popularity of food-on-a-stick, the *Minneapolis Star Tribune* gave away fans with Fairground maps, or "maps-on-a stick," in 2003. A museum on the Fairgrounds, open to the public during the fair, displays everything from vintage tickets and prize ribbons to posters, photographs, and programs for events such as horse races and, later, automobile races.

Politicians, both office holders and aspirants, usually have booths and make appearances and sometimes quite lengthy speeches at the fair. According to Dr. Marling the early fairs featured speeches by former governors and judges, but as the State Fair grew, the "demand for orators" encouraged planners to invite national political figures to Minnesota.[161] In 1878, when Minneapolis held its competing Northwestern Fair, President Rutherford B. Hayes was obliged to speak in both places. *Harper's Weekly* sent artist W. A. Rogers to cover the event and published his drawing of Hayes viewing prize cattle in their October 5, 1878, issue.[162] Hayes' visit was a "first," according to one local editorial writer. "Its [Minnesota's] whole political history is spanned by five presidential terms, and five presidents have approved the acts of Congress since Minnesota was represented in its chambers. Of these Buchanan was too old and foolish, Lincoln too busy, Johnson too distracted, and Grant too addicted to Long Branch and long nines to include Minnesota in the narrow circle of their summer wanderings."[163]

Vice President Teddy Roosevelt appeared at the State Fair in 1901, just four days before William McKinley was assassinated and Roosevelt became president. He came to the State Fair again in 1910 as a former president, and yet again in 1912, when he was a presidential candidate once again.

Attendance today is in excess of a million and a half persons, making it the second-largest state fair in the United States.

The signature annual events for the Twin Cities area are St. Paul's Winter Carnival (held in late January of each year since 1886, although not continuously), the Minneapolis Aquatennial (held in late July since 1940), and the Anoka Halloween Festival, inaugurated in 1920. Each of the three was organized in response to a problem. St. Paul was said

MINNESOTA STATE FAIR.

TWENTIETH EXHIBITION

HELD IN ST. PAUL.

SEPTEMBER 2, 3, 4, 5, 6, 7, 1878.

THURSDAY'S PROGRAMME.

11 A. M. Arrival of Rutherford B. Hayes, the President of the United State, and his party upon the Fair Grounds.

Address by President Hayes, at such time as suits his convenience, probably before 11.30 A. M.

12 M. Capt. Bogardus, the Champion Wing Shot of the World, will shoot 100 Glass Balls in seven minutes.

12.15 P. M. Dr. Carver will give an exhibition of his skill with the rifle.

2 1-2 P. M. Exhibition Trot by the famous trotters Edwin Forrest and Great Eastern, the latter to be ridden by Dan Mace, for a Special Purse and Five Hundred Dollars added if 2.14 is beaten, and an additional Five Hundred Dollars if 2.13 is beaten.

FOLLOWED BY

RUNNING RACES, HURDLE RACING, AND TROTTING IN THE 2.50 CLASS.

Pioneer Press.

Probably the most important day at the 1878 Minnesota State Fair was announced on this broadside. Rutherford B. Hayes was the first American president ever to visit Minnesota while in office, so his speech, whenever it happened, was a major event. Courtesy of the Minnesota State Fair History Museum.

to be too cold, so its answer was a winter festival complete with an ice palace. Minneapolis had suffered through labor turmoil and crime in the 1930s, so in an effort to reinvent its public image, a summertime Aquatennial was conceived and scheduled on what was deemed to be the best weekend in summer for fine weather. And a businessman in Anoka was annoyed by the vandalism that Halloween brought, so he suggested a citywide event. By organizing costumed parades and window decorating contests beginning in 1920, George Green changed the destructive pattern of Halloween tricks in Anoka.

Skiing, skating, and dogsled races have all been held during St. Paul's Winter Carnival. Minneapolis' Aquatennial highlights the sports of summer, and Anoka's Halloween festival has featured a football game, aptly named the "Pumpkin Bowl" by *Minneapolis Star* columnist Barbara Flanagan.

While the State Fair has its own buildings and permanent location, both the Aquatennial and Winter Carnival stage parades through downtown streets and host a long list of other activities. Thus, maps and schedules are vital. St. Paul newspapers published Winter Carnival supplements in the 1880s, when the

Carnival resumed in the winter seasons of 1916 and 1917, and then when it resumed almost continuously from 1937. Other printed materials and ephemera were produced for Carnival coronations, dinners, and for events such as pageants, horse shows, and concerts.

For the Aquatennial, begun in 1940, maps, schedules, programs for the Gene Autry rodeos, and the famed Aqua Follies at Theodore Wirth Park were among the printed memories. The official program was called the *Pictorial*.

Other celebrations that take place every year throughout the state include Fourth of July parades, county fairs held before the Minnesota State Fair at the end of August, and community festivals. Robert Lavenda, who has studied these events with his students at St. Cloud State University, notes

A die-cut dog stood on store counters to advertise the first annual bench show of the American Kennel Club at the 1912 Minnesota State Fair. Courtesy of the Minnesota State Fair History Museum.

Each year the Winter Carnival program lists sponsors and events. In 1990 Snoopy, the famous cartoon beagle, was selected as the celebrity mascot. Charles Schulz's *Peanuts* cartoon strip was then forty years old. Costumed *Peanuts* characters appeared at carnival events and rode in the parades. Courtesy of the authors.

Majorettes were expected to high step their way in parades by the 1930s. This sticker comes from the Aquatennial's second year. Courtesy of Bob Jackson.

Other Events

500-Mile Paul Bunyan Canoe Derby
Five-Mile Inaugural Parade, July 20
Girls' Diamondball Tourney, July 20–21
Yacht Regatta, July 25–27
Fireworks Displays

National Outboard Motor Races, July 21
10,000 Lakes Swimming Meet, July 24–26
Open-Air Religious Services, July 21
Thrilling Rowing Races, July 27
Daring Inboard Motor Races, July 28

Miller-Jersey Diamondball Game, July 26
Championship Tennis Matches
Aqua Trot Street Dance, July 23
Spectacular Night Parade, July 24
American Shows on Parade Grounds

Minneapolis Public Links Golf Finals, July 21
Lake Calhoun Pageant, July 21
Championship Archery Meet, July 23
Children's Playground Pageant, July 24–25
Hunters' Special Shoot, July 21

Senior Invitation Golf Tourney, July 26
Table Tennis Matches, July 20–21
Pro Golf Short Stop Tourney, July 22
State Skeet Shoot, July 26–27
Casting Contests, July 21

MINNEAPOLIS AQUATENNIAL
July 20 to 28

In slightly more than a week, planners for the 1940 Minneapolis Aquatennial managed to schedule races, pageants, parades, and fireworks. The Aqua Follies, an Air Show at Wold-Chamberlain field, and a rodeo starring Gene Autry were other attractions. Courtesy of the Hennepin History Museum.

Cover of the 1976 Minneapolis Aquatennial program. Courtesy of Nancy Viking.

launched as part of the wave of patriotism occurring at the time of the Bicentennial in 1976 and some were inspired by the statewide Celebrate Minnesota initiative of 1990.

Community festivals typically sponsor a parade, perhaps with a second parade for children, a street dance, a queen's pageant, and a race (often a 10K run). There may be other special events, depending on the energies and finances of the organizers and the theme of the festival. The festivals are often promoted through news stories and advertising in local newspapers. Programs, posters, schedules, postcards, and sheet music, clothing, coffee mugs, and buttons are typical festival souvenirs and ephemera. Sales of these items often partially fund a festival's events.

Some towns schedule their events in the fall or winter. During the 1930s winter festivals became popular means to emphasize sports venues in towns such as Duluth, Hibbing, Brainerd, and Bemidji. May, already crowded with end-of-school-year events, is also filled with festivals such as Cinco de Mayo in St. Paul's West Side, or District del Sol, and the Heart of the Beast MayDay parade in Minneapolis. One indoor festival with a long history is the Festival of Nations, begun in 1932 and sponsored by the International Institute of St. Paul.

The larger festivals and fairs usually provide maps and schedules with some description of the event's history and significant milestones. Often mentioned in connection with St. Paul's Winter Carnival is F. Scott Fitzgerald's short story *Ice Palace*.

that Minnesotans currently hold 200 community festivals between Memorial Day and Labor Day. He considers many of these to be outgrowths of the earliest Fourth of July events.[164] Others were

A set of oversized postcards printed by the Langwith Map Company honored the first Minneapolis Aquatennial in 1940. Other cards in the set showed a sailboat, a swimmer, and various Minneapolis landmarks. *Courtesy of Bob Jackson.*

For publicizing Anoka's Halloween event, the literary laurels go to Garrison Keillor. In an essay called "Halloween Capital of the World," Keillor wrote this about his hometown: "The highlight of all Halloweens to me was in 1957 when my older sister, Judy, rode in the parade as National Guard queen, very lovely in her white gown, sitting in the forward hatch of an Army tank, rumbling along Main Street, leaving deep tread-marks in the asphalt. When your sister rides a tank down the main street of the world's Halloween capital, there is not much higher a person can go."[165] Here Keillor perfectly captured the affection many people have for hometown festivals and why, often because of such a personal link, they collect its artifacts.

Christmas and Charity Seals

While the printing of poster stamps had essentially ceased by the time of the Great Depression, the concept of non-philatelic stamps or seals (called Cinderellas) continues to be popular in the direct mail world. Christmas Seals and Easter Seals, stamps issued by Boys Town, and wildlife conservation stamps, for example, are sent countrywide in bulk mail along with requests for donations to the charitable groups issuing them. In 1907 the American

National Red Cross issued its first Christmas Seals, an idea pioneered by the post offices of Denmark, Iceland, and Sweden as early as 1904.

In Minnesota, charity seals were issued by local authorities in several different places. On occasion, earlier national designs were utilized, but other designs were local works of art. Those who issued such seals included Blue Earth County Public Welfare Association, Mankato, 1925–1951; Marshall County Tuberculosis Association, 1926; Martin County Nursing Service, Fairmount, 1928–1936; McLeod County Public Health Association, Glencoe, 1927–1950; Willmar, Minnesota, Tuberculosis Association, 1951; and Pope County Public Health Association, of Glenwood, 1933.[166] The Christmas Seal and Charity Stamp Society is a national collectors' group that promotes the hobby of collecting tuberculosis and other charity seals.

Old Home Week

Family picnics and gatherings, all-class high school reunions, and Old Home Weeks were ways in which those who had remained in small towns encouraged those who had

Since 1932 the International Institute of St. Paul has presented The Festival of Nations every spring. This early program highlights the displays and entertainment drawn from the many ethnic groups in the city. Courtesy of the authors.

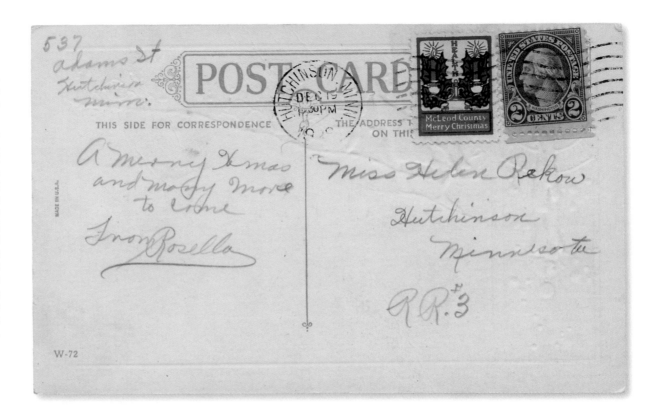

departed to return. The idea for an Old Home Week began in New Hampshire in 1899, suggested by that state's governor. According to Robert J. DuBois, Maine, Vermont, and Massachusetts all embraced the idea with celebrations of their own. Seals, cacheted envelopes, and special cancels were produced to mark these events.[167] In Minnesota, one Old Home Week celebration was a late summer event, held in 1909 just before the Minnesota State Fair opened.

Winona's 1909 Old Home Week was filled with varied events. A parade of boats on the Mississippi River; a ball with bands from Rochester, Rushford, and Lake City; a barbecue; and an automobile floral parade were all part of the welcome. As a newspaper reporter commented, "There are approximately 125 automobiles in Winona, including trucks and delivery wagons. Practically all of these are passenger machines and most of them ought to take part in the parade."[168] It was now easier to obtain

"They're Coming Back" reads the script on Winona's Homecoming seal of 1909. Five days' worth of festivities were planned. Courtesy of Tom Reiersgord.

bunting and paper flowers, so those vehicles could be decorated by "any one with an artistic sense." A major speaker at one of the Old Home Week events was former Governor Samuel Van Sant, who had become Commander of the Minnesota Grand Army of the Republic (GAR).

Printed envelopes and Old Home Week seals were mailed to former Winona townspeople. Evidently the response was considered a success, although the event apparently was not repeated. It is believed that the Winona event was the only Old Home Week celebration to occur in Minnesota.

Season's Greetings from Your Newsboy

Soon after newspapers made their appearance in Minnesota one custom was imported from other cities: the carrier's greeting card. Newsboys who delivered the newspapers presented their subscribers with a New Year's greeting card. Sometimes it was printed as a single folded sheet and sometimes the wishes expanded to six to eight pages. Usually the carrier's greeting offered a poetic summary of national and local events. Commenting on "Our City" in 1872, one verse of a poem in the Carrier's New Year Address read:

> Westward the Empire Star
>   taketh its way;
> Westward our city is strid-
>   ing to-day;
> 'On to the Falls!' the loud
>   greeting we send
> To the fair 'Dual Cities'—to
>   be our 'west end.'

Always printed in attractive fonts surrounded by decorative elements, these cards included drawings, calendars, and eventually photographs, all intended to bring a tip for the underpaid

On the front cover of the Daily Minnesotian's New Year's Address for 1856 is an engraving based on Joel Whitney's daguerreotype of Minnehaha Falls. The back cover gives subscribers both a calendar and another Whitney image of Father Ravoux's chapel, "the nucleus of St. Paul." Courtesy of the Minnesota Historical Society.

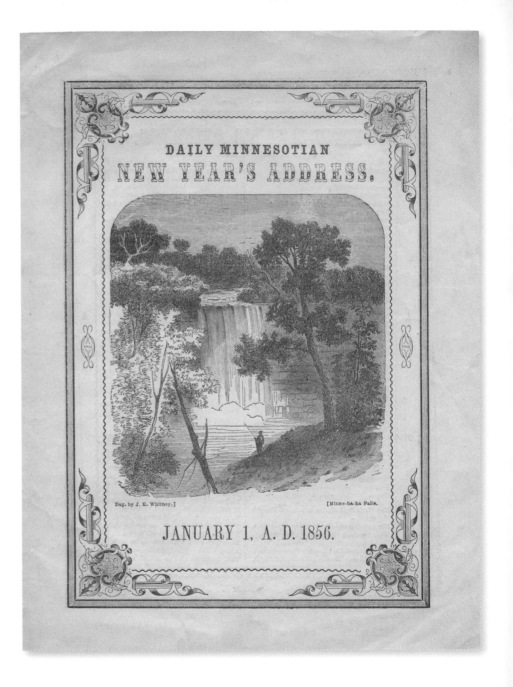

DAILY MINNESOTIAN
NEW YEAR'S ADDRESS.

Dag. by J. E. Whitney.]   [Minne-ha-ha Falls.

JANUARY 1, A. D. 1856.

newsboy. Some of the most elaborate cards were issued by the *Minneapolis Journal*, which used elegant covers and paper for poems and photographs.

Carrier's greeting cards were issued by every Twin Cities newspaper, and probably by most other larger newspapers through the state, from 1850 until about the time of World War I. June Drenning Holmquist, who wrote about these cards, believed that the custom died out when newspapers felt that subscribers had come to resent both paying for the paper and tipping the newsboys.[169]

It may be, also, that those newspapermen obliged to assemble the contents for the cards—poems and illustrations—were growing bored with the assignment. In 1895 a booklet sent to subscribers of the *St. Paul Pioneer Press* contained a letter addressed to Gentle Reader. It began, "We don't feel so full of poetry this year, so have thought it may prove as interesting to you if we tell in 'halting' prose something of ourselves." The letter noted

that carrier boys in the city numbered 115 and were aged from twelve to fifty. They earned from one to seven dollars per week, delivering from 40 to 230 papers daily. "We are not perfect," the letter continued. "We cannot make a paper stay in place on an exposed porch during a gale, we cannot prevent

A miniature front page of the St. Paul Daily Dispatch *was placed on a plate for the paper's New Year's Greeting in 1884. The plate suggests an offering with holly leaves and mistletoe sprigs as seasonal echoes.* Courtesy of the Minnesota Historical Society.

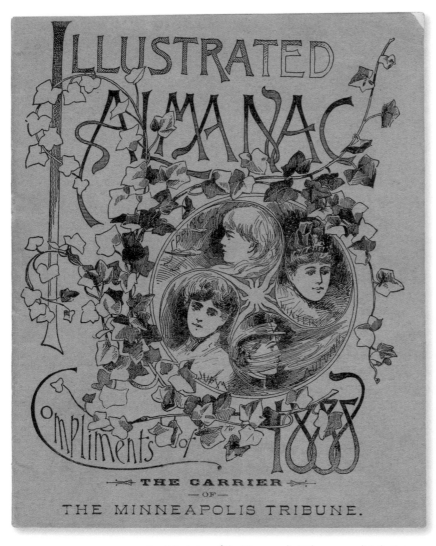

By 1888 carriers of the Minneapolis Tribune *were distributing a 36-page* Illustrated Almanac *containing advertisements, engravings, and a calendar. Courtesy of the Minnesota Historical Society.*

a dishonest pilgrim from carrying away a paper necessarily left within sight and reach, nor can we 'serve' with the poet and 'simply stand and wait' for the neighbor's dog to call that we may give him a stony reception and eradicate his appetite for wood pulp, cotton rags, printers' ink and 'general information'". Then, after concluding by wishing subscribers good health and happiness, the letter displays a small winged cherub wearing a top hat like a New Year's babe and, underneath, the word *Carrier*.

Nearly three dozen of these cards are in the collections of the Minnesota Historical Society, beginning with an 1858 card from the *Minnesota Pioneer & Democrat*. Edward D. Neill recorded what may have been the earliest example. Reverend Neill wrote that the *Minnesota Pioneer* had issued a carrier's New Year's greeting on January 1, 1850. The card's poem, which may have been written by the paper's editor, James Goodhue, concluded with the following lines:

> And ... above the village of Old Crow?
> Pig's Eye? Yes; Pig's Eye! That's the spot.
> A very funny name; is't not?
> Pig's Eye's the spot, to plant my city on.
> To be remembered by, when I am gone.
> Pig's Eye, converted thou shalt be, like Saul.
> Thy name henceforth shall be St. Paul.[170]

Pig's Eye was, of course, the original name for St. Paul.

Post Mortem

Many are the rituals of death, determined by faith, social and economic status, and custom. A religious service often requires a program so those who attend will know what is expected of them. There may be a mourning card as well. A funeral service will almost always take place soon after death has occurred, while a memorial service may take place weeks later. When a president dies, a state funeral normally is held in Washington, D.C., while burial may take place elsewhere. In the case of Abraham Lincoln, a funeral train carried his body from Washington to Springfield, Illinois, making stops along the way for memorial services in many cities.[171] Following that concept of national remembrance, services were held in Minneapolis following the deaths of both William McKinley and Ulysses S. Grant. Minnesota's governors are often mourned with services at the state capitol, as John A. Johnson was in 1909.

Messages of condolence are normally acknowledged by the family of the deceased with a handwritten note. When death involves an especially well-known person, a printed card may be sent in response to condolences, as was the case for Hubert H. Humphrey. Often monetary gifts are sent to charities in memory of the deceased, so those donations are acknowledged by cards and notes.

Nineteenth century funeral programs and cards were printed, sometimes in German or Swedish, if needed. Twentieth century programs were usually stock items or now may be desktop published,

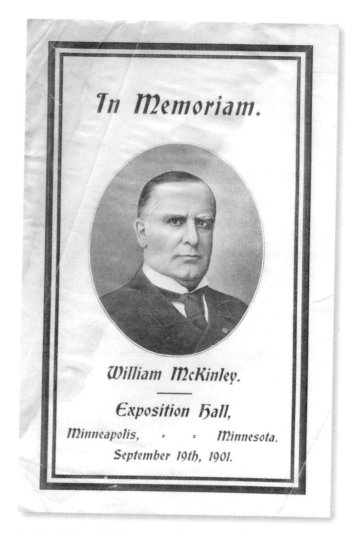

President William McKinley was assassinated at the Pan American World's Fair in Buffalo, New York, in 1901. Memorial services were held in Minneapolis and in other major cities. Courtesy of the Hennepin History Museum.

A black-bordered post card with a view of the state capitol served as a mourning message for Governor John A. Johnson, who died in 1909 while serving his third term. The view of the statehouse includes two empty pedestals. Each would later hold a bronze statue of a Minnesota governor: John A. Johnson on the left and Knute Nelson on the right. Courtesy of Floyd Risvold.

Gov John Albert Johnson
BORN JULY 28 1861
DIED SEPT. 21 1909
ELECTED GOVERNOR OF THE STATE OF
MINNESOTA 3 TERMS
1904-1909

Following the death of Hubert H. Humphrey in 1978, his widow, Muriel, mailed this engraved card to those who had sent condolences. At the time of his death Humphrey was serving as United States senator from Minnesota for the second time. Previously he was mayor of Minneapolis and vice president of the United States, serving with Lyndon B. Johnson. Courtesy of the authors.

Thank you so much for your warm message.

Our family is grateful for the countless expressions of compassion and goodwill extended to us. We have been sustained and comforted by the knowledge that Hubert's life and values and hopes have been shared and appreciated by so many friends. In his final days he was filled with joy, peace and gratitude.

Mrs. Hubert H. Humphrey

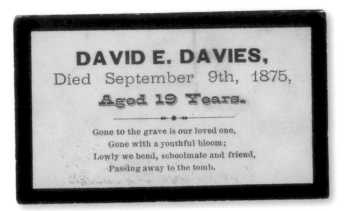

A black-bordered card served to remember a man who died at a very young age. Courtesy of the Ramsey County Historical Society.

using the computer's capacity to insert photographs, drawings, or decorative embellishments. Major players in corporate or philanthropic affairs have been remembered in elaborate booklets, such as those issued in 1915 for James J. Hill. Members of the boards of directors of both the First National Bank and Hill's own Great Northern Railway commissioned these forms of condolence to be sent to family members.

On June 3, 1916, members of the board of directors of the Great Northern Railroad sent this engrossed memorial (the front cover shown here) to the widow and family of James J. Hill, following his death. Courtesy of the James J. Hill Library (Hill papers).

A great bereavement has fallen upon the Great Northern Railway Company and upon all those connected with it

JAMES J. HILL

stood to it in the relation of a father to his child. This is no common loss; for both the relation and the man were unique in the history of this perhaps of any country. Mr. Hill himself called the creation of this railroad

In liebender Erinnerung an

FRAU LOUISE HAMM.

Werthe Leidtragende!

    Wir sind gekommen, der Verblichenen die letzte Ehre zu erweisen, den so schwer betroffenen Gatten, die Kinder und Verwandten zu trösten;—zu trösten unter Umständen ist schwer.

    Hier stehen die Hinterbliebenen wie betäubt, kaum fassend, daß die Mutter, die noch vor wenigen Tagen in voller Rüstigkeit mit warmem Herzen unter ihnen weilte, vom unerbittlichen Sensenmann niedergemäht wurde und in die kalte Erde gesenkt werden soll.

    Frau Louise Hamm, geborene Buchholz, wurde vor 63 Jahren zu Haßlach, Großherzogthum Baden, geboren.

    Im Jahre 1856 kam das junge Paar nach St. Paul. Frische, rüstige Schwarzwälder, Gestalten mit starken, arbeitswilligen Armen, der noch damals halben Wildniß muthig entgegentretend. Somit war sie ein Theil jener gewaltigen Schaffenskraft, die St. Paul zur jetzigen Blüthe verhalf, eine Pionierin im wahren Sinne des Wortes.

    Wie die Blume zum Erblühen, die Saat zum Gedeihen Sonnenlicht braucht, so braucht ein guter Mann eine gute Gattin, die Kinder eine gute Mutter. Sie war beides. Dem Manne, der anfangs in Armuth schwer schaffend, sich eine Existenz gründete, stand sie, mit starken Armen stets willig mitschaffend, zur Seite, und ihm ein fröhliches „Frisch auf" zurufend, zugleich ihren Kindern eine tüchtige Erzieherin bleibend. Das Resultat blieb nicht aus. Wohlstand und Glück zog im Hause ein. Vier Töchter sind Gattinen braver Bürger, der Sohn der tüchtigsten Bürger einer und eine ledige Tochter.

    Die Verstorbene hatte ein tief religiöses Gemüth, sie war eine fromme Katholikin. Was sie im Hause als Mutter war, war sie in der Kirche als Christin, ein leuchtendes Vorbild der Gemeinde. Trotz ihres Wohlstandes blieb sie eine einfache, bescheidene Frau, die Armen und Hülfsbedürftigen fanden in ihr stets eine unermüdliche Spenderin, sie ließ nie die Linke wissen, was die Rechte gab. Sie war nicht unduldsam, sie feindete Niemanden an, der in Religionssachen nicht glaubte wie sie, nur mußten alle, die in ihrem Kreise verkehrten, gute Menschen sein.

    Tiefgebeugter Mann, dem sie über 40 Jahre eine treue Gefährtin war, weinende Kinder, der unerbittliche Tod hat Euch plötzlich Euer Theuerstes geraubt, und gerade das **plötzlich** erfüllt Euch mit Schrecken, jedoch nur schrecklich für die Hinterbliebenen. Für eine Frau, die gelebt wie sie, konnte der Tod keine Schrecken haben. Werthe Leidtragende, ich möchte jetzt recht verstanden sein, ich spreche in dem Sinne, wie ich jeden glaubenstreuen Christen verstehe.

    Als der Todesengel an sie herantrat, war sie bereit, ihm zu folgen, er trug ihren Geist himmelwärts, wo ihr Heiland, ihr Erlöser, an den sie so innig glaubte, sie sanft in seine Arme schloß und sprach: Komm, meine Tochter, jetzt sollst du für alles belohnt werden, was du auf Erden Gutes gethan. Dort weilt sie, mild lächelnd auf Euch herniederschauend, und ihr guter Geist wird Euch für immer umschweben.

    Das sei Euer Trost.

Friede ihrer Asche!

Gestorben, St. Paul, Minn., 2. Feb. 1896.

When Louise Buchholz Hamm died in St. Paul in 1896, mourners at her funeral probably received both this large card, written in German, and a much smaller lithographed prayer card, also in German. Both noted that she was born in Hasslach, Baden, Germany, sixty-three years earlier, and had come to St. Paul with her husband, Theodore, in 1856. Courtesy of the authors.

CHAPTER EIGHT

Moving People

Explorers, fur traders, pioneers, and settlers came to what would become Minnesota in various ways. They walked, canoed, rode horses, and later journeyed on the rivers and the rails. Letters exist for some of the earliest travelers, but ephemera becomes more frequent when commercial travel begins.

The Steamboat

The age of the steamboat in Minnesota began on May 10, 1823, with the arrival of the *Virginia* at Fort Snelling, after a twenty-day trip up the Mississippi River from St. Louis. It was, wrote William J. Petersen, "the deathblow to the barge, the raft, the keel boat, the pirogue, and all other boats that hitherto had been the navigators of the Mississippi."[172] Sadly, the *Virginia* enjoyed its fame only briefly; it struck a snag on a trip between Louisville and St. Louis in September 1823 and sank.

According to Reverend Edward D. Neill, the summer of 1850 was the commencement of the navigation of the Minnesota River by steamboat. The *Anthony Wayne*, the *Nominee*, and the *Yankee* on which Reverend Neill traveled, all explored the Minnesota River that summer.[173] Navigation by steamboat on the St. Croix River was begun by the *Palmyra* when, in 1838, it carried men and machinery to the Falls to build sawmills.[174]

The 1850s were the boom years for steamboats. Each year, between April and November, settlers took passage to the north. Nathan Parker, who came to St. Paul in early June 1856 with 500 others aboard the *Northern Belle*, noted that "state-rooms were entirely out of the question, and bunks upon the floor or seats at the table were at a premium."[175]

One year later, J. Fletcher Williams noted that the spring of 1857 was one of the latest ever known. "The 'first boat' did not arrive at St. Paul until the morning of May 1. Once the barrier was broken, however, the season was inaugurated with a fleet of boats. On May 4th, eighteen were at the levee at one time, and a few days afterwards, twenty-four, the largest number ever seen at our landing. Each of these were crowded with passengers and their

CAMPBELL & SMITH,
FORWARDING AND COMMISSION MERCHANTS, GALENA, ILLINOIS.

Shipped, In Good Order and Well Conditioned, by CAMPBELL & SMITH

W. C. E. Thomas, Pr.

For account and risk of whom it may concern, on board the good Steam Boat called the *Redwing* whereof *Barger* is Master for the present voyage, now lying in the port of Galena, and bound for *St Piter* Being marked and numbered as below, and are to be delivered without delay, in like good order, at the Port of *St Piter* (unavoidable damages of the river and fire only, excepted,) unto *Fr. Steele* or to *his* assigns, he or they paying freight at the rate of *25¢/1000*

In witness whereof, the Master or Clerk of said Steam Boat, hath affirmed to *3* bills of lading, all of this tenor and date, one of which being accomplished, the others to stand void.

Dated at Galena, this *10* day of *July* 184*6*

MARKS.	ARTICLES.	WEIGHT.
	Ten pig Lead *Aa. Papin*	*185*

On July 10, 1846, Campbell & Smith of Galena, Illinois, shipped ten pigs of lead to Franklin Steele, the sutler at St. Peter (Fort Snelling). This bill of lading was folded much like a letter, addressed, and handstamped S. B. Red Wing. Less than three years later (on May 17, 1849) the Red Wing, a sternwheeler, was among twenty-one other steamboats that burned at St. Louis. Courtesy of Floyd Risvold.

Dan McLean, a passenger on the sidewheel steamboat Sucker State, departed Stillwater on July 25, 1869. This bill of lading notes the cost of his passage to Dubuque, Iowa ($13.00), and the cost of transporting his possessions (a stove, two skiffs, one boiler, two chests, three small kegs, and other goods) for $40.00. The Sucker State was built in Pittsburgh in 1860 for the Northern Line Packet Company, whose boats traveled between St. Paul and St. Louis. The steamboat burned and was abandoned in the Alton Slough in 1872. Courtesy of Floyd Risvold.

A detail of an invoice for goods carried by the steamboat Ariel from St. Paul, on May 11, 1865. This steamboat operated on the Minnesota River, with its sister ships the Mollie Mohler and Otter. Courtesy of Floyd Risvold.

A detail of a billhead of the Le Claire Navigation Company, dated April 16, 1887. The Le Claire Navigation Company ran three steamboats on the Mississippi River, towing log rafts. President of this firm was Samuel Van Sant, elected twice as Governor of Minnesota. Courtesy of Floyd Risvold.

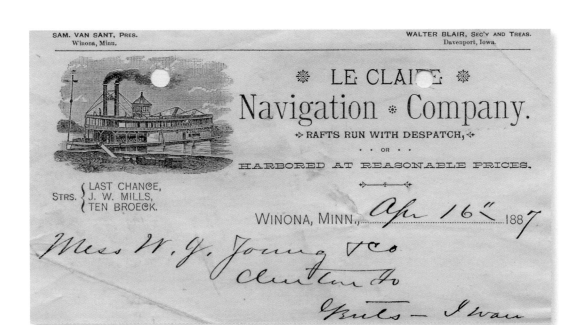

Envelope from the Grey Eagle, mailed from Hastings, Minnesota Territory, on September 18, 1857. The Grey Eagle, a side-wheeler, was one of the most famous steamboats to operate on the upper Mississippi River. Built in 1857, the Grey Eagle struck the Rock Island bridge in 1861 and was a total loss for its owner, Captain Daniel Smith Harris of Galena. Captain Harris retired from the business following the loss of his steamboat. Courtesy of Floyd Risvold.

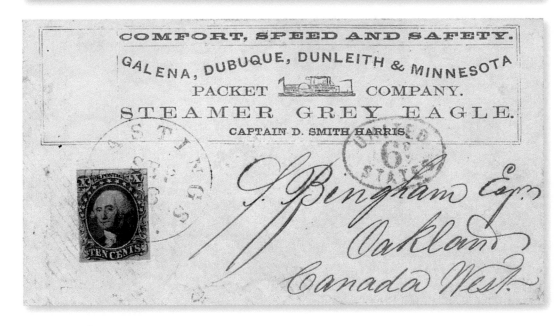

goods, so great was the rush of immigration that spring."[176]

The levee was an exciting place to be when the steamboats were chartered for excursions or when the circus came to town. On the St. Croix River, as Anita Albrecht Buck wrote, circuses such as the Spaulding & Rogers Great Monkey Circus and Burlesque Drama Troupe came to Stillwater on the *Banjo* and *James Raymond* in the 1850s.[177] Steamboats carried passengers and goods during their season, but they provided another important service to the logging industry. Working steamboats, such as those of Samuel Van Sant's Le Claire company, towed log rafts on the Minnesota, St. Croix, and Mississippi Rivers.

Passenger steamboats were defined as transients (single-owner independents), packets, and lines. The packets made regular trips between cities; several packets could be organized into a "line." One major line was the Galena, Dubuque, Dunleith & Minnesota Packet; another was the Northern Line Packet. Both were organized before the Civil War and merged by 1873. Their owner, William F. Davidson, then effectively controlled the steamboat trade on the upper Mississippi River.[178]

In 1854 the completion of the railroad connection from Chicago to Rock Island brought about a prime tourist opportunity named by its promoters, the Great Railroad Excursion.[179] Nearly 1,000 celebrities rode to the Mississippi river and then took passage on five large steamboats in order to reach the Twin Cities. Former president Millard Fillmore and

historian George Bancroft were among those who viewed the upper Mississippi's wonders from June third until their arrival in St. Paul on June eighth. Journalists filed the expected reports, but very little of an ephemeral nature has survived from this trip.

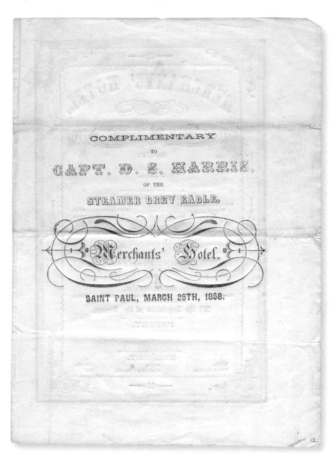

Menu for a dinner held on March 26, 1858, to honor *Daniel Smith Harris*, Captain of the *Grey Eagle*. Courtesy of the Minnesota Historical Society.

EXCURSION TICKET.

Chicago and Rock Island Rail-Road.

Mr. *William Evarts* is invited

to the Celebration of the Opening of the last link in the Rail-Road Line
between the Eastern Atlantic and the Mississippi.
By Railroad to the Mississippi, at Rock Island.
By Steamboat from Rock Island to the Falls of St. Anthony.

Leave Chicago on the 5th June 1854, at 9 A.M.

OFFICE OF THE CHICAGO AND ROCK
ISLAND RAILROAD COMPANY.
New-York, May 20, 1854.   Pres't.

COMMITTEE.

J. B. Jervis,   Thos. C. Durant,   Isaac Cook,
A.C. Flagg,   Jos. E. Sheffield,   L. Andrews,
Wm. Walcott,   Henry Farnham,   Eben. Cook.

*Ticket for the Grand Excursion trip from Chicago to St. Paul, 1854.
Courtesy of the St. Paul Riverfront Corporation.*

The excursion was, as Theodore Blegen wrote, the grandest of the Fashionable Tours that had become quite popular on the Mississippi since George Catlin suggested the idea in 1835. Blegen quotes Catlin's remark that he left it for the world to come and gaze upon for themselves. But Catlin hoped they would come soon while the experience was new.[180]

A century and a half later, the St. Paul Riverfront Corporation determined to commemorate the original excursion with a yearlong promotion involving all four neighboring river states and their

river towns. Art exhibitions, concerts, lectures, a bookshelf full of related histories, and many other events were scheduled around what was planned as a re-creation of the Excursion's Flotilla. Steamboats, led by the *Anson Northrup,* made their way to St. Paul while all manner of smaller craft filled the river from June 25 to July 4, 2004. The ephemera accumulation for the 2004 event was certainly greater than had been the case 150 years previously.

By the end of the nineteenth century the railroad had made steamboat travel obsolete. In the twenty-first century, paddle wheelers still offer seasonal tourist excursions on Minnesota rivers.

No. 1.   **FIRST DIVISION**   No. 1

ST. PAUL & PACIFIC R. R.

TIME CARD.

Into Effect July 2nd, 1862.

ST. ANTHONY AND MINNEAPOLIS TRAINS.

LEAVE.	A. M.	ARRIVE.	A. M.	LEAVE.	P. M.	ARRIVE.	P. M.
St. Paul	8:00	St. Anthony	8:45	St. Anthony	12:20	St. Paul	1:00
St Anthony	8:50	St. Paul	9:40	St. Paul	3:45	St. Anthony	4:30
St. Paul	11:30	St. Anthony	12:15	St. Anthony	4:35	St. Paul	5:20

Extra trains will meet all Steamboats for the accommodation of Passengers living in St. Anthony.

Special trains will be run on Sunday and Evenings by special arrangement.

No Engines allowed on the road except on order of the Superintendent or Master Mechanic.

Irregular Trains slow on curves, and look out for Section men.

In case of doubt, follow the safe course.

The St. Paul & Pacific Railroad was granted its charter in 1857 by the Minnesota legislature, but financial problems initially kept construction from proceeding. Tracks were eventually completed by June 28, 1862, so that the first engine, the William Crooks, which was named for the railroad's chief engineer, could make the hour-long trip from St. Paul to St. Anthony. Courtesy of Floyd Risvold.

One side of this carte de visite is a photograph of St. Anthony Falls, while the other side carries a promotional message for the West Wisconsin and Chicago & Northwestern Railroads and their elegant new Pullman sleeping cars. In the background can be seen the Winslow House, then the largest building in Minneapolis, which was built 1856–1857. Courtesy of Floyd Risvold.

Among Minnesota's major industries, railroads may well have generated the most forms of ephemera. For the passenger there were tickets, schedules, luggage labels, menus, postcards, brochures, and passes. For the railroad employees there were maps, more detailed schedules, and handbooks. For the investor or shipper there were more and different lists, billheads, stationery, schedules, and forms. Railroads advertised via posters, calendars, playing cards, matchbooks, and blotters. Trains,

This pass was issued in 1869 for travel on the St. Paul & Pacific Railroad. By that date passengers could ride from St. Paul to St. Cloud, Wayzata, and Willmar. Courtesy of Floyd Risvold.

However, they are no longer powered by steam and instead use diesel engines.

Paper ephemera for the steamboat era includes bills of lading, letterheads, and advertising envelopes, most of which are quite rare today.

The Railroad

"Railroads had a magical appeal for frontier people," wrote Theodore Blegen in his 1963 history of Minnesota.[181] Trains were faster, more economical, more efficient, and less weather dependent than the steamboats and wagons that travelers previously had used. By 1872 fifteen railroads had been established in the state; 2,000 miles of track had been laid. Not only could passengers reach the Twin Cities from Chicago, but they could take the train to reach Duluth, Sioux City, and the Red River Valley of the North.

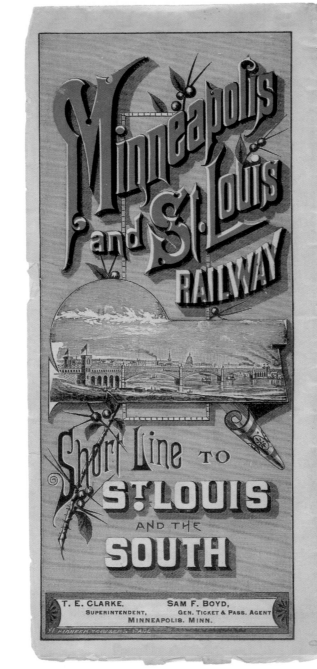

MOVING PEOPLE

depots, scenic views, and landmarks along the way and, especially, the Native American people who lived near Glacier National Park and Yellowstone National Park, were featured in attractive railroad paper souvenirs, often printed by Brown & Bigelow.

As each railroad link was forged, and ceremonial golden spikes were hammered into the railroad ties, special programs, tickets, menus, and invitations marked the occasion. Almost thirty years after the Grand Excursion excursed, Minnesota witnessed more railroad celebrations when Henry Villard's line, the Northern Pacific Railroad, completed its westward expansion. In 1893 James J. Hill's Great Northern tracks crossed the northern plains to the Pacific Ocean. Dinners, huge industrial parades, special trips with the requisite invitations, menus, programs, maps, and schedules marked these achievements.

When Henry Villard's Northern Pacific Railroad completed its tracks to the Pacific ocean, St. Paul festivities in September 1883 included a gala dinner, an enormous parade through downtown streets decorated with elegant welcoming arches, and a train trip west. A small ninety-six page booklet written by J. H. Hanson and printed by Brown & Treacy was produced for the event. Courtesy of Ramsey County Historical Society.

Collectors commonly preserve railroad memorabilia sorted by railroad company, or type (schedules and postcards are especially popular). The National Railroad History Society and the Railroad Collectors Association are among the groups aiding members interested in railroadiana, or as it is usually called, railroad paper. In St. Paul the Minnesota Transportation Museum is located in the former Great Northern Railway round house. The museum

Proctor & Hamilton, printers in Minneapolis, took advantage of the hoopla associated with the 1883 golden spike celebration of the Northern Pacific Railroad to create an unusual trade card. Courtesy of the Minnesota Historical Society.

Public officials, candidates for public office, and celebrities of all kinds rode the rails, with their passages preserved in typeset ephemera. As a candidate departed a town so small it was known as whistle stop, a traditional newspaper photograph would depict him waving from the platform of the last passenger car.

Through the efforts of Louis W. Hill, James J. Hill's son and successor, the railroads were important supporters of the Saint Paul Winter Carnival in 1916 and 1917, marking their participation with many attractive bits of printed ephemera, such as menus, tickets, and programs.

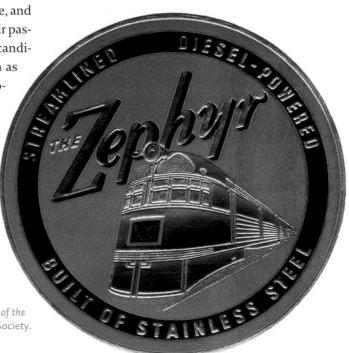

Window sticker for the stainless steel Zephyr train of the Burlington Road. Courtesy of the Minnesota Historical Society.

began with the idea of restoring a streetcar. Now on view are engines and ephemera relating to transportation.

The Airplane

Carl M. Becken was an amiable downtown Minneapolis postage stamp dealer who introduced three generations of young Minnesotans to postage stamp collecting. Becken was also a specialist in aerophilately (items related to airmail), and the source of philatelic materials for many advanced collectors. But the reason he is remembered in this context was for his assistance to a then-emerging new ephemera craze, the study and collection of air transport labels.

The so-called aerotelist hobby, or "ABLS" for short, began in the late 1920s, and consisted of three categories: passenger baggage, air express, and air freight labels. By 1933 there were in existence approximately 300 label varieties from 60 American airlines and from airlines in 38 foreign countries. The quantities printed in most cases were 5,000 or less. Northwest Airways was the only Minnesota-based airline at the time, and had issued two known varieties of labels.

In 1934 Becken published the first catalog listing air transport labels from the world's airlines.[182] In his publisher's note, Becken noted that he was pleased "… to offer this new catalog, which not only is a checklist of labels and values, but contains much valuable information about the airlines which have passed into history. The authors have spent four years of research, traveling in many foreign countries to obtain data at first hand, on the labels used by airlines operating in every quarter of the globe." On the front cover of this catalog is the first baggage label of what was then called Northwest Airways.

Northwest Airways transported its first passenger, St. Paul businessman Byron G. Webster, on a flight from the Twin Cities to Chicago on July 25, 1927. It was a one-way, 12½-hour flight, flown by Charles "Speed" Holman, for whom the downtown St. Paul airport is named.[183]

Air transport label collecting continues to this day, quite often being classified as collateral material to aerophilately. The most recent definitive listing of this material is in the six-volume *Air Transport Label Catalog,* published by the Aeronautica and Air Label Collectors Club and the Aerophilatelic Federation of the Americas.

Those interested in airline memorabilia also collect schedules, tickets, menus (from the days when meals were actually served), playing cards,

Nearly 300 baggage labels for airlines were known by 1933 when the first catalogue for collectors appeared. Northwest Airways used this label between 1927 and 1930. Courtesy of the authors.

Bus schedule for travel to the vacation areas of northern Minnesota by the Greyhound lines. Courtesy of the Minnesota Historical Society.

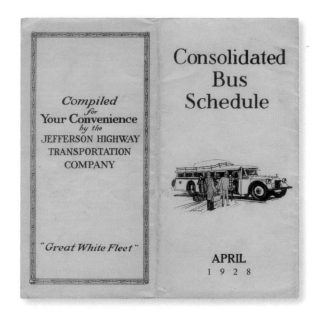

postcards, and in-flight magazines. Security concerns since September 11, 2001, have made other sorts of signs and notes (such as the polite memos that appear in luggage to inform a traveler that the luggage has been inspected) part of the airline ephemera collection.

The Bus

Once a system of reasonably paved highways was in place, comfortable travel by motor bus between cities and towns in Minnesota became feasible. The Mesaba Transportation Company began taking passengers from Hibbing to Grand Rapids in 1915. One of that company's partners, Carl Wickman, moved to Duluth where he purchased the White Bus Line, offering service to Grand Marais. Wickman incorporated Northland Transportation in 1929.[184]

Edgar Zelle began the Red Bus Line with service from the Twin Cities to St. Cloud in 1918. He sold this venture to Northland Transportation after buying the Jefferson Highway Transportation Company in 1925. Jefferson's lines served southern Minnesota, eventually connecting with other routes to Iowa, Kansas City, and St. Louis.[185] Northland would later become part of the Greyhound Corporation.

And, of course, along with buses came a new category of transportation ephemera: Minnesota bus ephemera includes schedules, posters, postcards, brochures, and tickets.

The Streetcar

Before there were streetcars, travelers were met by wagons at the steamboat landings and offered transport to nearby towns and beyond. J. Fletcher Williams wrote that some of these conveyances were neither reliable nor comfortable, but in territorial days that was perhaps to be expected. He noted that the first stage ever run in Minnesota Territory, in 1849, was by Amherst Willoughby and Simon Powers. "They had a nice span of horses and a two-seated open wagon, but not much else.... The first winter the traveling was very rough. There were no regular stations to stop at, and at night they would sometimes encamp on the snow."[186]

A 1913 brochure for the Twin City streetcar lines was a guide and schedule, with fold-out maps of the various routes. The small steamboat on the cover, the Como, was operated on Lake Minnetonka. Produced by the American Bank Note Company. Courtesy of the Ramsey County Historical Society.

Horse-drawn streetcars were the first major improvement in city transportation. The Minneapolis Street Railroad Company was organized in 1873, while its St. Paul equivalent preceded it by a year. Tracks were laid for the streetcar wheels and power was provided by a single horse. On hilly St. Paul routes where a horse-drawn car was not practical, the cars were pulled by an underground cable, much like the famous cable cars of San Francisco. Electricity, introduced in 1890, and the construction of the Selby Avenue tunnel in 1906 made the cable system obsolete. By 1900 both St. Paul and Minneapolis had streetcars powered by electricity.[187]

The first streetcar lines connected both downtowns (the Interurban Line) with the University of Minnesota and with Colonel King's vast south Minneapolis properties. Other streetcar lines carried passengers to various stops at Lake Minnetonka and Stillwater on the St. Croix River. At Lake Minnetonka steamboats owned by the transit company were available during the season for trips to Big Island and other vacation spots. The connections between the Twin Cities and tourist destinations meant that eventual advertising would stress not only the convenience for the commuter but the recreational opportunities available at the destination. The Twin City Rapid Transit Company operated most of these lines under the direction of Thomas Lowry until his death in 1909. By 1954 the streetcars were gone, about eighty years after they first appeared. Tracks were ripped up and sold for scrap. The streetcars, which were built and main-

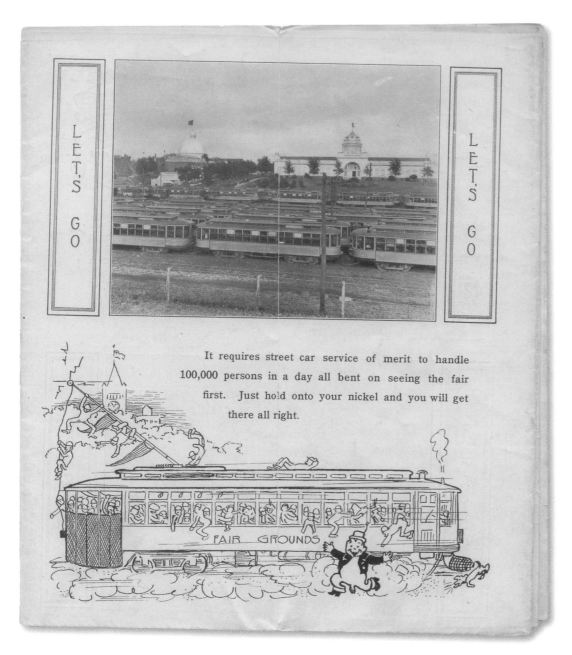

It requires street car service of merit to handle 100,000 persons in a day all bent on seeing the fair first. Just hold onto your nickel and you will get there all right.

FAIR GROUNDS

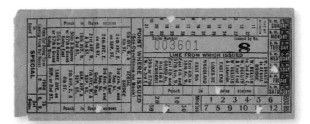

John Borchert noted in his discussion of Minnesota towns, by 1920 Moorhead, East Grand Forks, St. Cloud, Winona, and Mankato all had streetcar lines, linking their downtowns with neighborhoods, college campuses, parks, and fairgrounds.[188]

On June 26, 2004, Metro Transit opened its Hiawatha light rail system, which runs from the

For passengers with non-direct destinations, it was necessary to transfer between streetcar lines. The Interurban Line (an electric streetcar in 1912) connected the St. Paul and Minneapolis business districts. The name on the ticket is that of Horace Lowry, son of the company founder, Thomas Lowry. By 1944 some of these streetcars were replaced by buses, as they all would be within a few years. Courtesy of the authors.

tained at the Snelling Avenue shops, were sold abroad.

There were other streetcar lines. The St. Paul Southern Electric Railway's trolley linked Hastings and St. Paul until that line closed in 1928. And as

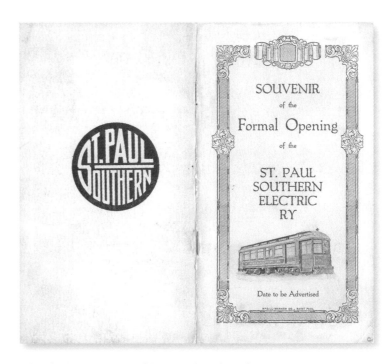

Folder for the inauguration of the St. Paul Southern Electric Railway, whose streetcar line ran from South St. Paul to Hastings. Lithographed by McGill-Warner, St. Paul. Courtesy of the Minnesota Historical Society.

THIS TRADE-MARK

WILL REMIND YOU THAT
THERE'S MONEY IN PAN FOR YOU

For a short period of time (1917–1923) St. Cloud was home to an automobile manufacturing company, the Pan Motor Company. Its trademark appears in a 1917 advertisement. Courtesy of Stearns History Museum.

downtown warehouse district to Fort Snelling, the Minneapolis-St. Paul International Airport, and the Mall of America. Schedules and other paper ephemera marked this development.[189]

Several of the original streetcars are now owned and maintained by the Minnesota Transportation Museum. These cars operate from May through November on tracks near to the east shore of Lake Harriet in Minneapolis. Another of the Museum's transit possessions is a summer visitor to Excelsior. The *Minnehaha*, one of the transit company's streetcar-looking steamboats, was restored in 1996. It carries passengers on Lake Minnetonka just as the original fleet did beginning in 1906.

Ephemera with a streetcar connection includes tickets, transfers, passes, posters, postcards, and schedules, as well as the banner advertising cards on the car walls.[190]

The Automobile

While Minnesota is not usually considered as being the home of automotive ingenuity, an insurance man from Mississippi once thought it should be. Samuel Pandolfo launched his Pan Motor Company in St. Cloud. He built a factory and homes for his workers (Pan-Town-on-the-Mississippi) and issued thousands of shares of stock for his new venture; success, it seemed, was in his grasp. Federal authorities, however, accused Pandolfo of mail fraud in the sale of his stock. He was convicted of this and served two and one-half

Each year a new Winter Carnival Vulcanus Rex, or Fire King, is selected. He is dressed in black and the members of his krewe are in red. All of these 2000 Vulcans ride a 1932 Luverne fire truck, photographed on this business card, on visits and in parades during the year. Courtesy of the authors.

The Exploits of PAUL BUNYAN

Price 10c
Mails for 1¼c with no writing

Distributed by Paul Bunyan Oil Co., Inc.
Conoco Dealers. • Dealer list inside

Paul Bunyan Mailer Copyright 1940 Lakeland Color Press, Brainerd, Minn.

years in prison. The Company manufactured several hundred automobiles over a six year period, from 1917 to 1923.[191]

Samuel Pandolfo's venture in St. Cloud was one of the more ambitious, but, as Alan Ominsky discovered, by the mid 1920s more than forty-five different car and truck models had been built in Minnesota, with more than half of the manufacturers hoping for serial production.[192] One business, that of the Leicher brothers of Luverne, began by building trucks in 1905, before specializing in fire engines a few years later. A Luverne fire engine is one of the prized possessions of the St. Paul Winter Carnival's Vulcans, and is often depicted on their Fire & Brimstone memorabilia.

Gas stations have offered many forms of ephemera to their customers. Highway maps, postcards, matchbooks, calendars, and toys for children such as a Paul Bunyan booklet, were typical offerings.

In a small postcard booklet entitled The Exploits of Paul Bunyan, *the Paul Bunyan Oil Company dealers in Aitkin, Bay Lake, Bemidji, Brainerd, Garrison, and Pine Center advertised their services. The booklet was printed by Lakeland Color Press in Brainerd in 1940. Courtesy of the authors.*

CHAPTER NINE

Public Affairs

The Land

THE ORGANIZATION OF MINNESOTA AS A STATE followed the signing of various treaties with the Native American peoples residing in the area. Before land could be legally homesteaded it then needed to be surveyed. Federal government land offices also had to be established. Among the paper records that facilitated settlement were plat maps, deeds, mortgages, and, eventually, real estate tax receipts. While most individuals did not preserve these tax receipts beyond a short span of time, one family did. One receipt for real estate taxes is illustrated here. These receipts give a clear indication of St. Paul history over a fifty-year span.[193]

Stock Certificates and Currency

Since early territorial days Minnesota companies have issued stock certificates. This form of security printing, like that of banknotes, was usually accomplished by specialized printers, such as the American Bank Note Company of New York or Goes Lithographers of Chicago. However, various

NOTICE!!

Of the removal of the Land Office from Chatfield to Winnebago City, in the State of Minnesota.

In accordance with the provisions of the act of Congress, entitled "An act authorizing changes in the location of Land Offices," approved March 3, 1853, it is hereby declared and made known, that the office for the sale of public lands at Chatfield, in the "Root River District," in the State of Minnesota, will be removed to Winnebago City, in Faribault county, in said State at as early a day as practicable.

Further notice as to the precise time of closing the office at Chatfield, preparatory to its removal, and of its opening for business at Winnebago City, will be given by the Register and Receiver for the Land District.

Given under my hand, at the City of Washington, this thirteenth day of August, A. D. 1861.

By order of the President

J. M. EDMUNDS,
Commissioner of the General Land Office,

Land Office, Chatfield, Minn.
Sept. 1st, 1861.

In accordance with the above instructions we hereby give notice that the Land Office at Chatfield, will be closed for business at 12 o'clock M., on Wednesday, the 16th day of October, 1861, and will be opened for business at Winnebago City at 12 o'clock M., on Monday, November 4th, 1861.

J. H. WELCH, Register.
H. W. HOLLEY, Receiver.

Poster notifying interested persons of the removal of the federal land office to Winnebago City in 1861. Courtesy of Rob Rulon-Miller.

Receipt for real estate taxes due to the city of St. Paul, dated 1857 and signed by Daniel Rohrer, city treasurer from 1854 to 1859. Printed by the Minnesotian Printing Company. Courtesy of the authors.

Minnesota printers, including the Pioneer Press; Brown, Treacy & Company; and H. M. Smyth, all of St. Paul, produced stock certificates in the first few decades following statehood.

The border of a stock certificate was normally an engraved, ornamental design. Along the top edge was usually the statement of incorporation under the laws of the relevant state. The certificate number and amount of shares flanked a vignette in the top third of the document. The secretary and president of the company signed their names above the border at the bottom edge. Vignettes could be stock designs (a seated Columbia or an eagle with outstretched wings, for example) or they could reflect the nature of the company's business. The St. Paul and Duluth Railroad Company, for example, utilized stock certificates with three vignettes: two sternwheelers, a train, and a depot.

Banking in Minnesota and in all other states once had a very local character.[194] The National Currency Act of 1863 was enacted to establish national banks, which were required to place a certain percentage of their assets in government bonds. In

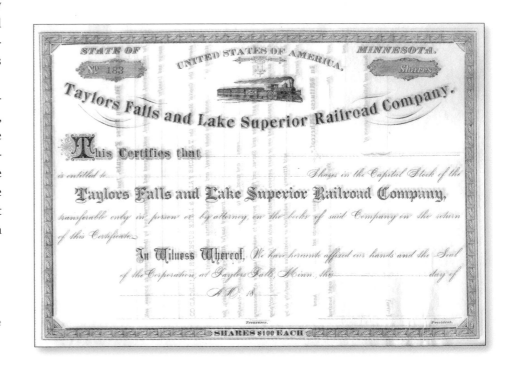

Unused stock certificate for a railroad line that connected Taylors Falls and Wyoming, Minnesota, from 1880 to 1948. The TFLS became part of the Northern Pacific in 1900. Courtesy of the Minnesota Historical Society.

PUBLIC AFFAIRS

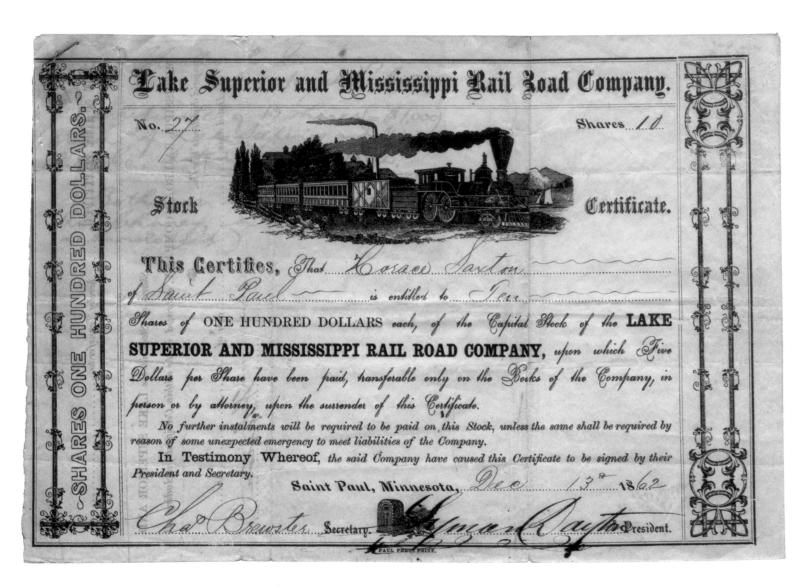

Horace Sexton invested $1,000.00 in shares of this railroad in 1862. Lyman Dayton, real estate investor, was president. The certificate was printed by the St. Paul Press Printing Company. Courtesy of the Minnesota Historical Society.

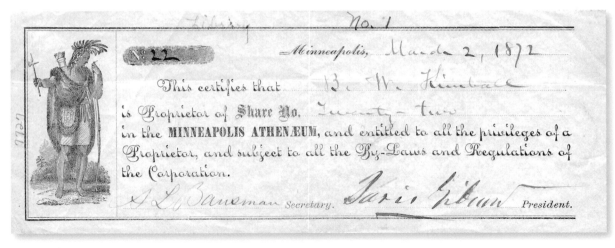

Stock certificate issued for the Minneapolis Athenaeum. This private library was founded in 1859, some years before the city had its own public library, and is located in the downtown Minneapolis library. Courtesy of the Minnesota Historical Society (Museum collections).

return they received national charters to operate, and special currency was issued for their use. These national notes were slightly larger (3⅛ by 7½ inches) than the Federal Reserve banknotes in use today. The name of the issuing bank appeared on the face of the bill, and there were spaces for the bank's officers to sign.

Designs on the national notes appeared on one side of the bill. Paper money today usually bears the portraits of former presidents or cabinet officers, but prior to the National Currency Act of 1863 many other images appear on currency circulated by local banks. Farmers and their families, winsome lasses, the Minnesota state seal, or Liberty with her flag were early design choices. Bank notes were typically printed by eastern security printers such as the American Bank Note Company.

Collectors of stock certificates save both issued and unissued shares, which are customarily bound together in a company's stock book. When the shares are eventually redeemed, they are often perforated and stamped *canceled*. Collectors may join the International Bond and Share Society, whose journal is *Scripophily*.

The Treasury Department supplied banknotes for local banks after 1900. The 1902 series bears the signatures of J. W. Lyons (register of the Treasury) and Ellis H. Roberts (Treasurer of the United States). Beneath the name of the Stockyards National Bank of South St. Paul (which opened for business on April 11, 1903) are the pen and ink signatures of its cashier (W. E. Briggs) and its president (John J. Flanagan). Banknotes were printed in numbered sheets and then cut apart. This bill is number 1. Courtesy of the authors.

An order for payment and receipt, dated 1887, establishes that Michael Maning was paid for the 3½ days he worked for the St. Paul Union Depot Company. Maning's acknowledgment appears with his mark, an X, at the lower right. The first Union Depot was built in 1881, and rebuilt in 1884, following a fire. Courtesy of the authors.

THE NEW CATHEDRAL FUND

TEMPORARY RECEIPT

No._____

St. Paul, Minn., _Sept. 6th_ 19_03_.

RECEIVED of _Joseph Steppan_ the sum of

$ _5 00_, this being the _5th_ installment upon his subscription

of $ _25 00_ to the Fund for the erection of the new Cathedral in the

city of St Paul,

_____
J. J. Slevin Collector.

N. B. A formal receipt for this sum will be given in due time, signed by the Treasurer of the Fund and the Secretary of the Executive Committee.

Many Thanks

(LEFT):

In 1913 Joseph Steppan paid the final installment of his $25.00 pledge toward construction of the new cathedral in St. Paul. Designed by Emmanuel L. Masqueray, construction of the cathedral began in 1906 and was completed in 1915. Courtesy of the authors.

(BELOW):

Prior to redemption, this unemployment scrip certificate from the Great Depression had to have twenty five-cent stamps signed and attached to the reverse side. The 1934 certificate was printed by the Goes Company, a Chicago security printer that specialized in stock certificates. Courtesy of the Stearns History Museum.

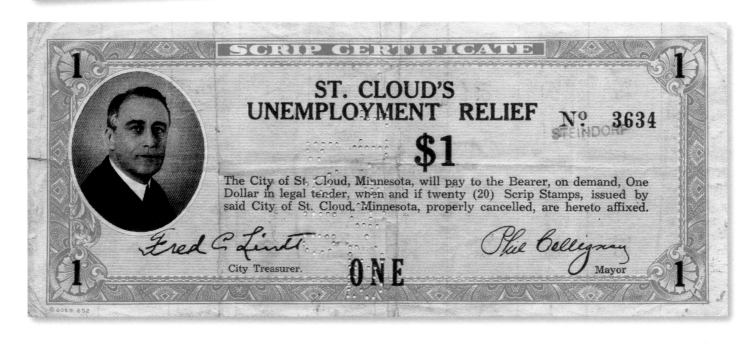

SCRIP CERTIFICATE

ST. CLOUD'S
UNEMPLOYMENT RELIEF

N̄o. 3634
STEINDORF

$1

The City of St. Cloud, Minnesota, will pay to the Bearer, on demand, One Dollar in legal tender, when and if twenty (20) Scrip Stamps, issued by said City of St. Cloud, Minnesota, properly cancelled, are hereto affixed.

Fred C. Lintt
City Treasurer.

ONE

Phil Collignon
Mayor

© GOES 652

Receipts

From the earliest days of the state it was customary to issue receipts for payment made, either for wages or for donations made to a favorite charity.

Scrip, Coupons, and Trading Stamps

Small paper squares, perforated to tear away or gummed to affix in booklets, are yet another means businesses and governmental entities have used for various purposes. Like regular currency, scrip is used to purchase goods, but usually only in designated stores or for the product shown on the coupon. The Fosston Co-op dairy coupon scrip entitled its user to purchase other goods and produce in their store, thus gaining the nickname of milk money.[195] Christmas stamps such as those issued by Fandel's Department Store in St. Cloud, were another variation.

Trading stamps became popular with the green and red Sperry & Hutchinson (S & H) stamps in 1896. In Minnesota Curt Carlson launched his Gold Bond

Increasing customer loyalty has long been a concern for businesses. During the 1950s the Fosston Co-op Creamery Association issued $2.00 coupon books with individual tickets in penny, nickel, and fifteen-cent denominations. Customers were requested to leave the coupons in the empty bottles that they returned to the deliveryman. Courtesy of the authors.

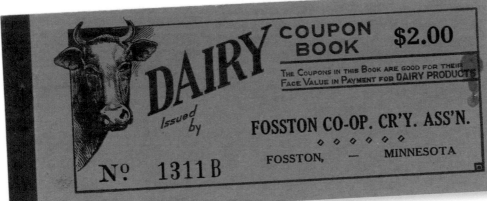

The Yellow Cab Company of St. Cloud issued coupon books, redeemable for rides, in books worth five dollars. Courtesy of Stearns History Museum.

Manufacturers' coupons and store coupons may be found in newspapers and magazine advertisements or in direct mail packets. Both types restrict their use to a particular product or a particular business, and are often limited by date. Cash registers in grocery stores and supermarkets now record the use of discount coupons and then inform the customer that he or she has saved a total amount or percentage of the bill by using the coupons.

Patriotism

While Minnesota's territorial history began after the country's first armed conflicts, it is not until the beginning of the Civil War that a military paper trail commences. The Dakota Conflict of 1862, the Civil War, the Spanish-American War, World Wars I and II, Korea, Vietnam, and the others, all produced documents with a Minnesota connection. Recruiting posters, draft notices, and food and gasoline ration stamps for civilians were among the results.

After the Civil War ended, veterans who returned home founded a group that became important politically while offering its members support and camaraderie. The Grand Army of the Republic (GAR) units met locally, in state and in national conventions. The thirtieth national convention of the GAR met in St. Paul in 1896. GAR posts (and related service organizations) were often the sponsors of commemorative memorials. Invitations, tickets, and programs exist for the dedication of such sculptures.

Stamps in 1938. Consumers acquired these stamps when they made a purchase, but could spend them only in the Gold Bond or S & H redemption stores or catalogs.[196] Through the 1960s trading stamps proved to be a popular store incentive to increase customer loyalty and sales for the Gold Bond Stamp Company. Trading stamps were phased out in 1973 as the Carlson Companies (its current name) moved into the hospitality industry, with a focus on hotels, travel agencies, and cruise ships.[197]

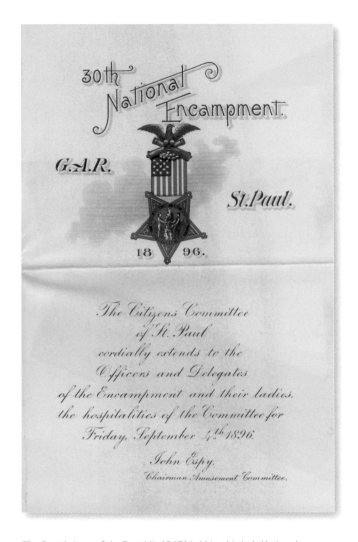

The Grand Army of the Republic (GAR) held its thirtieth National Encampment in St. Paul during September 1896. The officers and their ladies were invited for dinner and a steamship ride on Lake Minnetonka. The program was printed by the Banning firm. Courtesy of the Minnesota Historical Society.

Proclamation

WHEREAS, Company I has received Orders to leave for the War To-morrow, Friday Morning, April 29, and whereas the people desire to signify to the Company their appreciation of their brave and patriotic action in volunteering in their Country's Cause, Now therefore, I recommend that all business houses be closed between the hours of 4 and 6 o'clock this afternoon, and that all citizens, laying aside all other affairs, close their places of business and attend the Reception at the Opera House at 4 o'clock to be given under the auspices of Robson Post, G. A. R.

And all citizens are requested to assemble at the M. & St. L. depot to-morrow morning at 5:45 and join in the "Good Bye" to the Company.

C. M. WILKINSON, Mayor.

Albert Lea, April 28, '98.

STANDARD PRINT, ALBERT LEA.

Late in April 1898, President McKinley called upon the states to volunteer troops for a war against Spain. Minnesota's quota was three regiments. The Second Regiment, including Albert Lea's Company I, came from the southern part of the state. Saluted when they left home, they were greeted by ovations in St. Paul as they assembled at the State Fairgrounds. The Second Regiment was mustered out in September, never having seen duty abroad. Courtesy of Floyd Risvold.

Crime and Punishment

As new communities established laws and established incarceration as punishment for those who break those laws, they soon needed to build jails. The state reformatory at Stillwater was built in the 1850s, while the larger prison at St. Cloud was opened thirty years later. The police blotter included here provides information on one accused man, while the small twine booklet was an indication of how a life might be spent behind bars.

A small ink-stained booklet records another aspect of prison life. In 1901 the superintendent of the Minnesota State Reformatory at St. Cloud offered $25.00 as a reward for the capture and

Charles Crawford (or W. D. Rounds, or Rogers, or Stanley) of "everywhere," was arrested by the St. Paul police department in 1904, accused of being a bunco artist and swindler. This wasn't his first encounter with the law. The record listed earlier arrests in Seattle, San Francisco, and Omaha. He was sentenced to five years in Stillwater prison. Courtesy of the authors.

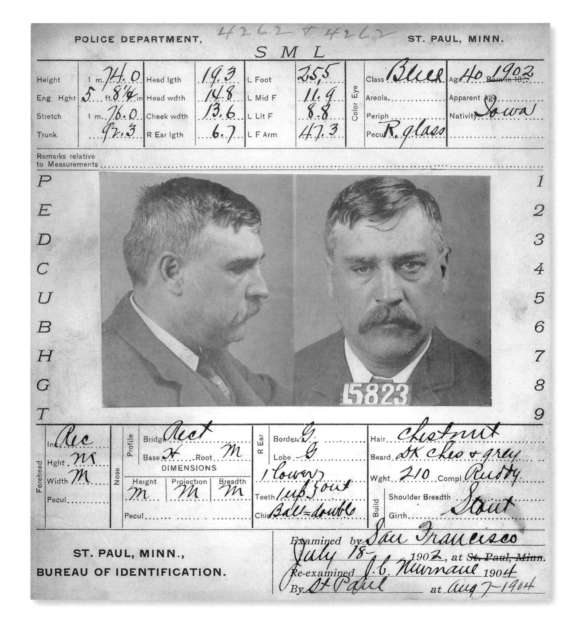

The manufacture of twine has long been a prison industry. Inside this note pad, a former user has carefully written rules for card games. Courtesy of the authors.

This small bounty hunters' booklet from the Minnesota Reformatory at St. Cloud listed forty men who had either broken parole or had escaped as of March 1, 1901. Courtesy of the authors.

Minnesota State Reformatory.

~~~~

St. Cloud, Minn., March 1, 1901.

The men whose names and descriptions are published herein, are fugitives from justice, having broken their parole, or escaped from this institution.

$50 REWARD will be paid for the capture and delivery of either of these men into the hands of an authorized officer of the Reformatory.

In correspondence by mail or wire, state whether or not the man admits identity, and if not, whether his description corresponds in every particular with that given in this book.

If the man is held for another crime, state when he can be delivered to an officer of this institution.

Yours truly,
FRANK L. RANDALL,
Supt.

$25 REWARD

JAMES SAVAGE.

Age, 30; height, 5 feet 8½ inches; weight, 230 pounds; complexion, sandy; eyes, slate blue; hair, sandy; nationality, American, occupation, engineer. While in the Reformatory corresponded with R.A. Savage, corner Third and Walker Streets, New Orleans, La.; and Mrs. W.A. Savage, Dakota, Minn.

Marks: Round white scar inside right forearm; scrofula scar on both sides of neck; long scar over knuckle of left first finger; three vaccine scars on left arm; small scar on left side upper lip; right toe has been split, bad nail; solid build; full face; large nose; double little toe on each foot. Escaped Aug. 23, 1896.

21

"DON'T SPIT!"

SPITTING SPREADS TUBERCULOSIS

✝ISSUED BY THE ANTI-TUBERCULOSIS SECTION OF THE IRISH RED CROSS SOCIETY

The Minnesota Public Health Association circulated this poster as a part of a campaign to stop "a disgusting, filthy and unnecessary habit." Courtesy of the Minnesota Historical Society (Museum collections).

delivery of any of the forty men shown and described in the booklet's pages. Most of the men had been released from prison but had broken the terms of their paroles. The crimes for which they had done time are not mentioned, but their physical descriptions, the names of probable family contacts, and habits (for example, "Intemperate. Smokes") are outlined. Most men were young, less than thirty years old, and had been imprisoned from five to ten years earlier.

Minnesota State Board of Health

WARNING!

WHOOPING COUGH

EXISTS ON THESE PREMISES

Dated _____ Health Officer _____

Local health departments once posted signs such as this on the front doors of residences where diphtheria, typhoid fever, scarlet fever, or chicken pox had struck. Used circa 1920. Courtesy of the Minnesota Historical Society (Museum collections).

Health

Quarantine signs were once nailed to front doors by the local health departments. They indicated danger to anybody who had not yet contracted measles, mumps, or other contagious ailments. Other health department signs warned against visiting beaches or public places where polio might be present, or against spitting and thus spreading tuberculosis.

Education

Like all of the subcategories of this chapter, printed paper items relating to education are numerous. The registration of students, the reporting of their grades, certificates of achievement, diplomas, invitations to graduations, baccalaureate ceremonies, and their programs are all part of this class of ephemera. Minnesota's institutions of higher learning generate their own voluminous ephemera. As any visitor to a dentist, doctor, or lawyer's office will attest, diplomas and membership in professional organizations are typical wall art, but also are ephemera.

Electoral Messages

From the moment a man or woman decides to run for office the campaign leaves a paper trail. Flyers and direct mail appeals go to potential voters in Minnesota's caucuses and state conventions, and then standards are waved at the convention for the candidates. Finally, for the nominee come yard signs, flyers to mail or hand out to voters, bumper

Ruby Curtis's parents signed their names on the back of this report card for the 1905–1906 school marking period. Eighth-grader Ruby was present each day, never late, but did badly in arithmetic. Courtesy of the authors.

PUBLIC AFFAIRS

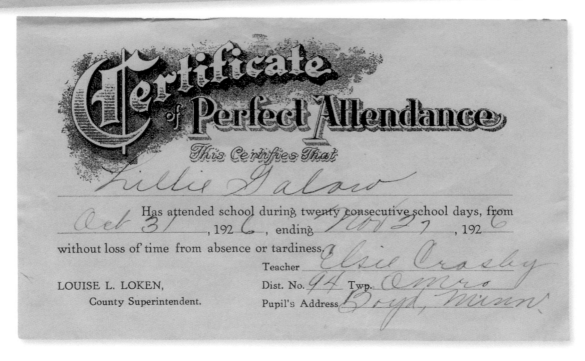

The State of Minnesota
STEARNS COUNTY

COMMON SCHOOL EXAMINATION
CERTIFICATE

This Certifies, that _Gertrude W. Krause_

passed an examination in _Reading_

for the School Year of 1914 with a standing of _85%_

Dated at St. Cloud, Minn.

May 1st 1914

Superintendent of Schools
Stearns County, Minnesota

MADE IN ST. CLOUD BY THE FRITZ CROSS CO

Certificate of Perfect Attendance

This Certifies That

Lillie Galow

Has attended school during twenty consecutive school days, from
Oct 31, 1926, ending _Nov 27_, 1926

without loss of time from absence or tardiness.

Teacher _Elsie Crosby_

LOUISE L. LOKEN,
County Superintendent.

Dist. No. _94_ Twp. _Omro_
Pupil's Address _Boyd, Minn._

Results from
the Stearns
County public
school reading
examination
were set forth
in printed
certificates
(top, 1914).
A perfect
attendance
certificate
from the Boyd,
Minnesota
schools
(bottom, 1926).
Courtesy of
the authors.

Folded graduation invitation, Clinton High School, 1929. The class of fourteen students celebrated the end of senior year with four major events. Courtesy of the authors.

The Class of Nineteen Hundred Twenty-nine

Clinton High School

invites you to its

Commencement Exercises

Friday evening, May thirty-first

Opera House

Clinton, Minnesota

Calendar

Junior-Senior Banquet	Baccalaureate Sermon
Saturday, April 13th	Rev. Paul Reque
Masonic Temple	Sunday, May 26th
	Big Stone Lutheran Church
Class Play	**Commencement Address**
Friday, April 26th	Benjamin Youngdahl
"Cheer up, Chad"	Friday, May 31st
Opera House	Opera House

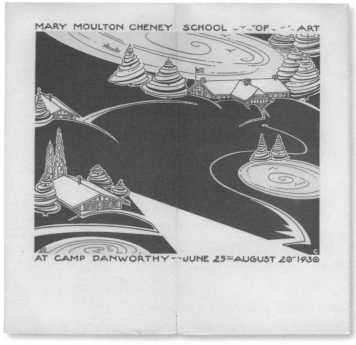

Brochure for Mary Moulton Cheney's summer art school located near Walker, Minnesota. Camp Danworthy, a girls' camp, had the usual recreational facilities, which the art students could use when they were not sketching at Star Island or Itasca Park. Courtesy of Ramsey County Historical Society.

stickers, decals, and posters. Roger Fischer, professor emeritus of American history at the University of Minnesota–Duluth, studied the memorabilia generated for presidential campaigns from 1824 to 1984. In his book Fischer noted that using material objects to catch the attention of voters began with the 1828 and 1832 presidential campaigns of

DEMOCRATS, ATTEND!

All democrats, good and true, who are interested in the Post Office at St. Anthony, are requested to meet at the School House, in Lower Town, FRIDAY EVENING next, at half past 6 o'clock for the purpose of recommending some suitable person for Post Master.

(BY ORDER OF THE PRECINCT COMMITTEE.)

D. STANCHFIELD, Chairman.

Feb. 15, 1853.

Andrew Jackson. Tokens, buttons, ribbons, bandannas, pitchers, and plates were among the items bearing that candidate's name. The 1840 election that brought William Henry Harrison to the White House "inspired a harvest of souvenir items seldom if ever surpassed in quantity and variety in nearly two centuries of American politics."[198] These campaigns took place before Minnesota had even become a territory but the precedent was set: political giveaways help win elections.

From 1920 until 1948, Fischer states, "an unprecedented variety and volume of political paper" appeared.[199] These

The appointment of postmasters was a presidential prerogative. This 1853 broadside urges democrats, "good and true," to attend a meeting for the purpose of recommending a new postmaster for the St. Anthony post office. The first postmaster, in 1849, was Ard Godfrey. Courtesy of Floyd Risvold.

Only one national political party has ever held its nominating convention in Minnesota. The Republicans met in June 1892 in the Minneapolis Industrial Exposition Building. The incumbent, President Benjamin Harrison, secured the nomination but lost the general election to Grover Cleveland. Courtesy of Patrick Coleman.

DINNER
TO
HONORABLE WILLIAM H. TAFT
SECRETARY OF WAR
BY
CITIZENS OF MINNEAPOLIS
AT THE
MINNEAPOLIS CLUB
ON
THURSDAY, JUNE 13TH
1907

included poster stamps, post-cards, noisemakers, blotters, and posters. In presidential campaigns postcards were mainly used before World War I, while matchbooks were introduced in 1928, replacing the earlier matchboxes. Fans have been a recent introduction, especially during the warm summer months. Blotters were a frequent giveaway until the invention of the ballpoint pen. Finally, when candidates spent time knocking on doors, attempting to meet voters face-to-face, flyers or door hanging leaflets became popular.

Citizens of Minnesota assembled at the Minneapolis Club on June 13, 1907, to honor "presidential possibility," Secretary of War William Howard Taft. Illustrated is the State, War and Navy Department building in Washington, D.C., now named the Executive Office building, which stands next to the White House. Speakers at the dinner also included University of Minnesota President Cyrus Northrop, Archbishop John Ireland, and Governor John A. Johnson. Secretary Taft also gave the twenty-fifth annual commencement address at the University of Minnesota that day. Courtesy of the James J. Hill Library (Hill papers).

A small booklet with spaces to affix coupons, much like a trading- or savings-stamp container, represents an early stage in Minnesota politics. The Working People's Nonpartisan Political League was organized by union leaders in 1920 as the equivalent of a similar group supported by farmers. Both groups would work together before officially merging into the Farmer-Labor Association in 1924. Candidates supported by the Farmer-Labor Association were selected by dues-paying members of the group's clubs.[200]

In the ephemera files of the Stearns County Museum in St. Cloud, the evolution of political paper items can be noted. Candidates for local offices usually began by handing out printed cards. Larger than a business card but smaller than a postcard, these carried a photograph and, in one-color type, the office sought and the candidate's name. Blotters, followed by leaflets, flyers, and bumper stickers in vivid color, came next. The most recent

The Three Supreme Court Justices
NOW ON THE BENCH AND CANDIDATES TO SUCCEED THEMSELVES

HOMER B. DIBELL   I. M. OLSEN   CHARLES LORING

The Justices are not nominated by political parties.
Their names appear on the white state ballot as "nominated without party designation."

VOTE FOR THESE THREE

47

Prepared and circulated by and in behalf of Justices Homer B. Dibell, Duluth Minn., I.M. Olsen, New Ulm, Minn., and Charles Loring, Crookston, Minn., each a candidate to succeed himself as Associate Justice of the Supreme Court of Minnesota, by their Personal Campaign Committes, Thomas D. O'Brien, Chairman; John K. Fesler, Secretary and Treasurer, E. 1508 First National Bank Building, St. Paul, Minn.

Justices Homer B. Dibell (of Duluth), Ingevall Olsen (of New Ulm), and Charles Loring (of Crookston) ran together as incumbent justices of the Minnesota Supreme Court in the 1932 general election. Their campaign effort included this giveaway blotter, printed at a union shop. Courtesy of the authors.

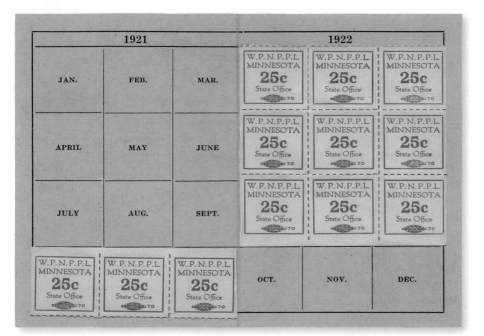

1921			1922		
JAN.	FEB.	MAR.	W.P.N.P.P.L. MINNESOTA 25c State Office 70	W.P.N.P.P.L. MINNESOTA 25c State Office 70	W.P.N.P.P.L. MINNESOTA 25c State Office 70
APRIL	MAY	JUNE	W.P.N.P.P.L. MINNESOTA 25c State Office 70	W.P.N.P.P.L. MINNESOTA 25c State Office 70	W.P.N.P.P.L. MINNESOTA 25c State Office 70
JULY	AUG.	SEPT.	W.P.N.P.P.L. MINNESOTA 25c State Office 70	W.P.N.P.P.L. MINNESOTA 25c State Office 70	W.P.N.P.P.L. MINNESOTA 25c State Office 70
W.P.N.P.P.L. MINNESOTA 25c State Office 70	W.P.N.P.P.L. MINNESOTA 25c State Office 70	W.P.N.P.P.L. MINNESOTA 25c State Office 70	OCT.	NOV.	DEC.

Membership dues for the Working People's Nonpartisan Political League were acknowledged with these small stamps, 1921–1922. Courtesy of the Minnesota Historical Society (Museum collections).

Bumper Stickers

While political giveaways have changed over time, many items have been used at every level from the presidential election down to the most local of campaigns. Signs or posters—whether carried, glued to walls, wrapped around telephone poles, or dug into yards—are now part of every campaign. One type of sign, the bumper sticker, carried proudly on its moving standard, exhibits the candidate's message wherever the car travels and is seen even when the car is motionless or parked. Depending on the driver, the bumper sticker

innovation is the sticker mounted on a toothpick, usually the size of a business card, and mimicking a candidate's yard sign in color and print style.

Shopping bags are another political giveaway. In 1920 Jacob Preus, who was running for governor of Minnesota, used a bag with his slogan "It's Jake with Me" on one side and Warren G. Harding's image on the other. These bags were printed by Jackson Printing Company, and examples may be found in the Museum Collection of the Minnesota Historical Society.

The World's Smallest Lawn Sign says:
☑ PICK
Larry
HAWS
for Stearns County Commissioner
Primary Election: 9/15/98   General Election: 11/3/98

An unusual and tiny campaign sign, mounted on a toothpick, names the candidate, the office sought, and the dates on which to vote. Courtesy of the Stearns History Museum.

PAUL WELLSTONE

FOR STATE AUDITOR

INVEST MINNESOTA'S
MONEY IN MINNESOTA

While teaching at Carleton College, Paul Wellstone ran for State Auditor in 1980. This pamphlet cover was a part of his losing campaign. Courtesy of Barry Casselman.

I WANT YOU
TO JOIN
THE REFORM PARTY

Ever since James Montgomery Flagg's World War I poster, many artists have used the finger-pointing "I want you" image of Uncle Sam for other purposes. This eye-catching version was part of Jesse Ventura's 1998 campaign for governor. Courtesy of Barry Casselman.

The color for Tim Penny's Reform Party campaign for Governor in 2002 was orange. This cartoon was drawn by the candidate's son, Jamison. Courtesy of the authors.

Repealing the Eighteenth Amendment was the cause that motivated this group to attach bumper messages to an automobile. In 1932 the shape of the bumper made tying on the card a necessity. George Luxton, photographer. Courtesy of the Minnesota Historical Society.

might be seen by more people than a button on a lapel, a yard sign, or even a billboard.

Metal license plate attachments were first used on automobiles in the 1924 presidential campaign when the car became integral to the vote-getting efforts.[201] While decals for car windows were also used at that early date, the bumper sticker only became a major cultural factor in the 1956 Presidential campaign between Dwight D. Eisenhower and Adlai E. Stevenson. In that campaign more than fifty different versions were noted. The bumper

sticker is, of course, not expensive, is easy to apply, although sometimes hard to remove, and has the great advantage of being highly visible. According to Fischer, the bumper sticker quickly developed into "the most significant avenue of personal political expression for the last 50 years."[202] Yet bumper stickers have not been the subject of any scholarly research or study, and apparently only the University of Texas has a major collection of this material.[203]

Since the 1960s the bumper sticker has been used for political campaigns as well as to indicate support for other ideas and causes, such as hunting and fishing rights, abortion rights (pro and con), and gun control (again, pro and con). The problem of removing the sticker once the campaign ended was solved by the 1970s. Fischer notes that they made newer stickers of vinyl material.[204]

One phrase has become ubiquitous on bumper stickers since it first appeared in 1977. Graphic artist Milton Glaser designed the I Love New York logo for the New York State Department of Commerce.[205] With the word *love* represented by a heart, the logo was an immediate success and was quickly imitated on decals and bumper stickers throughout the country.

LEGALIZE LUTEFISK NOW
VOTE MONDALE-GROWE

PAID FOR BY BILL WHITE – FRIEND OF GROWE/MONDALE CAMPAIGNS – 2243 BUCHANAN ST. NE., MPLS., MN. 55418, 1-612-781-4498

YOUR GOVERNOR IS
sMARTER
THAN MY GOVERNOR

UNION-BUILT
We're Building
Minnesota With
Quality & Pride
...and for less
MINNESOTA AFL-CIO BUILDING TRADES UNIONS

CRAM YOUR SPAM

(THIS PAGE, FROM TOP TO BOTTOM):

Bumper sticker from 1984 when two Minnesotans of Norwegian descent, Walter Mondale and Joan Growe, ran for office. Courtesy of Barry Casselman.

A bumper sticker printed during Jesse Ventura's administration. Courtesy of Barry Casselman.

Some bumper stickers indicate pride in belonging to a group, such as the building trades unions. Courtesy of Barry Casselman.

Spam, Hormel's luncheon meat, became widely known during World War II, both with the military and on the home front. The bumper sticker carries the message of a bitter strike in 1985–1986. Members of United Food and Commercial Workers Local P-9 confronted management of the Geo. A. Hormel Company plant at Austin, over working conditions and wages. Courtesy of Barry Casselman.

Afterword

A STICKER WITH TWO PRINTED SIDES WAS once provided to airline passengers. They were directed to affix the appropriate side to the back of their seat. The sticker instructed the flight attendants to either "please do not disturb" or "please wake me for meal service." This sticker is both Minnesota ephemera (the airline is Northwest Orient) and a reminder that what once was the norm is now rare in the airline industry.

Products and industries vanish, and services are eliminated or changed. A restaurant that once offered imprinted matchbooks to diners now displays no smoking signs on its wall and on table tents. A children's museum (like most museums now) displays a sign on its entry that guns are banned in the premises, thus warning its toddler audience to leave their weapons at home. Ephemera witnesses how behavior changes over time.

Even the production of ephemera has changed, with computers often being used to electronically design and display messages that once were relegated to paper. Spam has always existed, and will continue to do so even though the media differs.

Ephemera, the stuff that pervades our lives, will always be with us in some way. Only its form and message changes. We may preserve only the most intriguing bits of ephemera as souvenirs, but what we save will always illustrate our history.

Notes

Introduction

Additional sources of information include Theodore Blegen, *Minnesota: A History of the State* (Minneapolis, Minn.: University of Minnesota Press, 1963); William W. Folwell, *A History of Minnesota,* 4 vols. (St. Paul, Minn.: Minnesota Historical Society, 1921–1930); Jack El-Hai, *Lost Minnesota: Stories of Vanished Places* (Minneapolis, Minn.: University of Minnesota Press, 2000); Larry Millett, *Lost Twin Cities* (St. Paul, Minn.: Minnesota Historical Society Press, 1992); Gene Rebeck, "100 Minnesota Business Firsts," *Twin City Business Monthly* (September 2003): 56–73; J. Fletcher Williams, *A History of Saint Paul and the County of Ramsey to 1875* (St. Paul, Minn.: Minnesota Historical Society Press, 1876); Jack El-Hai, *Minnesota Collects* (St. Paul, Minn.: Minnesota Historical Society Press, 1992); Minnesota Historical Photo Collectors Group, *Joel E. Whitney: Minnesota's Leading Pioneer Photographer* (St. Paul, Minn.: The Group, 2001); Hal Morgan, *Symbols of America* (New York, N.Y.: Viking Penguin, 1986); Maurice Rickards, *The Encyclopedia of Ephemera: A Guide to the Fragmentary Documents of Everyday Life for the Collector, Curator, and Historian* (New York, N.Y.: Routledge, 2000); David Stivers, *The Nabisco Brands Collection of Cream of Wheat Advertising* (San Diego, Calif.: Collectors Showcase, 1986).

1.   Printed paper ephemera is often part of museum exhibits and collections; on occasion ephemera is the sole subject, as it was in the 2001 exhibition "Ephemera. Les Imprimés de tous les jours. 1880–1939" at the Musée de l'Imprimerie, Lyon, France.

2.   Many breweriana collectors regard any collectibles in their field dated after the repeal of National Prohibition in 1933, or "post-Pro," to be of lesser interest. Postcard collectors may choose to save only cards that are "real" photos or were printed before the "linen look" became popular.

3.   Michael Falcone, "Preserving Ephemera of Recall Campaign," *The New York Times* (September 29, 2003): A10.

4.   Robert Opie, *The Art of the Label: Designs of the Times* (Secaucus, N.J.: Chartwell Books, 1987): 140.

5.   This handbill is reproduced in Mary Wheelhouse Berthel and Harold Dean Cater, "The Minnesota Historical Society: Highlights of a Century," *Minnesota History* 30: 4 (Winter 1949): 307. A reproduction of the handbill appears in the journal.

6.   Maurice Rickards, *Collecting Printed Ephemera* (New York, N.Y.: Abbeville Press, 1988): 48–49, 53–54.

7.   Michael Twyman, "Avant-propos," *Ephemera, les imprimés de tous les jours 1880–1939.* Lyon: Musée de l'imprimerie (2001), 5. It is interesting to note the current popularity of scrapbooking as a craft hobby, with numerous shops selling albums and materials, and even classes offering how-to guidance.

8.   Rick Nelson, "Flour Power," *Minneapolis Star Tribune* (September 11, 2003): T4.

1. Who Made Ephemera?

Additional sources of information include Mildred Friedman and Phil Freshman, editors, *Graphic Design in America, A Visual Language History.* Exhibition Catalogue. (Minneapolis, Minn.: Walker Art Center and Harry N. Abrams, 1989); Pamela W. Laird, *Advertising Progress: American Business and the Rise of Consumer Marketing* (Baltimore, Md.: Johns Hopkins University Press, 1998); John Lewis, *Printed Ephemera: The Changing Uses of Type and Letterforms in English and American Printing* (Ipswich, England: Antique Collectors Club, 1990); and Philip B. Meggs, *A History of Graphic Design.* (New York, N.Y.: John Wiley and Sons, 3rd ed., 1998); and Alec Wilkinson, "Man of Letters. Matthew Carter's life in type design," *The New Yorker* (December 5, 2005): 56–65.

9.   J. Fletcher Williams, *A History of the City of St. Paul and of the County of Ramsey, Minnesota* (St. Paul, Minn.: Minnesota Historical Society, 1876): 210.

10.   Ibid., 328.

11.   Mamie R. Martin, "History of Printing in Minnesota to 1866" (MLS thesis, Columbia University, 1931): 7–10.

12.   *Chisago County Press,* February 10, 1944. The first foreman for the weekly *Medborgaren* was John Richard Moberg (1869–1944), who had come from Sweden at fifteen to be a typesetter (*typografelev*) in St. Paul. Between 1898 and 1921, Moberg set 40,000 ems of type every single week for the *Chisago County Press,* which had become an English language weekly and acquired a linotype machine.

13.   The Goodhue press is on view in the Society's museum, along with other displays from the Territorial period.

14.   "Genealogy of the St. Paul Papers" (*St. Paul Pioneer Press,* April 25, 1999): 31H.

15. Marjorie Kreidberg, *Fragments of Early Printing: Being an Account of Book, Job, and Ornamental Printing, and Every Other Description of Printing and Blank Book Manufactory, 1849–1860, in the Territory and State of Minnesota* (St. Paul, Minn.: North Central Publishing, 1958): 20.

16. Robert Staehlin, "A History of Printing in Minneapolis and Saint Paul, Minnesota, with a Bibliography of Imprints, 1866–1876" (MA thesis, University of Minnesota, 1951): 57.

17. Charles F. Deutsch, Ramaley Printing Company. *Established 1863: A Glimpse at 128 Years of St. Paul's Printing Industry* (St. Paul, Minn.: Ramaley Printing, 1991): vii.

18. *Since 1871: 75th Anniversary* (Minneapolis, Minn.: Harrison & Smith, 1946).

19. Undated clippings in Peter J. Giesen Scrapbook, Minnesota Historical Society.

20. Speech by Harvey Blodgett to St. Paul Graphic Arts Association Dinner, January 1944. (Minnesota Historical Society: Brown, Treacy, Sperry files.)

21. Katherine Morrison McClinton, *The Chromolithographs of Louis Prang* (New York, N.Y.: Clarkson N. Potter, 1973): 13–17.

22. Alan E. Kent, "Early Commercial Lithography in Wisconsin," *Wisconsin Magazine of History* (Summer 1953): 247.

23. "Are Leaders in Engraving Trade," *Minneapolis Journal* (March 31, 1910): 24.

24. *McGill-Warner Type Specimen Book*: 6, 11, 33, 42. This undated volume is in the collection of Ernie Haemig.

25. Matthew Mirapaul, "Is It About to Rain? Check the Typeface." *The New York Times* (July 24, 2003): 6E. See also Deborah Littlejohn, editor, *Metro Letters: A Typeface for the Twin Cities* (Minneapolis, Minn.: University of Minnesota Press, 2003).

26. Frederick W. Goudy, *Typologia* (Berkeley, Calif.: University of California Press, 1940, reprinted 1977): 169.

27. Juliann Sivulka, *Soap, Sex and Cigarettes: A Cultural History of American Advertising* (Belmont, Calif.: Wadsworth Publishing, 1998): 35.

28. Moira F. Harris, *Louise's Legacy* (St. Paul, Minn.: Pogo Press, 1998): 76.

29. *CM: Our First Fifty Years* (Minneapolis, Minn.: Campbell Mithun, 1983).

30. For examples of the firm's work, see the files of the Mac Martin Advertising Agency in the collections of the Minnesota Historical Society.

31. *Your Future* (Minneapolis, Minn.: Bureau of Engraving, circa 1937).

32. In 1948 the Institute of Commercial Art, later to be known as Famous Art Schools, opened in Westport, Connecticut, offering a similar course of mail instruction.

33.   Patricia C. Johnson, "Edward Brewer: Illustrator and Portrait Painter," *Minnesota History* 47:1 (Spring 1980): 4.

34.   An early example of Mac Martin's own work is the coloring book, *Mother Goose Now-a-Days*, which he created for Foot Schulze Shoes (see chapter 5).

35.   Friberg praised the training he received in a 1951 letter sent to Art Instruction.

36.   *Your Future* (Minneapolis, Minn.: Bureau of Engraving, circa 1937): 11, 12.

37.   Dottie Enrico, "Top 10 Advertising Icons," *Advertising Age* supplement (March 29, 1999).

38.   Moira F. Harris, "Ho–ho–ho! It *Bears* Repeating: Advertising Characters in the Land of Sky Blue Waters," *Minnesota History* 57:1 (Spring 2000): 23, 25.

2. Ex Libris

Additional Sources of information include Fridolf Johnson, *A Treasury of Bookplates from the Renaissance to the Present* (New York, N.Y.: Dover Publications, 1977); Carole Nelson, "She Designs Personalized Bookplates," *St. Paul Pioneer Press* (March 25, 1972); and Harold Peterson, "John and Ethel Van Derlip, Minneapolis Institute of Arts Library," *Libraries and Culture* 29:2 (Spring 1994): 220–222.

39.   J. Fletcher Williams, *A History of the City of Saint Paul and of the County of Ramsey, Minnesota* (St. Paul, Minn.: Minnesota Historical Society, 1876): 5.

40.   Larry Dingman, *Booksellers Marks: An Illustrated Book.* (Minneapolis, Minn.: Dinkytown Antiquarian Bookstore, 1986).

41.   *Minneapolis Star Tribune* (April 3, 1999): E1, E3.

42.   St. Paul's Ruminator bookstore, now closed, was once known as the Hungry Mind, and its newsletter was called "Fodder."

43.   Maurice Rickards, *Collecting Paper Ephemera* (New York, N.Y.: Abbeville Press, 1988): 152–153.

44.   A scrapbook containing examples of Cleora Wheeler's bookplates is included in her papers at the Minnesota Historical Society (No. P1254). Examples of her prints and bookplates are in other museum collections as well. Her working papers, trade cards, postcards, and other collected bookplates can be found in the Cleora Wheeler Papers, Special Collections and Rare Books, University of Minnesota Library. Her small embossing press, which she used to print Christmas cards, was later purchased by John Parker, whose publishing company was called the Cleora Press.

45.   Ruth Thompson Saunders, *A Book of Artists' Own Bookplates* (Claremont, Calif.: Saunders Studio Press, 1933): 44.

46.   Marcia G. Anderson, "Art for Art's Sake: The Handicraft Guild of Minneapolis," in *Art and Life on the Upper Mississippi 1890–1915: Minnesota 1900*, ed. Michael Conforti (Newark, Dela.: University of Delaware Press, 1994): 122–163.

47.   Leonard Wells (1863–1933), longtime manager of the bookstore at Powers department store, prepared the small catalogue, found in the Cleora Wheeler Papers, Special Collections and Rare Books, University of Minnesota Library. For the obituary of Oscar Blackburn, see *Minneapolis Sunday Tribune* (April 29, 1956), Upper Midwest section: 6.

48.   Louis Hennepin, *Nouvelle découverte d'un trés grand pays situé dans l'Amérique, entre le nouveau Mexique et la Mer Glaciale* (Amsterdam, 1698).

49.   Rutherford Aris, *The Ampersand in Script and Print: An Essay in Honour of The Ampersand Club on the Occasion of its Semicentenary* (Minneapolis, Minn.: The Ampersand Club, 1980): 8.

50.   Maurice Rickards, *Collecting Printed Ephemera* (New York, N.Y.: Abbeville Press, 1988): 217.

51.   Gary Derong, "Give 'em the Nod," *St. Paul Pioneer Press* (July 14, 2002): D1, 10.

52.   Ruth Berman, ed. *The Kerlan Awards in Children's Literature: 1975–2001* (St. Paul, Minn.: Pogo Press, 2001). See in this volume Bette J. Portola, "The Kerlan Award: A Short History," xx-xxiv.

53.   Aris, 8.

54.   Emerson C. Wulling, "The Ampersand Club Retrospect and Prospect, 1965," reprinted in *The Ampersandpaper*, 1 (Fall 1970): 1–2.

55.   "Unser Jane," *The Ampersandpaper* 2 (Spring 1972): 1.

56.   Donald L. Empson, "North Central Publishing Company Christmas Books: An Introduction and a Bibliography," (MA thesis, University of Minnesota, 1965).

3. Through the Mails

Additional sources of information include Robert B. Spooner, "Lindy's Philatelic Followers," *The American Philatelist* (September 2001): 802–807; Richard B. Graham, *United States Postal History Sampler* (Sidney, Ohio: Linns Stamp News, 1992); *American Illustrated Cover Catalog: The Collection of John R. Biddle* (North Miami, Fla.: David G. Phillips Co., 1981); *Standard Airpost Catalog, 1933 Edition*, Donald E. Dickason, ed. (Wooster, Ohio: The Berkshire Exchange, 1933); Moira F. Harris, "Small Format, Big View: Curt Teich Postcards of Minnesota," *Minnesota History* 54 (Fall 1995): 304–315; George and Dorothy Miller, *Picture Postcards in the United States: 1893–1918* (New York, N.Y.: Clarkson Potter, 1976); James Ogland, *Picturing Lake Minnetonka: A Postcard History* (St. Paul, Minn.: Minnesota Historical Society Press, 2001); Bonnie Wilson, *Minnesota in the Mail: A Postcard History* (St. Paul, Minn.: Minnesota Historical Society Press, 2004).

57.   Esther 9:30.

58.   Maynard H. Benjamin, *The History of Envelopes: 1840–1900* (Alexandria, Va.: Envelope Manufacturers Association, 1997): 2.

59.   See the cover used for the Winona Old Home Week celebrations in chapter 7.

60.   Moira F. Harris, "Stamp Album: A Collection of Minnesota People, Places and Events." *Minnesota History* 55/3 (Fall 1996): 107, 112. Since this article appeared, two more stamps had first day of issue ceremonies in Minnesota. These were a 34-cent stamp honoring Roy Wilkins issued on January 24, 2001, in Minneapolis and the Minnesota stamp in the Greetings from America sheet of 50 stamps, issued on April 4, 2002, in St. Paul.

61.   *Standard Airpost Catalog, 1933 Edition*, Donald E. Dickason, ed. (Wooster, Ohio: The Berkshire Exchange, 1933): 52, 161 *et seq.*, 216.

62.   Lithographers that prepared the majority of Minnesota business letterheads from the 1880s through the 1920s included I. Monash Lithographers, Crown Lithograph and Publishing Company, and the Cootey Lithographic and Printing Company in Minneapolis, and Berlandi & Bott (later to be William Berlandi & Company), McGill-Warner Company, and the *Pioneer Press* newspaper under various of its corporate or trade names in St. Paul.

63.   Those earliest commercially produced Chicago views were not the first postcards; earlier government-issued cards went on sale in 1873.

64.   Kim Keister, "Wish You Were Here," *Historic Preservation* 44: 2 (March/April 1992): 54.

65.   Warren Watkins, "How Curt Teich Postcards Are Presented," *Deltiology* 14 (1974): 4.

66.   Patricia Albers and William R. James, "Images and Reality: Post Cards of Minnesota's Ojibway People 1900–80," *Minnesota History* 49/6 (Summer 1985): 229.

4. For Boxes, Bottles, Barrels, Bags, and Cans

Additional sources of information include Frédérique Crestin-Billet, *La Folie des Etiquettes de vins* (Paris, France: Flammarion, 2001); Alec Davis, *Package and Print: The Development of Container and Label Design* (New York, N.Y.: Clarkson N. Potter, 1968); Keith Osborne and Brian Pipe, *The International Book of Beer Labels, Mats and Coasters* (Secaucus, N.J.: Chartwell Books, 1979); Robert Hajicek, "History of the Glencoe Brewing Company," *The Breweriana Collector* 80 (Winter 1993): 20–24; Herbert A. and Helen I. Haydock, *The World of Beer Memorabilia: Identification and Value Guide* (Paducah, Ky.: Collector Books, 1997); Bob Kay, "Early Minnesota Labels," *The Breweriana Collector* 122 (Summer 2003): 16–18; and Kate Roberts and Barbara Caron, "To the Markets of the World: Advertising in the Mill City, 1880–1930," *Minnesota History* 58 (Spring/Summer 2003): 308–319.

67.   Alfred J. Kolatch, *The Jewish Book of Why* (Middle Village, N.Y.: Jonathan David Publishers, 1981): 94 *et seq.*

68.   Moira F. Harris, "Breweries, Medals, and Three World's Fairs," *American Breweriana Journal* (January–February 2000): 12–17.

69.   Bob Kay, "Beer labels changed with the times—a simple guide to dates," *American Breweriana Journal* (March–April 2002): 21–25.

70.   George Klann, *Beer Coasters of Minnesota* (Rochester, Minn.: Self-published, 1998) : 17.

71.   Ibid., 39.

72.   "Pig's Eye Parrant for President" *St. Paul Pioneer Press* (June 21, 1992): 3B.

73.   Tony Kennedy, "From Cutout to Governor," *Minneapolis Star Tribune* (November 5, 1998): D1.

74.   Berit Thorkelson, "Products, Visits and Events Vary at Minnesota Wineries," *Minneapolis Star Tribune* (September 8, 2002): G9.

75.   Rudyard Kipling, *Rudyard Kipling's Verse—Definitive Edition* (Garden City, N.Y.: Doubleday, Doran and Co., 1945): 47. The widely quoted line is "And a woman is only a woman, but a good Cigar is a Smoke."

76.   *Commercial Bulletin and Northwest Trade* (Minneapolis, Minn.: The Commercial Bulletin Company, May 1, 1897): 12. Each manufacturer was assigned a tax number by the collector of internal revenue, and that number had to appear on each cigar box. Hence, reliable statistics abound.

77.   *Wisconsin & Tobacco: A Chapter in America's Industrial Growth* (Washington, D.C.: The Tobacco Institute, 1960): 2.

78.   *St. Paul City Directory for 1876* (St. Paul, Minn.: Campbell & Davidson, 1876): 332, and *The Minneapolis City Directory for 1888–1889* (Minneapolis, Minn.: Minneapolis City Directory Publishing Company, 1888): 1349.

79.   Thomas C. Somerville, "Beyond the Labels … Cigars and the Collector," *The Inside Collector* (March–April, 1996): 19, 20.

80.   One well-known German printing company that prepared cigar labels for Minnesota manufactories was Hermann Schött Actiengesellshaft, of Rheydt, near Dusseldorf. American companies that supplied Minnesota manufactories included Calvert Litho Co., Detroit and Chicago; Conover Engraving & Printing Co., Coldwater, Michigan; F. M. Howell & Co., Elmira, New York; Moehle Litho Co., Brooklyn, New York, and the (George) Schlegel Lithographing Corporation, New York City. Joe Davidson, *The Art of the Cigar Label* (Edison, N.J.: The Wellfleet Press, 1989): 28. Davidson lists the major lithographers and brokers who were active between 1880 and 1920, the so-called golden age of cigar label production.

81.   The Minnesota Historical Society has an extensive file with numerous examples of cigar advertising for this company. See MHS Museum files: J. W. Pauly & Co., 1989.230.

82.   1908 *Wholesale Cigar List of Winecke & Doerr* (Minneapolis, Minn.: Minneapolis Drug Company, 1908).

83.   Davidson, *Art of the Cigar Label,* 31.

84.   Chapter 24, General Laws of Minnesota for 1893. Complete trademark protection is a medley of the common law, state statutes, and an overriding federal statute, the Lanham Act of 1946, 15 USC 1501 *et seq.*

85.   Minnesota Historical Society files 112.F.11.6F and 112.H.11.5B. See Vol. 5: pages 1, 17, 24, 41, 58, 71, 96, 251, and 286 and Vol. 7: pages 66, 89, 90, 219, 317, 318, 354, 386, and 499.

86.   Marjorie Kreidberg, "Corn Bread, Portable Soup, and Wrinkle Cures," *Minnesota History* 41: 3 (Fall 1968): 112.

87.   David Stivers, *The Nabisco Brands Collection of Cream of Wheat Advertising Art* (San Diego, Calif.: Collectors' Showcase, 1986): 9.

88.   A majority of artifacts on display in the Mill City Museum are on loan from the Richard Ferrell Flour Milling History Collection. Mr. Ferrell is a retired mining engineer.

89.   James Gray, *Business without Boundary: The Story of General Mills* (Minneapolis, Minn.: University of Minnesota Press, 1954): 168.

90.   "Remarkable Growth and Success of the J. R. Watkins Company Due to Good Products, Attractive Packaging and Sound Merchandising," Winona County W.P.A. files, Minnesota Historical Society.

91.   Ibid., 3.

92.   National advertising was handled by the Erwin, Wasey Agency. Leslie Kouba was one of the artists they selected to prepare advertising that appeared in magazines such as the *Saturday Evening Post* during the 1950s.

93.   *Winona Daily News* (September 24, 1988): 1. The printing facility was closed and its staff laid off as a budget-cutting move.

94.   A special booklet, *Watkins 125th Anniversary* by Sandie McIntire, was published by the *Winona Daily News* in 1993 to mark the event.

95.   Mark M. Sheehan, "Kidspace: Stuck on stickers," *The Christian Science Monitor* (November 19, 2002): 18; and Janet Starr Hull, "Sticky Fruit Labels," *The Philadelphia Inquirer* (June 26, 2002).

5. Merchant Giveaways

Additional sources of information include Marcia Anderson. "Munsingwear, An Underwear for America," *Minnesota History* 50/4 (Winter 1986): 153–161; Evadene Burris Swanson, "Don't Say 'Underwear,' Say 'Munsingwear,'" *Hennepin County History* 45:4 (Winter 1987): 3–19; *Billboard: Art on the*

Road, Exhibition Catalogue (North Adams, Miss.: MassMoCa, 1999); Christopher DeNoon, *Posters of the WPA* (Los Angeles, Calif.: The Wheatley Press, 1987); Dave Cheadle, *Victorian Trade Cards: Historical Reference & Value Guide* (Paducah, Ky.: Collectors Books, 1996); David Latham, "John Henry Bufford: American Lithographer," *Proceedings of the American Antiquarian Society* 86: 1 (October 1976): 47–73; William G. McLoughlin, "Trade Cards," *American Heritage* 18 (February 1967): 48–63; "MHS Collections: Minnesota Trade Cards," *Minnesota History* 43 (Winter 1973): 270–274; David Anger, "Wrap It Up: Holiday Bags, Boxes, and Ephemera from the Nicollet Mall," *Hennepin History* (Fall 1994): 4–15; Judi Radice and Jackie Cornerford, *The Best of Shopping Bag Design* (Glen Cove, N.Y.: PBC International, 1987); Stephen C. Wagner and Michael L. Closen, *Shopping Bag: Portable Art* (New York, N.Y.: Crown Publishers, 1986); Sue Weiner and Fran Michelman, *Shopping Bag Secrets: The Most Irresistible Bags From the World's Most Unique Stores* (New York, N.Y.: Universe Publishing, 1999); Moira F. Harris, "They are Gone … We Remember," *Public Art Review* 7:2 (Spring/Summer 1996): 26–27; Gustav Niebuhr, "More than a Movement: The Spiritual Dimension of These Hallowed Walls," *The New York Times* (November 11, 1994): A8; Yosh Kashiwabara, *Matchbook Art* (San Francisco, Calif.: Chronicle Books, 1989); and H. Thomas Steele, Jim Heimann, and Rod Dyer, *Close Cover Before Striking: The Golden Age of Matchbook Art* (New York, N.Y.: Abbeville Press, 1987).

96. Bettie McKenzie, *The People's Art. 1889–1989* (Red Oak, Iowa: Montgomery Historical Society, 1991): 4.

97. E. W. Draper, "The Story of Our Paper Line," *The Quality Park News* (May 1927): 2. This publication was Brown & Bigelow's monthly newsletter, begun in 1927.

98. "Calendar Art," *Saturday Evening Post* 216:9 (August 28, 1943): 26–29, 38.

99. Patricia Condon Johnson, "Edward Brewer: Illustrator and Portrait Painter," *Minnesota History* (Spring 1980): 9, 12.

100. Ron Waataja, "Print Firm Founder Recalls Start," *St. Paul Pioneer Press*, February 9, 1963.

101. Moira F. Harris, "Minnesota Calendars: Daily Galleries," *Minnesota History* 58: 7 (Fall 2003): 353–365.

102. Karal Ann Marling, *Looking North: Canadian Mounted Police Paintings from the Northwest Paper Company Collection* (Afton, Minn.: Afton Historical Society Press, 2003).

103. The term *police blotter* is perhaps derived from this usage. The term came to mean both a desk where a police sergeant wrote and a register or sheet of information concerning a person who was arrested.

104. Robert Jay, *The Trade Card in Nineteenth Century America* (Columbia, Mo.: University of Missouri Press, 1987): 3.

105. Luna Lambert Levinson, "Images That Sell," in *Aspects of American Printmaking, 1800–1950,* James F. O'Gorman, ed. (Syracuse, N.Y.: Syracuse University Press, 1988): 85–92.

106. The set of cards is in the museum collection of the Minnesota Historical Society (1995.346.77–81.).

107. Herbert Manchester, *The Romance of the Match* (New York, N.Y.: The Diamond Match Co., 1926). This book is a major source of information concerning the history of fire and matches.

108. These include Westco (Minneapolis); Leslie Paper Company; Walt Peabody Advertising; Matches Unlimited (Minneapolis and Brooklyn Center); Fergus & Company (Albert Lea); Kruger Novelty (Fairfax); Schwartz Enterprises (Oakdale); Warren Company (Minneapolis); Elton Gujer (Duluth); MR Specialty Company (Cottage Grove); Gifts Unlimited (St. Cloud); Midwest Specialty Co., (Minneapolis); Schager Specialty (Minneapolis); Haugen Advertising (Minneapolis); Bagco Manufacturing (Moorhead); Shedd Brown (Minneapolis); and Valley Wholesalers (Winona).

109. These companies include Atlas Match; American Match & Prtg. Co. (Chicago); Chicago Match Co. (Chicago); Crown Match; Federal Match (New York); Lion Match Co. (Chicago and New York); Maryland Match Co. (Baltimore); Ohio Match (Wadsworth, Ohio); Superior Match Co. (Chicago); and Universal Match Corp. (St. Louis).

110. Robert Opie, *The Art of the Label: Designs of the Times* (Secaucus, N.J.: Chartwell Books, 1987): 140.

111. From a speech by Byron A. Johnson, Vice President, Diamond Match Division, Diamond International Corporation at Cloquet, Minnesota, November 10, 1977. The full speech is contained in the vertical files of the Cloquet, Minnesota, Historical Society.

112. Audrey Warren, "As Demand Wanes, Restaurants, Bars Assess Value of Matches," *St. Paul Pioneer Press* (July 27, 2003): F1.

113. E. J. Couper, "Munsingwear's Successful Cultivation of Dealer-Agents," *Printer's Ink* (April 30, 1914): 4.

114. Minutes of Supervisory Board of the Northwestern Knitting Company, March 6, 1918: 4. Munsingwear Papers P1454, Minnesota Historical Society.

115. Lagretta Metzger Bajourek, *America's Early Advertising Paper Dolls* (Atglen, Pa.: Schiffer Publishing, 1999): 103, 109, 110.

116. Abbey Klaassen, "First Lady of Fashion," *Mpls-St.Paul* (March 2003): 80–83, 126.

117. From text inserted on the flyleaf of a poster stamp album published by Brown & Bigelow Company, circa 1915. Collection of the Minnesota Historical Society, Folio NC 1280.B8.

118. H. Thomas Steele, *Lick 'em, Stick 'em: The Lost Art of Poster Stamps* (New York, N.Y.: Abbeville Press, 1989): 14.

119. Milton Wright, "How a Piece of String, Plus a Paper Bag and Idea, Equaled a Nation-Wide Business," *Scientific American,* (November 1927): 414.

120. Later the Deubeners established a foundation that funds college scholarships in Minnesota. Following Deubener's death in 1980, the St. Paul Area Chamber of Commerce instituted a small business award for entrepreneurship and innovation named for Deubener and his wife. See also Gareth Hiebert, *City on Seven Hills* (St. Paul, Minn.: Pogo Press, 1999): 17–19.

121. Catalogue No. 100 (1928), Walter H. Deubener Papers, Minnesota Historical Society.

122. Richard B. Oliver, *Bandboxes and Shopping Bags* (New York, N.Y.: Cooper Hewitt Museum, 1978): 3.

123. Lori J. Gilbertson, "The Historical Development of the Shopping Bag," in *Shopping Bag Design: People, Process, Product* (St. Paul, Minn.: Goldstein Gallery, 1992): 8.

124. Barbara Flanagan, *Minneapolis Star Tribune,* July 13, 1984.

125. The enclosed shopping center or mall, a huge box of stores surrounded usually by acres of parking, was pioneered by Victor Gruen & Associates in their design for Southdale (1956). The apotheosis of such construction, the Mall of America in Bloomington, Minnesota, at times has offered mallwide shopping bags for special promotions.

126. *New York Times* (April 14, 2002), Education Life Section: 42.

127. Billie Young and David Lanegran, *Grand Avenue—The Renaissance of an Urban Street* (St. Cloud, MN: North Star Press of St. Cloud, 1996) 95–100. Also, Billie Young, *Mexican Odyssey* (St. Paul, Minn.: Pogo Press, 1996): 7.

128. Gareth Hiebert, "Memories Museum Recalls Swedish Immigrant Farm," *St. Paul Pioneer Press,* June 19, 1977.

129. Ted Shaffrey, "Signs of Grief," *St. Paul Pioneer Press* (September 1, 2002): 17A.

130. Peggie Autin Schommer, "Strong but Silent: Witness Impact Spreading Across Country," *Minnesota Women's Press* (December 14–27, 1994): 2.

131. Richard Chin, "Lost Pets, Found Art," *St. Paul Pioneer Press,* June 13, 2004, F1. A Toronto man, Ian Phillips, was the collector whose interest led to a book, *Lost: Lost and Found Pet Posters from Around the World* (Princeton Architectural Press, 2002).

132. The 1835 painting, *Fantasy of a Billposter,* is by John Parry.

133. Ellen Lipton and J. Abbott Miller, "A Timeline of American Graphic Design, 1928–1989," in *Graphic Design in America: A Visual Language,* ed. Mildred Friedman and Phil Freshman (Minneapolis, Minn.: Walker Art Center and Harry N. Abrams, 1989): 32, 36.

134. Michael E. Zega and John E. Gruber, *Travel by Train: The American Railroad Poster 1870–1950* (Bloomington, Ind.: Indiana University Press, 2002): 12.

135. Neil Cockerline, "Ethical Considerations for the Conservation of Circus Posters," *WAAC Newsletter* 17:2 (May 1995): 5, 10–12.

136. Geoff Weedon and Richard Ward, *Fairground Art: The Art Forms of Traveling Fairs, Carousels and Carnival Midways,* 5th ed. (New York, N.Y.: Abbeville Press, 1994): 198–199. The Von Wagner painting, the Calvert lithograph, and various fairground imitations appear in *Fairground Art.*

137. *Travel by Train,* the Zega and Gruber book concerning train posters noted previously, shows the wide range of styles selected. One especially interesting example was done by W. W. Denslow for the Chicago Burlington and Quincy railroad. Denslow soon left the field of railroad art for his monumental work with L. Frank Baum in the *Wizard of Oz* books.

138. To see the University of Minnesota posters, visit "A Summons to Comradeship: World War I and II Posters," at http://digital.lib.umn.edu/warposters.

139. Kirby Lambert, "The Lure of the Parks," *Montana* 46:1 (Spring 1996): 45, 50–51.

140. David Kunzle, "From the Poster of Protest to the Poster of Liberation," in *Graphic Design in America: A Visual Language,* ed. Mildred Friedman and Phil Freshman (Minneapolis, Minn: Walker Art Center and Harry N. Abrams, 1989): 180.

141. Ibid., 190.

142. John W. Merten, "Stone by Stone Along a Hundred Years with the House of Strobridge," *Bulletin of the Historical and Philosophical Society of Ohio* 8:1 (January 1950): 28.

143. Ibid., 30.

6. Eat, Drink, and Be Merry

144. John Seabrook, "The Money Note: Can the Music Business Survive?" *The New Yorker* (July 7, 2003): 54.

145. While printers' names are usually given on sheet music covers, those who created these images are not credited. Information concerning artists responsible for record album covers seems to be much more readily available.

146. Kevin Kious and Donald Roussin. "Sheet Music and Beer: American Beer History as Traced through the Song Sheet Music of Tin Pan Alley." *American Breweriana Journal* (May–June 2003): 176.

147. May 6, 2003 lecture by Kate Roberts, exhibits developer for the new Mill City Museum of the Minnesota Historical Society. See also Kate Roberts and Barbara Caron, "To the Markets of the World, Advertising in the Mill City, 1880–1930," *Minnesota History* 58/ 5 & 6 (Spring-Summer 2003): 308–319.

148. Moira F. Harris. *Fire & Ice: The History of the Saint Paul Winter Carnival* (St. Paul, Minn.: Pogo Press, 2003): 114–117.

149. Kenneth Carley, "Lindbergh in Song." *Minnesota History* 45 (Spring 1977): 192–194.

150. Philip D. Jordan., "Some Sources for Northwest History, Minnesota Sheet Music," *Minnesota History* 26:1 (March 1945): 52–54.

151. J. Fletcher Williams, *A History of the City of Saint Paul and of the County of Ramsey, Minnesota* (St. Paul, Minn.: Minnesota Historical Society, 1876): 153.

152. Ibid., 172.

153. Anthony Trollope, *North America* (Philadelphia, Pa.: J. P. Lippincott, 1862): 158.

154. An excellent book by Kathryn Strand Koutsky, Linda Koutsky, and food writer Eleanor Ostman, *Minnesota Eats: An Illustrated History* (St. Paul, Minn.: Minnesota Historical Society Press, 2003), traces the state's dining history through ephemera, recipes, and photographs.

155. Frank M. Whiting, *Minnesota Theatre: From Old Fort Snelling to the Guthrie* (St. Paul, Minn: Pogo Press, 1988): 58, 59.

156. Randall Hobart, "Aim for Magazine Empire," *Minneapolis Star* (March 17, 1964).

157. Bertha L. Heilbron, "Christmas and New Year's on the Frontier," in *Selections from Minnesota History*, ed. Rhoda Gilman and June Drenning Holmquist (St. Paul, Minn.: Minnesota Historical Society Press, 1965): 103.

158. The British Festival of Minnesota program was published by Group 7 and edited by Bette Hammel.

159. *St. Paul Pioneer Press* (April 28, 2002): 10A.

7. Holidays and Rites of Passage

Additional sources of information include John Baule, "Ahhhquatennial—Fifty Fabulous Years," *Hennepin County History* 48: 3 (Summer 1989): 23–27; Moira F. Harris, *Fire & Ice. The History of the Saint Paul Winter Carnival* (St. Paul, Minn.: Pogo Press, 2003); Colleen J. Sheehy, editor, *25 Years in the Heart of the Beast* (Minneapolis, Minn.: University of Minnesota Press, 1999); Alice L. Sickels, *Around the World in St. Paul* (Minneapolis, Minn.: University of Minnesota Press, 1945); "A History of Halloween in Anoka," *Anoka County Union* (October 28, 1960); and Sheri Fiegehen, "Extra! Extra!" *History Magazine* 5: 1 (October–November 2003): 44–45.

160. Karal Ann Marling, *Blue Ribbon* (St. Paul, Minn.: Minnesota Historical Society Press, 1990): 27.

161. Ibid., 154.

162. Reproduced in "Campaigning in Minnesota," *Minnesota History* 41: 3 (Fall 1968): 126.

163. *St. Paul & Minneapolis Pioneer Press* (September 5, 1878): 2.

164. Robert Lavenda, *Corn Fests and Water Carnivals: Celebrating Community in Minnesota* (Washington, D.C.: Smithsonian Institution Press, 1997): 3, 12. The first Fourth of July celebration in Minnesota took place in 1849 in St. Paul. A parade of about 500 people marched through hazel brush and scrub oaks to Rice Park. There they heard speeches, then went to the American House for dinner, followed by a grand ball. The day ended with fireworks, wrote J. Fletcher Williams in his *History of St. Paul* (1876): 227.

165. Garrison Keillor, "Halloween Capital of the World," *The New York Times* (October 31, 1991).

166. *Green's Catalog of the Tuberculosis Seals of the World Part II: U. S. Local Seals and National Back of the Book* (Granville, Ohio: Christmas Seal and Charity Stamp Society, 1998): 69, 98, 99–101, 107.

167. Robert J. DuBois, "Vermont Old Home Week Seals of 1901," *The American Philatelist* (November 2002): 1,018–1,019. See also Terence Hines, "The Seals of Old Home Week," *The American Philatelist* (November 1997): 1,022–1,027.

168. *Winona Herald* (July 20, 1909): 6.

169. June Drenning Holmquist, "Greetings for the New Year," *Minnesota History* (Winter 1952): 168. See also, Bertha Heilbron, "Christmas & New Year's on the Frontier," *Minnesota History* 16:4 (December 1935): 373–390.

170. Rev. Edward D. Neill, *The History of Minnesota*, 4th ed. (Minneapolis, Minn.: Minnesota Historical Company, 1882): 523.

171. Jack El-Hai, *Lost Minnesota* (Minneapolis, Minn.: University of Minnesota Press, 2000): 12. Many years after the Lincoln funeral railroad car, called the United States, made its cross-country journey, it was purchased by Thomas Lowry in 1905. Lowry, owner of the Minneapolis and St. Paul streetcar companies, hoped it could become a museum, but six years later it was destroyed by a fire.

8. Moving People

172. William J. Petersen, "The 'Virginia,' the 'Clermont' of the Upper Mississippi," *Minnesota History* 9: 4 (December 1928): 347.

173. Rev. Edward D. Neill, *The History of Minnesota*, 4th ed. (Minneapolis, Minn.: Minnesota Historical Company, 1882): 534.

174. Ibid., 456.

175. Nathan Parker, *The Minnesota Handbook for 1856–1857* (Boston, Mass.: John P. Jewett & Co., 1857): 10.

176. J. Fletcher Williams, *A History of the City of St. Paul and of the County of Ramsey, Minnesota* (St. Paul, Minn.: Minnesota Historical Society, 1876): 374.

177. Anita Albrecht Buck, *Steamboats on the St. Croix* (St. Cloud, Minn.: North Star Press of St. Cloud, 1990): 39–40, 126.

178. Louis C. Hunter, *Steamboats on the Western Rivers* (Cambridge, Mass.: Harvard University Press, 1949): 630–631.

179. Williams, *History of St. Paul,* 352 and William J. Petersen, "The Rock Island Railroad Excursion of 1854," *Minnesota History* (December 1934): 405–420.

180. Theodore C. Blegen, "The Fashionable Tour on the Upper Mississippi," *Minnesota History* 20: 4 (December 1939): 377–396.

181. Theodore C. Blegen, *Minnesota: A History of the State* (Minneapolis, Minn.: University of Minnesota Press, 1963): 295.

182. S. F. Martin, *Martin's Air Transport Label Catalog* (Minneapolis, Minn.: Carl M. Becken, 1934): 3.

183. "75 Years of Service," *Northwest Airlines World Traveler* (July 2002): 16, 32.

184. Margaret Walsh, "Tracing the Hound: The Minnesota Roots of the Greyhound Bus Corporation," *Minnesota History* 49:8 (Winter 1985): 312, 316.

185. Margaret Walsh, "Minnesota's 'Mr. Bus': Edgar F. Zelle and the Jefferson Highway Transportation Company," *Minnesota History* 52: 8 (Winter 1991): 307–322.

186. Williams, *History of St. Paul,* 295–296.

187. *St. Paul Pioneer Press,* November 1, 1953.

188. John R. Borchert, "The Network of Urban Centers" in *Minnesota in a Century of Change,* ed. Clifford E. Clark Jr. (St. Paul, Minn.: Minnesota Historical Society Press, 1989): 61–64.

189. "Catch the Train," *St. Paul Pioneer Press,* June 20, 2004.

190. James Ogland, *Picturing Lake Minnetonka: A Postcard History* (St. Paul, Minn.: Minnesota History Press, 2001). Materials produced for the streetcar-steamboat venture on Lake Minnetonka are well illustrated in *Picturing Lake Minnetonka.*

191. John A. Dominik, "Sam Pandolfo: Minnesota's Almost Auto Magnate." *Minnesota History* 48: 4 (Winter 1982): 138–152.

192. Alan Ominsky, "A Catalog of Minnesota-Made Cars and Trucks," *Minnesota History* 43: 3 (Fall 1972): 93.

9. Public Affairs

193. Leo J. Harris, "The Aches and Pains of St. Paul Property Ownership: Taxes, Assessments and Fees Between 1856 and 1904," *Ramsey County History* 35: 3 (Fall 2000): 17–23.

194. Claudia J. Nicholson, "Bankers with Shotguns and Other Minnesota Banking Stories," *Minnesota History* (Winter 2000–2001): 184. The Minnesota Historical Society received a collection of Minnesota banknotes from the Minnesota Bankers Association in 1989. Both the national currency and earlier locally issued bills are included.

195. Edward Rochette, "Got Milk Money?" *Numismatist* (September 2003): 115–116.

196. Jeff R. Lonto, "The Trading Stamp Story (or When Trading Stamps Stuck)," 2004: www.Studioz-7.com/stamps1.shtml. Somehow it seems appropriate to cite an article currently appearing on the Internet, and thus fully ephemeral, in a book concerning ephemera.

197. Stephen George, *Enterprising Minnesotans: 150 Years of Business Pioneers* (Minneapolis, Minn.: University of Minnesota Press, 2003): 102–104.

198. Roger A. Fischer, *Tippecanoe and Trinkets Too: The Material Culture of American Presidential Campaigns* (Urbana, Ill.: University of Illinois Press, 1988): 33.

199. Ibid., 194.

200. John E. Haynes, "Reformers, Radicals, and Conservatives," in *Minnesota in a Century of Change,* ed. Clifford E. Clark Jr. (St. Paul, Minn.: Minnesota Historical Society Press, 1989): 372–373.

201. Fischer, *Tippecanoe and Trinkets Too*, 194.

202. Ibid., 236.

203. Ibid., 313.

204. Ibid., 236.

205. *The New York Times*, July 28, 1991.

Illustration Sources and Page Numbers

Stearns History Museum: 124, 171, 179, 181, 192

University of Minnesota Libraries, Special
Collections: 23

Nancy Viking: 143

Glenn Wiessner: 10, 76, 82, 89, 90, 92, 115

Watkins Inc.: 46, 69

*For design and layout reasons many of the objects in this
book are not shown in their actual size.*

Index

U

V

W

Y